Also by Anne Bianchi

From the Tables of Tuscan Women: Recipes and Traditions

ZUPPA!

ZUPPA!

Soups from the Italian Countryside

ANNE BIANCHI

Photographs by Douglas Hatschek

THE ECCO PRESS

Copyright © 1996 by Anne Bianchi
Photographs © 1996 by Douglas Hatschek
All rights reserved

THE ECCO PRESS
100 West Broad Street
Hopewell, New Jersey 08525
Published simultaneously in Canada by
Penguin Books Canada Ltd., Ontario
Printed in the United States of America

Library of Congress Cataloging-in-Publication Data
Bianchi, Anne.
   Zuppa! : soups from the Italian countryside / Anne Bianchi ; photographs
by Douglas Hatschek. —1st ed.
      p.   cm.
   Includes index.
   ISBN 0-88001-513-6
   1. Soups—Italy—Garfagnana. 2. Cookery, Italian—Tuscan style. 3. Food
habits—Italy—Garfagnana.   I. Title.
   TX757.B46   1996
   614.8'13'09455—dc20   96-19067

Designed by Barbara Cohen Aronica
The text of this book is set in Bembo

9   8   7   6   5   4   3   2   1

FIRST EDITION

To Sandra, colleague and friend.
Grazie.

Contents

INTRODUCTION *xi*

ABOUT SOUPS *xv*

CHAPTER ONE *Understanding Life's Priorities*
Broths
3

CHAPTER TWO *The Importance of Play*
Vegetable Soups
27

CHAPTER THREE *A Sense of Community*
Bread Soups, Purees, and Cream Soups
59

CHAPTER FOUR *Two Points of View*
Grain Soups: Rice, Pasta, Polenta, and Chestnuts
91

CHAPTER FIVE *Drawn to the Land*
"Farro" Soups
121

CHAPTER SIX *Of Saints and Superstitions*
Lentil and Chickpea Soups
141

CHAPTER SEVEN *The Fruits of Isolation*
Bean Soups
163

CHAPTER EIGHT *Living with Poetry*
Fish Soups
195

Zuppa!

x

CHAPTER NINE *The Virtues of Mountain Air*
Meat Soups
223

ACKNOWLEDGMENTS *255*

INDEX *257*

Introduction

*T*his book focuses on the Garfagnana, a largely undiscovered region of northern Tuscany hidden away between the perennially snowcapped Apuan Alps and the stark, jagged pinnacles of the Apennines. The Garfagnana is a naturalist's dream come true, with deep rocky gorges, wide panoramic plains, evergreen forests, raging rivers, and protected parklands that include the enormous Parco Regionale delle Alpi Apuane —the Apuan Alps Regional Park—and the smaller Parco dell'Orecchiella —Orecchiella National Park.

There are over one hundred villages in the Garfagnana, each with terra-cotta–roofed houses piled one on top of the other and narrow cobblestone streets that wind their way under arches and passageways and clotheslines hung with colorful laundry. There are castles and fortresses and Romanesque churches and natural cave sanctuaries and a host of quaint museums like the Museo de Don Pellegrino housing over 4,000 artifacts testifying to the area's agricultural and pastoral past.

Above all, the area's charm lies in its traditions that, unlike the more visited areas of Tuscany—Florence, Siena, Chianti—continue intact as part of everyday life. It is not unusual, for example, to see chestnuts drying on roofs, to see people baking bread outdoors in community ovens, to see men making pecorino cheese in huge iron vats hung over stone hearths.

For me, the Garfagnana also has a personal dimension, one that springs instantly to mind whenever I see a rustic stone house or smell the blistering fragrance of charred chestnuts. I see my family bundled into a car and careening around endless mountain curves en route to a holiday, en route to—as my mother put it—"take in deep healthy breaths of fresh mountain air." We would journey from our home near the seaside town of Viareggio, and when we rounded the final bend and I saw the house, I would leap out of the car and run to the edge of our property and stand there, taking in the 180-degree view of mountain peaks and magnificent green valleys.

But it was only as an adult that I realized how much the Garfagnana's people figured in my profound love for the area; they were different from the people I knew in Viareggio, more affectionate, more

naively loving, more likely to hand you an armful of freshly picked tomatoes just because you had wandered by their garden at that particular
moment.

From the shepherds who still wander the area's mountain pastures
with herds of moufflon sheep, to the marble miners who spend their days
extracting pure white marble for modern-day Michelangelos, to the
pork butchers, knife sharpeners, and chimney sweeps who wander from
village to village offering their specialized services, the people of the
Garfagnana are unique and timeless.

This is a cookbook containing soup recipes and, as such, focuses
largely on individual ingredients. In my mind, however, to truly recreate
the foods of a specific geographic region, it is necessary to understand
the people who live there, for people are as essential an ingredient as any
combination of herbs and spices. Food is an inherent and indivisible part
of a region's culture and to attempt to make the soups of the Garfagnana
without knowing something about its remote location and how its people have historically dealt with poverty would be impossible.

Ultimately, soups and the Garfagnana go together. For one thing,
the area's crisp mountain climate creates a palpable need for warm,
hearty foods. For another, its poverty lends itself perfectly to the tradition of simple one-dish meals that can be heated and reheated any number of times. And finally, there is the matter of lifestyle, the fact that most
of the area's men worked either as shepherds or marble extractors—oc-
cupations that required long hours and a lack of certainty about when
the workday would end. A hearty soup could simmer on the burner for
two hours or five without losing any of its flavor; in fact, many of the
soups in this book are actually better the following day.

And so, I offer what I hope is a thorough view of an area's food tradition. The soup recipes that follow were all compiled during one winter
spent with the area's residents, a winter in which I ate and drank in homes
ranging from the humble kitchen of shepherd Alduino Cecchi whose
wife, Elda, made a wonderfully dense *zuppa sostanziosa*—Hearty Kale and
White Bean Soup, to the opulent restaurant of Garfagnana legend,
Carlino Andreucci, proprietor of Castelnuovo's *Da Carlino* where I enjoyed one of Carlino's own creations, *mescola alla garfagnana*, a soup made
with lentils, chickpeas, and red and black beans. In between came the
shopkeepers and bus drivers and pork butchers and fruit merchants whose
wonderfully hearty bowls of soup matched their gracious hospitality.

May you enjoy your stay in this area as much as I did. "For everyday, a soup" says an old Garfagnana proverb. It is my hope that the following recipes will demonstrate the truth of this statement.

On foot through Il Darco Regionale delle Alpi Apuane with Gianluca.

About Soups

$\mathcal{T}$here are many factors in creating an exquisite soup that are as essential as a good recipe and fresh ingredients. I have included the following for your consideration.

ZUPPE VERSUS SOUPS

The English language refers to anything liquid and eaten with a spoon as soup. Italians, however, take their soups more seriously and divide them into individual categories, each with the proper title. Thus, *zuppa* is a term reserved for those dense, full-bodied soups that are eaten over bread such as *zuppa alla frantoiana* (soup olive presser style) or *zuppa di fagioli* (bean soup). Generally these are considered to be one-dish meals, and many are so densely textured as to resemble risottos.

Farinate are yet another category of dense soups; these are thick vegetable soups to which polenta has been added, producing a robust consistency that would, in theory, lend itself equally well to being eaten with a fork, but is never consumed with anything other than a spoon.

Minestrone is a rather nebulous term reserved for "big soups," for soups that have many, many ingredients.

Minestre can also be dense and have many of the same ingredients as *zuppe,* but instead of being served over bread, they rely on either rice or pasta as their farinaceous ingredient and are first courses only.

Brodi—broths—are just that, and can be served over croutons or not. In some cases, a broth will be cooked with rice or a small-grain pasta like pastina and be called a *minestra*.

One chapter in this book is devoted exclusively to *pancotti, passate,* and *creme*—bread soups, purees, and creams—which are in their own categories and entitled as such.

THE PROPER POT

In choosing the proper pot, its size and weight are as important as the material from which it is made. Thin pots can develop hot spots and cause foods to stick; pots that are too small can inhibit cooking, cramp the flavors, and inadequately distribute heat.

A good soup pot should be of fairly heavy gauge—not so heavy as to prevent ease of handling but heavy enough to diffuse heat evenly. Aluminum has good diffusion properties, but tends to become discolored, which eventually affects the flavor and color of foods. Copper, especially in the heavier gauges, distributes heat evenly, but unless it is lined with stainless steel on those surfaces that come in contact with food, it can be adversely affected by acids and even prove poisonous.

Iron pots are both heavy and low in heat conductivity. They also rust easily and discolor acidic foods. Stainless steel also conducts heat poorly, unless there is an inner core of heat-diffusing copper or aluminum.

Ultimately, the best soup pot is one made of alloys combining the superior diffusion of aluminum, the quick conductivity of copper, and the noncorrodible quality of stainless steel. Although the ideal size is largely dependent on the desired number of servings, a good all-purpose soup pot comfortably holds a gallon of liquid.

Soup pots should also conform to the size of your burners. A pot that fits the size of the heating unit gives better cooking results, as well as being more economical. Be certain also that the lid fits snugly.

FLAVOR BASES

When flavoring food—soups or otherwise—Garfagnana's cooks rely mainly on an initial *soffritto*—a sauté—to create an underlying fragrance base that is then transmitted to whatever else is added. The process itself is called *insaporire,* which means "to give flavor to," and the ingredients used for the *soffritto,* the *odori.*

The *odori* consist of a few standard staples—diced or chopped carrot, onion, and celery—and then varies according to the dish in preparation. Included might be parsley or other herbs, pancetta, prosciutto, or pork fatback. It goes without saying that all are sautéed in the very finest oil—extra-virgin, and plenty of it.

THE USE OF BRICKS

Because the Garfagnana was so poor for so long, many of its old *massaie* (housewives who labored from morning till night cooking, cleaning, and taking care of the homestead) cooked their soup all day to compensate for the lack of refrigeration. They would start it in the morning, serve it at lunchtime, and then again for dinner. In order to keep it from burning or spilling over the edge, they placed a few bricks on the burner and laid the soup pot on top. Although it now sounds a bit arcane, this is an excellent technique to use when preparing soups that require long cooking times over low heat. It works both to avoid spills and to ensure an even dispersal of heat. Commercially-produced flame tamers can also be used.

CHEESE

The Garfagnini have a saying to indicate that something is exactly as it should be: *come il parmigiano sulla pasta*—like Parmesan cheese on pasta. They should have added "and soups" to that statement since many of the area's *zuppe* or *minestre* also require a final dusting of cheese. And if they had thought it through a little further, they would have stipulated that the cheese be of the very highest quality. A word to the wise: When purchasing Parmesan cheese, limit yourself to Parmigiano-Reggiano, which is well worth the extra cost. As Fulvia Bertolani of Castiglione says, "What good does it do to buy inferior ingredients and then use more of them because the flavor is not there?" In the case of pecorino, it is important to remember that there are many types of pecorino—from the dozens of soft varieties made to be eaten on their own, to the harder types used for grating. Never under any circumstances should you consider buying supermarket prepackaged, shaker-top pecorino. Again, the words of Signora Bertolani: "Use salt instead."

BREAD

Many of the following recipes call for thickly sliced peasant-style bread that is placed in the bowl and then covered with soup. The Garfagnini generally use either the type of bread that comes in long loaves, like rather corpulent baguettes, or the large round forms with thick hard crusts. In either case, the bottom of the soup bowl should be fairly covered with bread slices. *Focaccia,* croutons, and herb polenta can alternately be used.

SALT

While each of the recipes in this book leaves the amount of salt to the discretion of the individual cook, it is important to note that the Garfagnini usually flavor their soups with ¾ teaspoon per 4 servings.

DENSENESS

Many of the Garfagnana's soups have very little liquid and a denser consistency than most soups known to American audiences. And yet, as you go through this book, you will notice that the bean, legume, and *farro* recipes all say "add more water if necessary"—a direction that becomes meaningless unless you know the desired thickness of the finished product. Therefore, each of the recipes in this book contains one of three icons listed alongside the title to help clarify how much liquid, if any, should be added. The icons refer to the denseness of the broth—not to how many ingredients are suspended in it. Hence, the White Bean and Escarole Soup listed on page 182 carries an icon indicating that it is the least dense of the soups despite the fact that its ingredients include dense foods such as beans and escarole.

    ○ indicates a very liquidy base.

    ◕ indicates a thick but still fluid base.

    ● indicates a dense, risotto-like consistency that could just as easily be eaten with a fork.

TEMPERATURE

In addition to denseness, another feature that will sometimes seem strange is that many of the soups are eaten lukewarm. The reason has to do with optimal blending of flavors and the fact that, in some cases, the flavors blend best when allowed to sit for an hour or two.

FOOD MILLS

You will note as you meander through these recipes that many call for the use of food mills rather than food processors. Quintessential ingredient in every Garfagnino home, food mills create a dense, textured mash;

food processors, on the other hand, create aerated purees, which work very well for cream soups and *passate* but are too devoid of texture for many of the heavier recipes included here.

THE USE OF BROTH AS A SOUP BASE

Many of the recipes in this book are prepared using various broths as the liquid base. This is a fairly new phenomenon and speaks to the limited prosperity experienced by the Garfagnini in the last ten years. Before then, soups were generally made with water and depended for flavor on the ingredients themselves as well as the basic *soffritto* that underlies much of this area's cooking.

SOUP TERRINES

Except for a few cases in which I could not do otherwise, I have avoided suggesting that bread soups—*zuppe*—first be placed in terrines before they are served in individual bowls. Although there is not a kitchen in the Garfagnana that does not have a soup terrine no matter how poor the household, I know of few American homes stocked with such an item. Let me, however, speak in support of their purchase. *Zuppe* are meant to soak into the bread, to create a thorough blending of soup, bread, and oil while still retaining a certain temperature. In individual bowls, the soup is more likely to cool before attaining that melded flavor. A further consideration involves the sheer aesthetic and familial appeal of serving soup from a large, common bowl, preferably of terra-cotta.

QUANTITY

All recipes in this book are for four people. In many cases, there will be leftovers that are just as good, if not better, the next day.

RECIPE VARIATION

Unlike Americans whose diets vary from Mexican on Monday to French on Tuesday to Indian or Italian on Wednesday, Italians eat only Italian food. As a result, their culinary reputations rest not on creating vastly different recipes using extravagantly diverse ingredients, but on using what is available in their individual regions to create recipes different from each other in small, significant ways. Hence, a region such as the Garfagnana might have four different recipes for making Red Bean Soup and each might vary in what seems like minute and unimportant details. But as the saying goes, "God is in the details," and the proof is in the end result, in this case, in the fact that each of the four soups tastes wonderfully—and noticeably—different. Therefore, as you wander through the following soup recipes, adapt the mind-set of the Garfagnini who, like fine sommeliers, differentiate one flavor from another using exquisitely refined criteria.

ZUPPA!

Chapter One

UNDERSTANDING LIFE'S PRIORITIES

San Pellegrino in Alpe

BRODI
Broths

Chi mangia bene, bene dorme
Chi bene dorme, non pecca
Chi non pecca, va in Paradiso
Allora, chi bene mangia, va in Paradiso

Who eats well, sleeps well
Who sleeps well, sins not
Who sins not, goes to heaven
Therefore, who eats well, goes to heaven

San Pellegrino in Alpe is a tiny hamlet that straddles the border between Tuscany and Emilia-Romagna. Located at the summit of a long, winding drive through breathtaking alpine landscapes, the village is surrounded by mountain peaks (several over 2,000 meters) and serves as a natural starting point for treks into two nearby national parks: Parco dell'Orecchiella to the northeast and Parco Regionale delle Alpi Apuane to the southwest.

Spend a few minutes in discussion with any of the forty-three locals, however, and chances are you will not find yourself conversing about either nature or the scenery. What else would anyone want to talk about, you wonder incredulously.

Food, of course.

Like other villages in the Garfagnana, San Pellegrino is a place where you spend your days sitting down to traditionally splendid four-course feasts and do nothing during the entire meal but dissect other even more splendid meals past or future.

While eating a delectable bean soup, someone might prompt another's recollection of a fish broth made by Graciela the preceding Easter: *Com'era quel brodo di pesce che a fatto Graciela a Pasqua?* The reply might go something like this: *E quello di Omero che fa tutti l'anni quando ni porta il suo cugino le trote dal Serchio?* And what about Homer's, when his cousin brings him fresh trout from the Serchio River? Not a direct answer—merely a raising of the stakes.

Wherever one travels through this stunningly rugged country, food is the conversational glue that binds the area's residents one to another. In the colorful lexicon of the Garfagnini, food—not natural beauty—looms as the main conversational fodder, mealtime or any other time. How certain dishes are prepared. How much specific food items cost. How individual dishes were executed previously by other people. How they could benefit by certain alterations in the future. Even the perennially popular political discussions are deemed best reserved for after-dinner sessions at the café.

Gioacchino Rossini was one of Italy's greatest operatic composers. Although not from the Garfagnana, Rossini spent much time here on holiday—so much so that he was eventually adopted by the region as one of its own. According to local legend, the composer is said to have cried three times in his life: when his first opera was booed; when he first heard Paganini play; and when, during a short boat ride to the home of friends to whom he was bringing a small turkey stuffed with truffles, the turkey fell overboard.

Rossini's love affair with food and wine is etched in the region's mythology. Stories are still told of the items that arrived regularly from faraway places: prosciuttos from Seville, cheeses from Gorgonzola, panettones from Milan, a particular type of linguine from Naples. Supposedly, the gifts he appreciated most were cured meats—salamis, mortadellas, *zamponi*. Those and the frequent crates of Lafitte wines sent by the Baron de Rothschilds.

So central was food to Rossini's being, in fact, that the overture to his *Barber of Seville* carries these dicta: "After doing nothing, I know no better way to occupy my time than to engage in eating . . . the appetite is to the stomach what love is to the heart . . . the stomach is the choir master that governs and drives the great orchestra of our passions . . . a full stomach is like a pair of cymbals crashing in joy."

At the Spanish premiere of *Barber,* Rossini spoke to Queen Isabella of his particular love for Castillian *zamponi* (a type of pork sausage that is often boiled with lentils and served on New Year's Eve). Having planted the seed, he then waited for weeks in delicious expectation. What he received instead was a letter of commendation for the splendid opera "given as a gift to the grateful people of this distant shore." Enraged, he threw the document into the fire along with the yellow and white ribbon that adorned its face.

Gianluca Padovani lives on the outskirts of San Pellegrino in a charming stone house that dates back to the 1700s. Above the doorway hangs a block of wood etched with the first two lines of poet Umberto Monti's famous ode, "Canti di San Pellegrino in Alpe" (Chant to San Pellegrino of the Alps): *Fra i molti fior che vanta l'Appenino, il più bello sei tu, San Pellegrino.* Of all the flowers blanketing the slopes of the Apennines, the most beautiful is you, San Pellegrino.

Visiting Gianluca on this occasion is his brother Piero, proprietor of "In Garfagnana," a restaurant in Milan's fashionable financial district. "Piero went to Milan right after the war," Gianluca says. "At first he sold *castagnaccio*—chestnut bread—which he cooked in a restaurant kitchen near his apartment. He would get to the kitchen by three A.M. so as to be finished when the restaurant's owner arrived at six. In time, and after selling thousands of *castagnacci,* Piero opened his own small place." Today, it is one of dozens that offers food cooked in the style of the Garfagnana.

Piero breaks in: "In the last few years, it has become stylish to say that Tuscans—and to a large part, Tuscans from the Garfagnana—taught the Milanese to cook. The truth, however, is that we had little to teach, only the lessons learned from our persistent hunger. From the beginning, we cooked in a style that was simple in both ingredients and methodology. Perhaps what the public appreciates today is that our cooking has remained simple. Look, for example, at what we use as ingredients— everything, even stale bread. Nothing gets thrown away, merely reinvented with fantasy.

"Of all the cooking styles in Italy, ours is one of the few that has not become Milanizzati, which refers to a transformational process I think you in your country call nouvelle cuisine. If anything, the Milanese have become Garfagnizzati!"

He returns to the topic of poverty. "It is true I have done well and I have no regrets over the way my life has been lived. But I must at the same time be honest. If at home I had had one meal every day, I never would have gone to Milan."

One memory prompts another. "I remember the way we used to make minestrone—*ti ricordi, Gianluca?* A pot of water, many many beans, and a little seasoning. What a pleasure to make it now the way God intended, with fresh vegetables and an ample piece of pancetta."

Gianluca smiles and nods his head. "We were four brothers in our house. Soups and broths were the mainstay of our diet, and there was no such thing as not liking what had been prepared. *O mangi la minestra, o salti la finestra,* our mother used to say, only partly in jest. You either eat what is on the table or you jump out the window.

"Only when you were sick could you have an egg, so naturally we all played at being sick every once in a while. *Dio,* the laments: I am exhausted; my stomach hurts; I have a headache, this last said while holding our heads as if they would split apart. Our grandmother was the easiest to trick—not that she was ever truly fooled. It was a bargain: She gave us the egg only if we promised not to tell our father. *Nonna beata,* she emigrated to Milan nine times to keep house for rich people, returning with a few *centesimi* and a suitcase filled with discarded clothing. And with that suitcase, she dressed the entire family."

Gianluca is an old friend and a park ranger who works for Il Parco Regionale delle Alpi Apuane, the lush national preserve created by the Italian government in 1985 to protect the flora and fauna of the Garfagnana. Covering hundreds of square miles, the park has recently become a cherished haven for naturalists and adventure travelers drawn to the excellent opportunities for hiking, birding, mountain biking, river rafting, rock climbing, and skiing.

I joined Gianluca last November for a four-day trek along old mule trails that wound through the valleys just south of San Pellegrino. Along the way we encountered falcons, eagles, foxes, one wild boar, a flock of sheep, two baby owls that may or may not have fallen from the nest, and a ski area where a group of small children were practicing their snowplowing.

At one point, we also encountered two hunters standing on the side of a path dressed in full regalia and talking on cellular phones. Ever alert for people photographs, I began looking through the eyepiece of my camera to frame a picture I envisioned labeling "The Call in the Wild." Whereupon the two men began running toward us, one jabbering nervously about how he had no bullets in his rifle and we were free to check if we doubted his word, the other—a significantly darker figure—threatening to rip the film from my camera if he heard a click.

It was obviously not their day. To my great surprise, Gianluca pulled out his own cellular phone and called the main ranger station, where he reported the two *bracconieri*—poachers—and gave their exact location. After flashing his badge before their astonished faces, he asked to see some identification, which they reluctantly produced. Thirty minutes later, we heard a four-wheel drive on the distant road, and within minutes two uniformed rangers appeared on the scene. We left at that point, Gianluca explaining that the men had been hunting out of season and without the proper licenses, serious offenses in a national preserve. He also suspected—because of the phones—that they might be part of an organized and illegal hunt for wild boar. Regardless, they would be taken to the ranger station and, at the very least, fined heavily.

Adventure concluded, we resumed our hike, arriving eventually at the summit of a wide plateau from which we had an unobstructed 360-degree view of jagged, snowcapped peaks. As I stood there marveling at the rugged beauty of the Apennines, I found myself wanting to break into an Italian rendition of "The Sound of Music." Instead, I merely remembered something my mother had once told me: *Il più vicino che siamo a Dio, il più bello che doventa le vedute.* The closer one gets to God, the more beautiful the view becomes.

At night, we slept in rustic mountain huts placed strategically along a weblike network of trails. Any assumptions I ever had about cooking our own food and eating like Spartans were disallowed from the start by Gianluca, who was firm in his conviction that two people who had spent a hard day hiking deserved at the very least a modest meal at a village trattoria—a slice or two of prosciutto with pickled mushrooms and onions, a bowl of semolina *gnocchetti* in broth, a plate of grilled trout with roasted potatoes, and a few glasses of '92 Chianti. *Bravo Gianluca!*

We arrived back in San Pellegrino on a Thursday, and on Friday, the last night of my stay, we went to Albergo Ristorante L'Appenino, one of the oldest family-owned restaurants in Italy. Before dinner we stopped at one of the village's main attractions, the Ethnographic Museum of Don Luigi Pellegrino. The museum houses over 4,000 artifacts displayed in fourteen rooms inside an ancient hospice, all culled from the slopes of the Apennines by the late Don Luigi Pellegrino. From the weaving room with its dozens of two-hundred-year-old looms, to the cobbler's room with its sewing machine and shoe forms, to the kitchen with its stone hearth hung with iron pots and molds for making bread, the museum serves as a remarkable testimony to the area's agricultural and pastoral past.

At my request, we also stopped at the village church. I had heard before coming that of the two saints whose remains are housed behind the altar, one had been stolen. But in fact there they both were, Saint Pellegrino and Saint Bianco, lying side by side in their gilt-edged glass tomb. Alongside were raffia baskets filled with hand-written requests. From Antonio: Please help me win the ski race this Saturday. From Alessio: I would very much like a brother, but I will leave the rest of the details to you.

We arrived at L'Appenino well before our seven-thirty reservation so that I could be introduced to Angela Marche-Lunardi, the restaurant's proprietor, and her son Paolo. The smell of food permeated the dining rooms, whose dark wood walls were blanketed with Lunardi family history: a portrait of Count Lunardi, who served as an ambassador to London in 1775; a family crest from 1221, its half-moon symbolizing the family's participation in the Crusades; a picture of Michaele Lunardi, Duke of Modena, who in 1759 was the first Italian ever to go ballooning.

Signora Lunardi exuded pride both in her ancestors and in the numerous awards accorded her establishment over the years, the most prestigious being La Croce d'Oro, a gold star citation that hung over the entrance to the main dining room in acknowledgment of *cinquant'anni di cucina eccezzionale*—fifty years of exceptional cooking.

Of the stories she told, one of the most interesting involved how she came to be named Marche-Lunardi. It seems that four generations ago, when there were no male Lunardi children to carry on the restaurant's name, her great-great-grandmother married a man named Marche, and had to apply to Rome for permission to hyphenate her name in order to continue the tradition. She was one of the first Italians ever to be allowed to do so.

For dinner we had a multicourse feast, and Gianluca sighed with happiness at *finalmente* being able to sit down to a verifiable meal, not the *piatti semplici*—simple foods—of the preceding four days. Afterward we were taken through a subterranean tunnel that connects the restaurant with the Lunardi family bar. The bar straddles the line between Tuscany and Emilia-Romagna, and prompted by Paolo, the Signora's son, we had blueberry liquer in the province of Lucca and then walked a few paces across the marble floor and paid for it in the province of Modena.

ABOUT BROTHS

Throughout Italy, broths have always been served as a *primo piatto* (first course) on holidays. As such, they are refined, delicate dishes, served sometimes as a clear liquid in round porcelain cups, but more often either over croutons fried in oil or butter, or cooked with small cuts of pasta, tortellini, or dumplings.

Removing Fat from Broths

Whether a basic broth will be used as the foundation for another soup or as a delightfully satisfying soup in its own right, its presentation is considerably more pleasing if the fat is first skimmed from the surface. Following are three methods for accomplishing this maneuver.

1. Chill the soup. The fat will rise to the top and coagulate, at which time it can be scraped off with a knife and discarded.
2. Float a paper towel over the top. When the towel is saturated, discard and repeat the process. An alternate method involves rolling a few paper towels into a kind of wand. Drag the end of the wand across the surface until it becomes saturated. Using scissors, cut off and discard the end and repeat the process until the wand is used up.
3. Use a meat baster with the bulb as a suction device.

Clarifying Broths

Although the Garfagnini of old never gave a thought to whether or not their broths and stocks were clear, today's heightened culinary awareness requires a word or two about this technique designed to enhance the soup's appearance.

Before starting, make sure the soup to be clarified has been well degreased and is at room temperature. For each quart of broth, you will need 1 slightly beaten egg white, 1 crumbled egg shell, and—unless the soup is already cold—a few ice cubes.

Add the egg white, egg shell, and ice to the soup, stirring until well blended. Bring the soup very very slowly to a simmer without any further stirring. As the soup heats, the egg will cause a heavy, crusty foam more than an inch thick to rise to the top. This should not be skimmed, but pushed very gently to one side of the pot. Under no circumstances should the soup be allowed to boil. Continue simmering in this fashion for 10 to 15 minutes, without stirring.

Now move the pot away from the heat source and let it stand for 30 minutes. In the meantime, soak a large piece of cheesecloth in hot water, wring it out and use it, doubled, to line a large strainer. Suspend the strainer over a second pot.

Push the foamy crust once again to the side of the soup pot and ladle the soup carefully through the cheesecloth until all the soup has been strained. At this point the soup should be sparklingly clear. Cool, uncovered; then, if not using immediately, cover tightly and refrigerate.

Basil Pesto

To make approximately ¼ cup basil pesto, you will need 2 cups fresh basil, washed and dried, 4 tablespoons extra-virgin olive oil, 1 ounce pignoli nuts, 2 cloves peeled garlic, and salt. Place all ingredients in a food processor and process until smooth.

Herb "Battuto"

To make approximately ¼ cup herb *battuto,* you will need 2 cups mixed fresh herbs (equal amounts of oregano, sage, basil, parsley, rosemary, and thyme), 2 ounces shelled walnuts, 4 tablespoons extra-virgin olive oil, 1 tablespoon heavy cream, and salt. Place all ingredients in a food processor and process until smooth.

BRODO DI CARNE
Basic Meat Broth   ○

Signora Padovani recalls Christmas Eve 1944: "Our family had long been with-
out meat, eating bean soups and chestnut polentas and plates of pasta. The day
before, I had finally managed to buy some beef bones and a kilo of beef sides to
make a good broth which had simmered all day on the stove. At one point just as
the subtle fragrance had reached its peak, my husband came running through the
door. 'The Germans are coming!' he screamed. 'Take what is most important and
come now—we must leave for the hills immediately!' Well, I clamped the lid on
the pot and ran out the door. 'They can take my house,' I told him, 'but I am not
leaving without my broth!'"

> 2 pounds beef with bone (different cuts will render different tastes,
> but any cut will produce a good broth)
> 4 cups water
> 1 clove garlic
> 1 onion
> 1 carrot
> 1 stalk celery
> 3 tablespoons minced fresh parsley
> ¼ teaspoon dried thyme
> ¼ teaspoon dried rosemary
> Salt to taste
> 8 sprigs fresh watercress, cleaned and with stems removed

1. Place all the ingredients except the salt in a soup pot. Heat to boiling
over high heat. Reduce the heat to medium, cover, and cook for 1½
hours, salting the water at the 45-minute mark. Skim the grease from
the top four or five times during the cooking process.

2. Strain the broth (see Note), adjust for salt, and serve hot garnished
with the watercress. Or freeze and use as the base for other recipes.

*The boiled beef and vegetables make an excellent second course when
arranged on a platter and served with *Salsa Verde,* a green sauce made from
pureed parsley, olive oil, and salt.

BRODO DI POLLO

Basic Chicken Broth

○

Italians say this of chicken broth: Abbraccia lo stomaco. *It hugs the stomach.
The Garfagnini put it a bit differently:* Fa resuscitare i morti. *It resuscitates the
dead. In olden days, chicken broth was reserved for the royals, who consumed it
from beautiful porcelain bowls and called it "consommé." Today, in Garfagnana,
chicken broth is made with* pollo ruspicante—*a free-range chicken that has been
raised on nothing but grass and corn. When I explain to Signora Padovani that
most Americans buy their chicken from a supermarket, she narrows her eyes and
looks at me crossly.* Ma scherzi? *she says.* You must be kidding.

    1 whole chicken, preferably free-range, skinned
    2 small carrots
    1 stalk celery
    2 medium onions
    3 tablespoons minced fresh parsley
    8 cups water
    6 fresh basil leaves
    Salt to taste

1. Place all the ingredients except the salt in a soup pot. Heat to boiling
over medium heat. Reduce the heat to low, cover, and cook for 2
hours. Skim the grease from the top four or five times during the cooking process.

2. Strain the broth (see Note), add salt, and serve hot in small porcelain
cups. Or freeze and use as the base for other soups.

★The boiled chicken and vegetables make an excellent second course when
arranged on a platter and accompanied by mashed potatoes and pickled *peper-
oncini*.

★★This basic broth can be frozen and used as the base for other recipes.

BRODO DI PESCE
Basic Fish Broth

To make a good fish broth, it is important to use the very freshest fish. In most cases the quantity does not matter as long as there is a proper balance between the odori (carrot, celery, onion, parsley, and garlic) and the quantity of fish (hence the following recipe can be doubled or halved). "At this point," says Paolo Marche-Lunardi, proprietor of L'Appenino, which is known for its superb fish broths, "I don't think we have to say that frozen fish should be avoided, do we?"

   8 cups cold water
   2 very ripe Italian plum tomatoes
   2 small carrots, scraped
   1 small onion
   3 tablespoons minced fresh parsley
   2 cloves garlic, peeled
   Salt to taste
   1½ pounds mixed fish chunks (haddock, pollock, halibut—the
      greater the mix, the more tasty the soup)

1. Place the water in a soup pot along with the tomatoes, carrots, onion, parsley, garlic. Heat to boiling over medium heat. Reduce the heat to low.

2. Clean the fish well under cold running water and add it to the pot. Poach over low heat for 30 minutes, or until the fish begin to flake. Strain the broth, returning the liquid to the pot.

3. Discard the fish bones, pass the remaining fish and vegetables through a food mill, and add the puree to the broth. Discard the solids.

4. Heat the broth and serve over croutons. Or freeze and use as the base for other soups.

BRODO DI VEGETALI ○
Basic Vegetable Broth

Vegetable broth is a year-round staple in the Garfagnana, although its flavor depends on the season. In winter, for example, it is made with butternut squash, while in summer zucchini are used. The one factor that never changes, however, is that the fresher the vegetables, the better the broth.

8 cups water
2 small carrots, scraped
1 medium onion, halved
1 stalk celery
2 potatoes, peeled and halved
3 tablespoons minced fresh parsley
6 fresh basil leaves
⅓ cup dried peas or beans, soaked according to directions on page 169
3 pounds chopped vegetables (the greater the variety, the richer the broth—spinach, lettuce, Swiss chard, broccoli rabe)
2 ounces gorgonzola cheese, crumbled (optional)

1. Place all the ingredients in a soup pot. Heat to boiling over medium heat. Reduce the heat to low, cover, and cook for 2 hours, stirring occasionally with a wooden spoon. Crush the vegetables against the pot when stirring to release their full flavor.

2. Strain the broth and discard the vegetables. Cook the strained broth for another 20 minutes and serve hot sprinkled with the crumbled cheese. Or freeze and use as the base for other soups.

BRODO AI FUNGHI O

Mushroom Broth

Mushroom broth is the most delicate of all the broths and depends completely on the type of mushroom used. Although the following recipe calls for creminis, other varieties will also work well, albeit creating a far different flavor. The best advice comes from L'Appenino's Paolo Marche-Lunardi: "Experiment!"

4 ounces cremini mushrooms
4 cups Basic Chicken Broth (see page 12)
1 bunch watercress, rinsed, thickest stems removed, remainder
  chopped
Salt and freshly ground black pepper to taste

1. Separate the mushroom caps from the stems. Add the stems to the broth in a saucepot. Heat to boiling over medium heat and cook, un-covered, for 10 minutes. Using a slotted spoon, remove and discard the stems.

2. Slice the mushroom caps into thin slivers. Add to the broth, return to boiling and cook, uncovered, over medium heat for another 10 min-utes. Add the watercress and mix well.

3. Add salt and pepper and serve hot.

BRODO DI CEREALI

Broth Made with Cereal Grains

O

Piero Padovani prepares this broth in his restaurant in Milan when he feels nostalgic for what he refers to as quei bei tempi—*the wonderful days of yesteryear. "Its preparation dates back to when we were all very poor," he says. "But every now and then it does the soul good to remember those days when we had to make do with nothing."*

> 1 tablespoon extra-virgin olive oil
> 1 chunk (4 ounces) smoked pancetta or bacon, diced
> 8 cups Basic Chicken Broth (see page 12)
> 1 cup rolled oats
> ⅔ cup pearled barley
> 1 tablespoon lemon juice
> Salt and freshly ground black pepper to taste

1. Heat the oil in a skillet (over medium heat). Sauté the pancetta or bacon until it is browned and crispy. Drain on paper towels and crumble when cool.

2. Place the broth in a soup pot and heat to boiling over medium heat. Add the oats and barley, cover, and cook for 40 minutes or until the barley is tender.

3. Stir the lemon juice into the broth. Add salt and pepper and serve hot, sprinkled with the bits of crisp pancetta.

BRODO DI VONGOLE

Clam Broth

One morning, while in a local market, I overheard a conversation between two women, one of whom complained that her family had tired of the same foods day in and day out. "Listen," the other one replied. "Yesterday I made a wonderful clam broth that took no time at all. You can serve it over croutons or cooked with small cut pasta." I continued to stand there, unapologetic, until the complete recipe had been revealed and, later that day, enjoyed the fruits of my thievery.

    4 pounds clams, scrubbed thoroughly under cold running water
    5 tablespoons extra-virgin olive oil
    8 cups water
    Salt and freshly ground black pepper to taste
    16 croutons fried in oil (see page 68)

1. Place the clams in a soup pot along with the oil and cold water. Bring to a boil, cover, and cook for 15 minutes.

2. Remove the clams from the broth with a slotted spoon, discarding any that did not open, and pour the broth through a fine-mesh strainer to filter out any residue sand. Return the broth to the pot.

3. Separate the clams from their shells. Pass the clams through a food mill and blend the resulting puree into the broth. Add salt and pepper.

4. Divide the croutons among 4 bowls. Pour the soup over and serve hot.

BRODO ESTIVO

O

Summer Broth

The following recipe blends the lightness of broth with the richness of egg yolks and cream. Slivers of lettuce add the final touch, rendering a delicate, colorful broth that is generally served on holidays throughout the Garfagnana.

> 8 cups Basic Chicken Broth (see page 12)
> 2 egg yolks
> ½ cup heavy cream
> 1 head *lattuga* (Boston-type lettuce), washed and cut into small slivers
> 3 tablespoons unsalted butter
> 8 fresh basil leaves, slivered

1. Heat the broth to boiling in a soup pot over medium heat.

2. Beat the eggs with the cream. Whisk into the broth and simmer for 5 minutes, stirring constantly.

3. Add the lettuce, cook for 1 minute longer, and remove from the heat.

4. Stir the butter into the broth and place in the refrigerator for 30 minutes before serving. Garnish with the basil slivers.

GNOCCHETTI DI SEMOLINO
IN BRODO

Chicken Broth with Tiny Semolina Gnocchi

This wonderfully delicate broth is served for Christmas dinner at L'Appenino, where it is followed by a secondo consisting of roast loin of pork with potatoes and braised fennel. Says owner Angela Marche-Lunardi: "I also offer other choices for a primo, but only once did someone request something else. It was a Frenchwoman, and she ordered onion soup. To this day I regret not telling her what a mistake she was making."

    1 cup whole milk
    ¾ cup semolina
    3 tablespoons unsalted butter, at room temperature
    1 egg yolk, lightly beaten
    ¼ cup freshly grated Parmigiano-Reggiano
    1 egg white, beaten to stiff peaks
    6 cups Basic Chicken Broth (see page 12)
    Salt to taste

1. Heat the milk in a saucepan until just before boiling. Remove from the heat.

2. Pour the semolina into the milk in a steady stream, whisking constantly. Return to low heat and cook, stirring constantly, until the semolina has achieved a thick, pastelike consistency. Cool to room temperature.

3. In a bowl, mash the butter, using a fork; add the egg yolk and the cheese and mash until thoroughly blended.

4. Stir the cooled semolina into the egg yolk and cheese mixture. Fold in the egg white.

5. In a soup pot, heat the broth to boiling. Reduce the heat to low and drop the semolina mixture into the boiling liquid, 1 teaspoon at a time. Cook for 10 minutes, add salt, and serve immediately.

BRODO DI VINO

O

Creamy Marsala Broth

In olden days, this soup was fed to children and convalescents with the hope that it would act to reinforzare—reinforce—*the blood. Today, its use is limited to the holiday table, especially at Easter, when it acts as both a wonderful first course and—because it is made from eggs—as a reminder of Christ's Resurrection.*

> 4 eggs, lightly beaten
> 1 cup marsala or vin santo
> 6 cups Basic Chicken Broth (see page 12)
> Salt and freshly ground black pepper

1. Whisk the marsala into the beaten eggs.

2. Place the broth in a soup pot, cover, and heat to boiling over medium heat. Remove the pot from the stove and whisk the marsala and egg mixture into the broth. Add salt and pepper and serve.

Piero Padovani. "In the Garfagnana nothing is thrown away, not even stale bread. Each ingredient is merely reinvented with fantasy."

BRODO CON TORTELLINI DI BASILICO
Basil Tortellini in Broth

Tortellini in broth have long been a staple of the Garfagnino holiday table where they are served as a delectable first course. The following version uses basil pesto for the filling instead of the traditional ground meat and can be easily incorporated into a vegetarian meal by substituting vegetable broth.

The filling

⅓ cup basil pesto (see page 10)
2 tablespoons heavy cream
½ cup unflavored bread crumbs
1 medium egg, lightly beaten
Salt and freshly ground black pepper

The dough

3 cups unbleached flour
4 large eggs, lightly beaten
6 cups Basic Chicken Broth (see page 12)
4 tablespoons freshly grated Parmigiano-Reggiano

1. Stir the cream, bread crumbs, and egg into the pesto until a paste has formed. Add salt and pepper.

2. Place the flour on a wooden board. Make a well in the center and fill with the eggs. Begin incorporating the flour into the eggs, a little at a time, until a slightly moist ball has formed. Knead for 5 minutes. Cover with a towel and let rest for 30 minutes.

3. Pick off a piece the size of an egg and roll flat with a floured rolling pin to a ⅛-inch thickness. Cut into 2-inch squares.

4. Place ½ teaspoon filling on each square, fold into a triangle, and seal by pinching the edges of the dough tightly together. Bend the triangle around an index finger and seal the dough on the two open sides. Continue until all the squares have been filled.

5. Repeat the process with the remaining dough.

6. Heat the broth to boiling in a soup pot over medium heat. Reduce to low, drop the tortellini carefully into the broth, and cook for 5 minutes. Remove with a slotted spoon and divide among 4 bowls. Pour the broth over the tortellini, dust with cheese, and serve.

All of San Pellegrino's streets end with a view of the surrounding mountains.

STRACCIATELLA

Egg Drop Soup

In the Garfagnana, stracciatella *is also used to connote a delicious type of vanilla ice cream. "In a way," says Piero Padovani, "it is the same thing, except that one is sweet and the other salted." I have tried numerous times since to understand what he might have meant by that statement, but to no avail.*

> 2 eggs
> 2 teaspoons unbleached white flour
> 2 tablespoons freshly grated Parmigiano-Reggiano
> ⅛ teaspoon grated nutmeg
> 8 cups Basic Chicken Broth (see page 12)
> Salt to taste

1. Place the eggs, flour, grated cheese, nutmeg, and salt in a food processor and pulse once or twice until the ingredients are well blended and soupy.

2. Heat the broth to boiling in a soup pot over medium heat. Pour the egg mixture, through a strainer, slowly into the soup, stirring constantly with a wooden spoon. Cook for 10 minutes over medium heat, add salt, and serve hot.

CAPELLI D'ANGELO IN BRODO   O

Angel-Hair Pasta in Vegetable Broth

There is not a house in the Garfagnana that does not serve this dish at least once a year on some holiday or other. In general it is followed by roasted meat served in its juices with potatoes and a salad. I once asked an old woman how she managed on hot days to conserve the broth until serving time. Her eyes shone with the pride of someone who has lived through very hard times. "We simmered it on the stove from morning until night."

    8 cups Basic Vegetable Broth (see page 14)
    4 ounces angel-hair pasta
    3 tablespoons chopped fresh parsley
    2 tablespoons unsalted butter
    ⅛ teaspoon grated nutmeg
    ⅓ cup freshly grated Parmigiano-Reggiano

1. Heat the broth to boiling in a soup pot. Add the pasta and cook for 5 minutes, stirring occasionally.

2. In a bowl, blend together the remaining ingredients and stir into the soup. Serve immediately.

BRODO CON BRICIOLETTI ○

Chicken Broth with "Crumbled Ricotta"

The following is a typical mountain broth—a favorite of shepherds, who always had access to fresh ricotta. In general it was eaten at night, as a rich, high-calorie reward for a hard day's work.

4 cups Basic Chicken Broth (see page 12)
4 ounces fresh sheep's milk ricotta (goat's milk ricotta can be
   substituted)
Salt and freshly ground black pepper to taste

1. Heat the broth to boiling in a soup pot. Add the ricotta, rubbing it between the fingers so that it drops into the soup one "crumb" at a time. Add salt and pepper and heat through. Serve hot.

Saint Pellegrino and Saint Bianco in their gilt-edged glass tomb, and the basket with special requests for their intercession.

Chapter Two

THE IMPORTANCE OF PLAY

Barga

ZUPPE DI VERDURE
Vegetable Soups

I have come to Barga to see the Della Robbia terra-cottas located in the Duomo's Chapel of the Holy Sacrament. "You have never before seen them?" my cousin Sandra asked incredulously when I said as much the other evening at the home of Tuscan painter and sculptor Giancarlo Cannas. We were discussing the changing face of terra-cotta sculptures, the insufficiency—as one of the dinner guests put it—of simply producing a visually beautiful work of art.

"There is no value to turning out pieces that merely engage the senses," said one of the other guests, summing up what was unfortunately the majority opinion. "To be of value today, you must engage the mind, the thinking process, the multidimensional layers of interpretation whose significance is founded on a respect for the considered response rather than the spontaneous reflex."

Cannas' own work falls, I think, somewhere in the middle. Both his paintings and sculptures portray the surrealistic nature of death and existence—the way the two twine inexorably around each other while, at the same time, maintaining a clear and defined separateness. It is the way he evokes "separateness," however, that I find particularly intriguing: his sculptures all come apart, like pieces of a puzzle. A pregnant woman distills into four fragments: a head, a body, a baby, and a hat. But beautifully so—magnificently rendered—albeit in what must be such a subversive manner that it seems not to offend the more "meaning-oriented" art critics at his table.

Eventually, most of Cannas' guests ceded a certain invaluable estimate to the work of Andrea and Giovanni Della Robbia. But they also turned the focus as soon as possible to those they considered more "substantial" artisans. All of which made me hunger to see the Della Robbia terra-cottas in a way that I know would not have been the case had I been seated at a dinner table with eight sixteenth-century *appassionatas.*

I arrive in Barga quite early and stop just outside the Porta Reale, which is one of three gates leading into this eleventh-century walled town. I'm very anxious to get inside, to see again that photogenic assembly of archways and little *palazzi* piled on top of each other.

But I point myself squarely to the Cafe Refugio, where I seat myself in the corner and order a steaming cup of *caffè macchiato.* I am to be joined here in a little while by my cousin Sandra, who was so thoroughly stunned by the gaps in my aesthetic education that she now does not trust me to close the breach myself.

Before leaving this morning, I made sure to buy the paper, anxious as I am to read about the ongoing trials of Italy's two most famous crooks: former Prime Minister Silvio Berlusconi, who resigned last year amidst allegations that he used his political power for financial gain, and former President Giulio Andreotti, who is accused of extensive comingling with the Mafia.

Instead, my attention strays toward a table of men playing cards. They are four in number, two teams, although they are often "advised" by others passing by. The men are playing *briscola,* a game that is as simple in its standard rules as it is complicated in the nuances of the associated behavior.

Briscola decks contain forty cards (no eights, nines, or tens) encompassing 120 points, of which the winners must take at least 61. Aces are worth 11 points, threes are worth 10, kings 4, queens 3, and jacks 2. In some towns (possibly those where men feel somewhat threatened?), jacks and queens exchange values.

At the beginning of the game, each man receives three cards; the rest of the deck is placed in the middle, facedown over an exposed *briscola,* or trump. The person to the right of the dealer throws the first card onto the table and each of the other players follow in suit. Trump may be used only when a player has no cards in the chosen suit.

Thus far, the rules approximate those of many other such card games. What makes this one uniquely Italian, however, is the accompanying set of words and gestures—most legitimized as a "standard" part of the game. For starters, *briscola* is not played in silence; far from it. Partners talk in a steady stream of suggestions and demands.

Gioca un carico, one man might order his partner. Play a valuable card. At another point, a man about to play a valuable nontrump card might query his partner in advance. *C'e l'hai delle briscole?* Do you have any trump? If the partner simply nods his head yes, the man might query further. *E vestita?* Is it dressed, meaning is it a jack, queen, or king? One of the more colorful expressions involves situations where one person wants his partner to trump higher. *Amazza quella briscola,* he'll say. Kill that *briscola,* a phrase that is, of course, spoken with the appropriate inflection and decibel level.

But there's more. Before the start of the very last hand, partners exchange cards so that they can even more effectively plan their strategies. And although this exchange is only supposed to take place at the end, some *briscola* players show their cards to their partner whenever they want.

As if that weren't enough, there are the gestures. A wink means you have an ace. Raising your eyes toward the heavens means you have a three. When you have a king, you shrug one shoulder.

And finally, there are the nonstandard, nonlegitimized, uniquely Garfagnini maneuvers. The yawning and bending sideways to see a neighbor's cards. Picking up of two cards instead of one and then apologetically returning the other card to the deck. Kicking each other under the table to indicate that what was said is untrue.

As my friend Valerio says: "Watching four Garfagnini play *briscola* is the very best way to understand everything you need to know about the way of life in this region."

He is correct in his underlying assumption, but I would expand the theory to include all games. What, for example, did I learn about the Garfagnana the night I accompanied a friend to his parents' home and saw his nieces and nephews playing bingo with beans? What about the children who I saw the other day making dolls out of rags? What about the group of schoolboys outside this very cafe engrossed in a simple game of marbles?

I finish my coffee and turn to stare out the window of the bar. In the distance, I can see Barga's Duomo rising majestically above the old town. Together with the Loggia del Podesta, it stands on a fortified hill-top around which the community expanded as it became more powerful. I make a mental promise to myself to come one July for the Barga Jazz Festival. The event draws musicians from all over the world who flood the city, playing in piazzas and open-air theaters and especially in the old Dei Differenti Theater, founded in 1600.

My thoughts are interrupted by the sight of two people racing across the stone walkway. It is my cousin and her boyfriend, Marco. The two are running and trying to trip each other and laughing so hard that they are nearly out of breath.

Marco is so good for Sandra, I tell myself for what is possibly the millionth time. Clearly her equal when it comes to talent and intelligence, but also possessing a playful streak that serves as an antidote to her overly cerebral existence.

"There is nothing more important than playing," I once heard him tell her when she scolded him for wanting to go swimming rather than continuing to work on a museum funding grant. "It frees up your mind and makes you even more productive in the long run." She listens, but only occasionally.

They sit down and I point out the card players, who are now finished with their game and in the process of ordering coffee. As luck would have it, Marco, who is originally from Barga, knows one of them. "*Ciao,* Carlo," he calls out.

Carlo turns out to be a friend of Marco's father, and before long he and two of his card-playing associates have joined us for coffee. I tell them how much I enjoyed watching their game, and eventually the conversation turns to Carlo's uncle Aldo, who, he says, "was not only the world's best card player but a master at *whatever* he played, whether it was soccer or the trumpet or the frequent jokes he played on people he disliked."

He launches into a story about Aldo and his friends deciding to get back at a particular teacher they hated. "They waited until it was dark and tied a thin string to the door knocker on the poor man's house. Now there were no streetlights then, so it was easy to lay the string across the street and leave it there without anybody finding out.

"When it was good and dark, the boys hid behind the bushes across from the teacher's house. At a certain point, they pulled the string and the door knocker started thumping. Pom, pom, pom. The teacher appeared on the balcony in his nightdress. *Chi e?* Who is it? The boys stayed silent.

"They waited until they were sure he had gone back to bed. And then they pulled the string again. Pom, pom, pom. The same response. The teacher in his nightdress out on the balcony. *Chi e?*

"They repeated the joke a third time, but when the teacher made his appearance on the balcony, he began shrieking so loudly that everybody came running out of their houses, thinking someone was being murdered. The boys were caught, and the next thing you heard were their own screeches as their fathers taught them the proper way to treat a teacher."

In the middle of our laughter, the taller of Carlo's two friends—Angelo—chimes in with a story of his own. *Allora c'era quella del Gaggini e la cioccolata. Ti ricordi il Gaggini?* The one about Gaggini and the chocolate. Remember?

The story concerns three boys—one named Gaggini—who waited until the village grocer received his annual order of bulk chocolate. "The chocolate was for the women of the village who needed it for the dense rice cakes they baked every year at Christmas. Since the grocer always stored the chocolate in the same place, the boys knew exactly where to go when they sneaked into the store after hours.

"There were over four kilos, and they ate it all—all of it! But that night when they got home, each one was sick. So sick that their parents had to call the doctor." Angelo pauses because Carlo has just remembered the story and is laughing and coughing hard enough to drown out the words. *O Dio, Gaggini!* he keeps saying. *O Dio, Gaggini!*

"Now, the doctor was a very smart man," Angelo continues. "And so he put two and two together. But to be absolutely sure, he went to see the grocer, to ask whether he was missing anything from the store.

"When the grocer—Pellegrini was his name, *ti ricordi, quel bastardo?* Remember that bastard?—realized what had happened, he started to scream about how he would seek reimbursement, about how he would have to pay for the chocolate regardless, about how he would take the boys' fathers to court. At a certain point, the doctor looked into the box and noticed a few remaining chocolate fragments. He picked them up and looked at them more closely. They were filled with little white worms.

" 'Is this the chocolate you plan to go to court over?' he asked. When Pellegrini said it was, the doctor gave him a good tongue-lashing, telling him how it had gone rancid and that he was lucky the boys had eaten it because he could have poisoned the entire town." Angelo finishes the story and is about to get up for another cup of coffee when he remembers what is obviously an important conclusion. "*Comunque*—however—the boys got a good beating anyway."

We say good-bye to the three men and are about to leave for the Duomo when Marco comes up with an important point. It is Sunday, and we can hardly go traipsing around the Chapel of the Holy Sacrament until Mass is over. His suggestion—readily accepted—is that we first have lunch. "We can go next door, to the Locanda Fuori Porta," he says. "The owners, Graciela Corsaro and Allesandro Manfredini, are friends of mine. They just bought it last year; before that, it had been another restaurant, La Luana, which was not very good."

He introduces us to Graciela and Allesandro and their three-year-old daughter, Giulia, who is too busy playing with her Barbie-like doll to notice our presence. Graciela, Marco adds, is also an amateur archivist, especially as regards the history of Barga. And so, at my request, she gives us a few facts about the town and its Duomo.

She tells us that the town was very successful in defending itself against invaders for more than three hundred years, until 1341. Then, she says, they got tired of such a besieged existence and decided to link their fortunes to those of Florence.

"The Duomo," she continues, "is built of a blond stone called *albarese di Barga,* and its facade is decorated with two leering lions. Over the portal, there's a strange relief of a scene from a banquet featuring a number of euphoric dwarfs. Inside there's a rather odd pulpit held up by four red marble pillars. One of the pillars sports a few more dwarfs; the others contain equally idiosyncratic figures: a lion grinning over a conquered dragon, and another lion being stroked and stabbed by a man."

We tell her that we're on route to see the Della Robbia terra-cottas and she nods in enthusiastic approval. "Don't forget to go around the back though, and see the gardens," she says. "There is a magnificent Lebanon cedar there, and if you go down the stairs, you will also see Barga's old corn measures—a medieval Bureau of Standards."

We eat a fabulous meal—everything from *zuppa di funghi porcini* (porcini mushroom soup) to *agnello con olive nere* (roast lamb with black olives). As we walk out the side door of the restaurant, we see Giulia, the owners' daughter, playing in the garden with a few of her friends. They are holding hands and twirling each other around in a circle. One chant is endlessly repeated: *O che bel castello, trullerille trullero.*

Out of the corner of my eye, I see Marco nudge Sandra. "Want to join it?" he asks. She grins and we are on our way.

ABOUT VEGETABLES

In the days when the Garfagnana was ruled by an assortment of dukes and counts, the land was divided into large vegetable fields that were all located along the Serchio River for purposes of irrigation. Each field was governed by laws prescribing what could be grown and in what quantity. Near Careggine, for example, each field had to produce at least four hundred cabbages, eight hundred onions, five hundred heads of garlic, and six hundred leeks. Family gardeners, however, could determine for themselves and most planted shell beans (many of which were dried for winter use), cabbages, onions, leeks, carrots, celery, winter squash, Swiss chard, a few heads of lettuce, and a few tomatoes.

Today the tradition of family gardens continues, with many people selling their excess produce at village markets.

Mushrooms

To the people of the Garfagnana, a "good" year is one in which the forests are blanketed with vast quantities of wild mushrooms. Prodigious gatherers, the Garfagnini rise early in the morning (no one has ever yet explained why mushroom gathering requires a three A.M. arousal) to comb the forest floor in hopes of filling their sacks with large quantities of the fifteen or so mushroom varieties that grow in this region. By law, Italians must use an open receptacle when gathering mushrooms to allow the spores to fall freely to the earth and repopulate the forest.

Mushroom caps are like sponges and should never be immersed in water. For the same reason, they should also never be placed under running water. The best method for cleaning (albeit laborious) is to use a mushroom brush or damp sponge and sweep the dirt away from the caps and stems one by one.

Parsley

While parsley is often used as an attractive garnish by American chefs, Italian cooks take this wonderful herb more seriously and consider it to be a quintessential ingredient. Since the dried variety is virtually useless, parsley—by which is meant the flat-leafed variety also referred to as Italian parsley—should always be bought fresh. After washing, it should be dried thoroughly before chopping to prevent it from becoming pulpy.

Lettuce

Tuscan recipes that include *lattuga* or lettuce as an ingredient generally intend the use of a Boston-type butterhead lettuce whose leaves are more tender than other varieties and light green in color. Other types that can be used include Bibb as well as the various types of loose-leaf or leaf lettuce (red, salad bowl, greenleaf). Crispheads and romaines or other cos types should be avoided.

Canned Tomatoes

Many of the recipes in this book require the use of canned tomatoes, by which is meant Italian plum tomatoes, which are sweeter than their American counterparts. Furthermore, canned tomatoes are like many other ingredients in that the best buy is generally the most expensive. More expensive varieties contain riper tomatoes and pack them in thicker liquid.

You will note also that recipes call for squeezing the tomatoes by hand rather than slicing them or otherwise shredding with a knife. The initial reason had to do with the reaction that took place when highly acidic canned tomatoes come in contact with non–stainless steel knives. Today, however, it is mainly an aesthetic consideration. When squeezing, rub the tomato back and forth so that it dissolves into long uneven shreds.

Dried mushrooms of the Garfagnana.

ZUPPA DI FUNGHI PORCINI

Porcini Mushroom Soup

Since, according to the Garfagnini, this soup should only be made with fresh porcini mushrooms, its appearance on their tables is restricted to the period between June and October, which is mushroom season. Generally only mushrooms that are 4 or 5 days old are used since, unlike "young" (2 or 3 days old) ones, those that are older impart a riper, richer flavor to this delicate soup.

   1 pound fresh porcini mushrooms (or substitute another type of
      wild mushroom such as shiitake, chanterelle, or morel)
   5 tablespoons extra-virgin olive oil
   2 cloves garlic, minced
   3 tablespoons minced fresh parsley
   1 teaspoon minced fresh mint
   Salt and freshly ground black pepper to taste
   ½ cup dry white wine
   6 cups Basic Meat Broth (see page 11)
   8 three-quarter-inch-thick slices peasant-style bread, toasted

1. Clean the mushrooms according to the directions on page 33 and cut them into rough three-quarter-inch-thick slices.

2. Heat the oil in a soup pot over medium heat. Sauté the garlic and parsley for 1 minute. Add the mushrooms, mint, salt, pepper, and wine and stir until the ingredients are thoroughly mixed.

3. Add the broth and heat to boiling. Cook, covered, for 15 minutes.

4. Divide the bread among 4 bowls, pour the soup over, and serve hot.

ZUPPA ALLA BOSCAIOLA

O

Woodcutter's Soup

The Garfagnini generally use coccore when making this soup. Coccore are small, very rare orange-colored mushrooms that look like eggs and grow in the forests throughout the area. Like porcini, they are prized for their pungent flavor and hunted religiously once mushroom season begins. Also like porcini, they are wonderful in both their fresh and dried form as well as pickled in vinegar or marinated in olive oil. Because coccore are largely unavailable in the U.S., the following recipe uses a variety of wild mushrooms to create a similar flavor, one that differs from the previous recipe for Porcini Mushroom Soup in both its heartier texture and more pungent fragrance.

> 12 ounces wild mushrooms (shiitake, chanterelle, or morel)
> 1 tablespoon unsalted butter
> 2 tablespoons extra-virgin olive oil
> 1 chunk (1 ounce) pork fatback, finely minced
> 3 tablespoons chopped fresh parsley
> 2 cloves garlic, minced
> 6 cups Basic Meat Broth (see page 11)
> 1 egg, lightly beaten
> ½ cup freshly grated Parmigiano-Reggiano
> Freshly ground black pepper to taste

1. Clean the mushrooms according to the directions on page 33 and then cut into rough chunks.

2. Heat the butter and oil in a soup pot over medium heat. Add the fatback, parsley, and garlic and sauté until the garlic is lightly browned.

3. Add the mushrooms and cook for 5 minutes, stirring often with a wooden spoon.

4. Add the broth and heat to boiling. Cook, covered, over medium heat for 15 minutes.

5. In a soup terrine, beat the egg with the cheese until a thick paste forms.

6. Pour the soup into the terrine and mix well to blend with the cheese paste. Add pepper and serve hot.

MINESTRA DI RISO
E PISCIALETTO
Rice and Dandelion Soup

The Garfagnini call dandelions piscialetto, *which literally means "piss in the bed," a reference to the greens' diuretic properties. "But they also make an excellent soup," says Velia Angelotti of Barga, "one that is perfect for early spring, not only because dandelions are at their most tender and succulent then, but also because that is when gardeners generally enter into their annual—and fruitless—battle to eradicate the persistent little plants." Perhaps by making such wonderful use of the greens, she says, "gardeners will develop an exalted place in their heart for dandelions and even grow them specially."*

    3 tablespoons unsalted butter
    1 pound dandelion greens, stems removed, cleaned and roughly
        chopped (reserve two or three leaves for slicing into slivers to
        use as garnish)
    1 medium onion, chopped
    2 leeks, white part only, washed, dried, and chopped
    1 celery stalk, diced
    8 cups Basic Vegetable Broth (see page 14)
    1 cup Arborio rice
    Salt and freshly ground black pepper

1. Heat the butter in a soup pot. Sauté the onion and celery over medium heat for 5 minutes or until the onion is soft. Add the dandelion greens and sauté for 3 minutes longer.

2. In a separate skillet, heat the remaining butter and sauté the leeks for 5 minutes. Place in a food processor and puree.

3. Pour the broth over the onion and dandelion mixture, add the pureed leeks, rice, salt and pepper, cover, and bring to boil. Reduce the heat to medium, and cook for 15 minutes or until the rice is tender.

4. Serve hot, sprinkled with the reserved dandelion slivers.

ZUPPA DI PORRI
Leek Soup

○

A delightful recipe prepared in the olden days by the Garfagnana peasants, leek soup is now once again in vogue, fueled by the demand for French onion soup or, even more, by its predecessor, carabaccia, *a Tuscan soup made with red onions and white wine. This particular version replaces the pungency of onions with the delicacy of leeks and advances the subtlety by adding tiny green peas.*

> 4 tablespoons extra-virgin olive oil
> 6 tablespoons unsalted butter
> 1 medium onion, diced
> 1 stalk celery, diced
> 6 cups Basic Meat Broth (see page 11)
> 5 leeks (white part only), washed, dried, and chopped
> 2 cups fresh or frozen peas
> 6 tablespoons minced fresh parsley
> Salt to taste
> 8 thin slices peasant-style bread (optional)
> ½ cup freshly grated Parmigiano-Reggiano

1. Heat 4 tablespoons of the oil and 2 tablespoons of the butter in a soup pot over medium heat. Sauté the onion and celery for 5 minutes, stirring frequently.

2. Add a ladleful of broth, as well as the leeks, peas, and half the parsley, and stir to mix well. Add salt.

3. Add the remaining broth to the pot and heat to boiling. Reduce the heat to low, cover, and cook for ½ hour.

4. Puree the soup, in batches, in a food processor. Return to the pot and heat until boiling.

5. Melt the remaining 4 tablespoons butter in a skillet. Toast the bread on both sides in the butter and divide among four bowls.

6. Pour the soup over the bread and serve hot, garnished with the remaining parsley, dusted with the grated cheese.

ZUPPA DI AGLIO

Garlic Soup

The ancient Egyptians were the first to realize the powerful medicinal qualities of garlic. They used it to lower blood pressure, to rid the body of parasites, and as an antibiotic. Graciela Corsaro, proprietor of Barga's Locanda Fuori Porta, also sees garlic as un disinfettante di sangue—*a blood purifier. "Every now and then,"* she says, *"a good garlic soup helps rid the blood of alien substances—if not because of any actual purifying properties, from the odor alone!"*

8 thin slices peasant-style bread
4 cloves garlic, sliced in half
4 cloves garlic, peeled and minced
7 tablespoons extra-virgin olive oil
2 very ripe Italian plum tomatoes, peeled, cored, and thinly sliced
8 fresh basil leaves, minced
6 cups Basic Chicken Broth (see page 12), heated
Salt and freshly ground black pepper to taste

1. Toast the bread and then immediately rub each side with the cut side of the garlic, 2 slices per garlic half. Place 2 slices in each of 4 soup bowls.

2. Heat 3 tablespoons of the oil in a soup pot. Sauté the minced garlic until golden. Add the broth, cover, and heat to boiling. Lower the heat and simmer for 5 minutes.

3. Divide the tomato slices among the 4 bowls, placing them on top of the bread. Sprinkle with the basil and drizzle 1 tablespoon olive oil over each portion.

4. Add salt and pepper to the hot broth. Fill each bowl with the broth, and serve.

ZUPPA DEI FRATI DI SORAGGIO ◖

Potato Soup in the Style of the Monks of Soraggio

The potato was introduced to the Garfagnana in 1815 by a monk from Soraggio, who had previously been a lieutenant in Napoleon's army. Its cultivation quickly spread to both mountain and valley regions, and by the mid 1800s the potato had become one of the Garfagnana's foremost food staples. Cut in half, potatoes were also used as a home remedy for scrapes and burns.

> 5 tablespoons unsalted butter
> 3 leeks (white part only), washed, dried, and chopped
> 2 pounds potatoes, peeled and cut into ½-inch chunks
> 4 cups Basic Chicken Broth (see page 12)
> 2 cups milk, heated
> Salt and freshly ground black pepper to taste
> 16 croutons fried in butter (see page 66)
> 4 tablespoons minced fresh parsley

1. Heat 3 tablespoons of the butter in a soup pot over medium heat. Sauté the leeks for 5 minutes, stirring frequently. Lower the heat. Add the potatoes, broth, and hot milk. Add salt and pepper, cover, and cook for 20 minutes.

2. Puree the mixture, in batches, in a food processor and return to the soup pot. Add 2 tablespoons of butter and simmer over low heat until the butter is melted. Stir to blend.

3. Divide the croutons among 4 bowls. Pour the soup over the bread and sprinkle 1 tablespoon parsley over each portion.

MINESTRA DI PATATE ALLA GARFAGNINA

Potato Soup Garfagnina-Style

In the Garfagnana, it has long been said that potatoes, butternut squash, and cabbages are the saviors of the winter kitchen. This recipe combines all three to create a thick hearty soup that is the perfect antidote to blustery winter winds.

8 cups Basic Vegetable Broth (see page 14)

6 potatoes, peeled and cut into tiny chunks

1 chunk (1 ounce) pork fatback, diced

8 ounces butternut squash, peeled, seeded, and cut into ½-inch chunks

8 ounces savoy cabbage, roughly chopped

6 fresh basil leaves, minced

2 cloves garlic, minced

¼ cup minced fresh parsley

3 tablespoons extra-virgin olive oil

2 tablespoons tomato paste

Salt and freshly ground black pepper to taste

8 ounces pastina

½ cup grated Pecorino Romano

8 sprigs fresh watercress, cleaned and with stems removed

1. Pour the broth into a soup pot and heat to boiling over medium heat. Add the potatoes, fatback, squash, cabbage, basil, garlic, parsley, oil, and tomato paste. Cook, covered, for 1½ hours. Add salt and pepper.

2. Add the pastina and cook for 7 minutes or until tender.

3. Serve hot, dusted with the grated cheese and garnished with the watercress.

ZUPPA D'INSALATA
O
Summer Salad Soup

The following recipe is a variation on the popular Tuscan soup called panzanella, *which is a mainstay of summer picnics throughout the province. The Garfagnini have added rice and broth to create a soup that is at once denser and more liquidy. Other summer vegetables can also be added and other kinds of broth, such as chicken and mushroom, would work just as well.*

3 cups Basic Vegetable Broth (see page 14)
8 ripe plum tomatoes, chopped
3 garlic cloves, crushed
1 small cucumber, peeled, seeded, and chopped
1 red onion, sliced into thin slivers
1 red pepper, cored, seeded, and chopped
1 yellow pepper, cored, seeded, and chopped
2 ounces red cabbage, sliced
4 ounces baby string beans, julienned
1 small carrot, scraped and grated
1 bunch watercress, thick stems removed and chopped
1 cup cooked Arborio rice, cooled
¼ cup extra-virgin olive oil
1 tablespoon balsamic vinegar
Salt and freshly ground black pepper
8 leaves fresh basil, chopped

1. Bring the broth to room temperature.

2. Place the tomatoes, garlic, cucumber, onion, red and yellow peppers, cabbage, string beans, carrot, watercress, and rice in a large bowl.

3. Whisk the oil and vinegar into the broth. Pour over the rice and vegetables and mix well. Add salt and pepper.

4. Ladle into 4 bowls and serve topped with the chopped basil.

ZUPPA DI ERBE LEGATE

Wild Herb Soup

This is one of the oldest recipes in the Garfagnana and, according to La Locanda Fuori Porta's Allesandro Manfredini, "one of the most unusual in that it depends for its substance not on an ingredient included in the soup, but on a light, airy omelet created from the very freshest herbs and greens." The omelet, he says, can either be sliced into wedges and placed in the soup as wedges or cut into smaller triangles and placed alongside the soup, a few to each bowl.

3 tablespoons unsalted butter

4 leaves fresh leaf lettuce, finely chopped

4 leaves Swiss chard, finely chopped

4 leaves spinach, finely chopped

1 bunch watercress, thickest stems removed, cleaned and chopped

1 cup fresh or frozen peas

8 ounces prosciutto, minced

⅛ teaspoon grated nutmeg

¼ cup chopped fresh parsley

⅛ teaspoon dried thyme

Salt and freshly ground black pepper to taste

2 tablespoons unbleached white flour

4 cups Basic Chicken Broth (see page 12)

2 tablespoons tomato paste

2 tablespoons unflavored bread crumbs

4 eggs, lightly beaten

1. Heat the broth to boiling. Lower heat, cover, and keep at a slow simmer.

2. Heat 2 tablespoons of butter in a skillet. Add the lettuce, Swiss chard, spinach, watercress, peas, prosciutto, and nutmeg. Sauté for 5 minutes or until the vegetables are wilted. Add the parsley, thyme, salt, and pepper and sauté for another 2 minutes, stirring constantly.

3. Sprinkle the flour over the mixture, then add a ladleful of broth and the tomato paste. Stir to mix well and cook for 20 minutes, stirring frequently.

4. Preheat the oven to 350 degrees. Grease an 8-inch square baking dish with the remaining 1 tablespoon butter and dust with the bread crumbs.

5. Add the beaten eggs to the vegetables, blend well, and pour the mixture into the prepared baking dish. Bake for 20 minutes or until lightly set. Cut into 4 wedges.

6. Ladle the remaining broth, into 4 bowls, top with a wedge of the herb omelet, and serve.

Barga's duomo rises majestically above the old town.

ZUPPA DELLA SIGNORA MATILDE ○

Matilda's Butternut Squash Soup

Originally cultivated by Native Americans, winter squashes were first introduced to Europe in the sixteenth century. But although there are many shapes and sizes grown in the rest of Italy, the Garfagnini restrict themselves to butternut squash, which they call simply zucca—*squash. Its culinary value is such that there is no such thing as a good vegetable soup made without butternut squash. This recipe is one I learned from Barga's Elena Malfratti who says it was named for her grandmother, Matilda. "Nonna was the type of woman who liked everyone to know what she accomplished," said Signora Malfratti. "We also have a* torta della Matilde *(Matilda Cake), a* Marmelata della Matilde *(Matilda Marmelade), and a* risotto della Matilde*."*

¼ cup extra-virgin olive oil

1 tablespoon unsalted butter

1 medium onion, diced

1 pound butternut squash, peeled, seeded, and cut into ½-inch chunks

Salt and freshly ground black pepper to taste

4 cups Basic Chicken Broth (see page 12)

8 ounces fresh spinach, cleaned and roughly chopped

3 tablespoons minced fresh parsley

¼ cup freshly grated Parmigiano-Reggiano

1. Heat the oil and butter in a large soup pot over medium heat. Sauté the onion until translucent. Reduce the heat to low. Add the squash and cook, covered, for 10 minutes. Add salt and pepper.

2. Add the spinach and broth and heat to boiling over medium heat. Reduce the heat to low, cover, and cook for another 30 minutes.

3. Pour the soup into the bowls and serve hot, dusted with the parsley and grated cheese.

ZUPPA ALLA POVERA
CON ERBE DI PRATO
Poor People's Soup Made with Field Herbs

According to Mario Venuti, longtime resident of Barga, this is very much a poor people's soup. In his day, he says, people gathered dozens of herbs from the surrounding hillsides and tossed them into the soup pot with confident abandon. He notes, however, that in his day everyone knew their herbs well enough to dispute the advantage of a little more wild radicchio or a little less mountain fennel. "Today no one knows anything about these personable plants that once were our very staples. They crush them with picnic cloths and then serve for lunch a soup made with herbs grown in glass-covered factories."

The following recipe modifies Mario's own in that it makes use of herbs that are more readily available. Those fortunate people with easy access to wild herbs and greens should, however, experiment with as many combinations as they dare.

> 10 cups Basic Chicken Broth (see page 12)
> 1 cup various fresh herbs (thyme, rosemary, oregano, fennel, parsley, sage, basil, etc.), washed, dried, and chopped
> 1 pound mixed greens (mustard, kale, dandelion, Swiss chard, watercress, spinach, etc.), washed, dried, and shredded
> 8 ounces fresh shelled *borlotti* (cranberry beans)
> Salt and freshly ground black pepper to taste
> 3 links fennel sausage, removed from casings and crumbled
> ¼ cup extra-virgin olive oil
> 4 teaspoons herb *battuto* (see page 10)

1. Place the broth, herbs, greens, beans, sausage, and oil in a large soup pot. Salt and pepper to taste. Heat to boiling over medium heat. Reduce the heat to low and cook, uncovered, for 2 hours, or until almost all the liquid has evaporated.

2. Pour the soup into the bowls. Stir 1 teaspoon of herb *batutto* into each bowl and serve hot.

ZUPPA DI VERDURA AUTONNALE

Autumn Vegetable Soup

In literally translating the term cavolo nero, *one comes up with "black cabbage," which connotes a round, dense head of tightly wrapped darkish leaves. When the Garfagnini use the term, however, what they* really *mean is* braschette, *a vegetable that is much like kale in both flavor and nutritional value, although its leaves are smooth edged, more wrinkled in texture, and darker in color. Since* braschette *is largely unavailable in the States, I have substituted kale, whose crispness and tang make a fine alternate.*

¾ cup dried *borlotti* (cranberry beans), soaked according to
  directions on page 169
1 tablespoon dried crumbled sage
1 red onion, minced
3 cloves garlic, sliced in half
5 tablespoons extra-virgin olive oil
1 chunk (1 ounce) pork fatback, diced
8 ounces kale, washed, dried, and chopped
12 ounces butternut squash, peeled, seeded, and cut into ½-inch
  chunks
12 ounces rutabagas, cleaned and chopped into ½-inch chunks
1 large fennel bulb, stalks and fronds removed, halved, cored, and
  sliced crosswise
Salt to taste
4 three-quarter-inch-thick slices peasant-style bread

1. Drain the beans. Place in a soup pot along with enough water to cover by 2 inches and the sage, onion, and garlic. Heat to boiling over medium heat. Cook, covered, for 1 hour, adding more water if the beans absorb too much of the liquid.

2. Drain the beans, reserving the liquid.

3. Heat 1 tablespoon of the oil in a heavy skillet over medium heat. Add the fatback and kale and sauté for 5 minutes, stirring constantly. Add the beans, the reserved bean liquid and the rutabagas. Cook, uncovered, for 20 minutes, stirring often.

4. Add the squash and fennel and cook, covered, for another 15 minutes. Add salt.

5. Divide the bread among 4 bowls. Pour the soup over and serve hot, drizzled with the remaining oil.

ZUPPA DI FIORI DI ZUCCA
Squash Blossom Soup

Squash blossoms are used for many of the quick summer soups generally served as a primo *at lunchtime. The reason, according to La Locanda Fuori Porta's Allesandro Manfredini, is that squash blossoms are picked in the morning when they're open and have a very short lifespan after they are picked. "If you are going to make this soup," he advises, "make sure the blossoms you buy are crisp and dry and picked that day, preferably in the early morning when they are still open. If there is any hint of wilting or a strong odor, make something else." Note also that although the soup is generically entitled, the ingredients call specifically for* zucchini *blossoms.*

> 2 tablespoons extra-virgin olive oil
> 1 clove garlic, halved
> 3 tablespoons chopped fresh parsley
> 6 zucchini blossoms, washed, dried, and cut into slivers
> 6 small zucchini, scraped and cut into thin rounds
> 4 cups Basic Meat Broth (see page 11)
> Salt to taste
> 8 sprigs fresh watercress, cleaned and with stems removed

1. Heat the oil in a heavy soup pot over medium heat. Sauté the garlic and parsley until the garlic is lightly browned. Remove the garlic with a slotted spoon.

2. Add the zucchini blossoms and zucchini rounds and continue to sauté, stirring often until the rounds are lightly browned.

3. Add the broth and heat to boiling over medium heat. Reduce the heat to low, cover, and cook for 35 minutes. Add salt.

4. Serve hot, garnished with the watercress sprigs.

ZUPPA DEI PRATI
Field Vegetable Soup

The culinary use of artichokes dates back to the ancient Romans, who called them cynara *because of the practice of sprinkling ashes, or* cenere, *over their growing fields to lend additional potash to the soil. The following recipe combines a number of flavors—the tartness of artichokes, the richness of prosciutto, and the delicacy of lettuce—to create a soup that, according to La Locanda's Allesandro Manfredini, "delights the eye, the nose, and, of course, the tongue."*

8 medium artichokes
¼ cup extra-virgin olive oil
1 chunk (2 ounces) pork fatback, diced
1 chunk (4 ounces) prosciutto, diced
Salt and freshly ground black pepper to taste
2 tablespoons dried mint
2 heads *lattuga* (Boston-type lettuce), washed, dried, and cut into
   crosswise slices
4 cups Basic Chicken Broth (see page 12)
16 croutons fried in oil (see page 66)
8 sprigs fresh parsley, cleaned and with stems removed

1. Remove the tough outer leaves of the artichokes and, using scissors, cut the spiny tips off the rest of the leaves. Cut the artichokes into four sections lengthwise and remove and discard the hairy inner core (the "choke"). Peel the stems and cut the artichoke sections into small chunks. Set aside.

2. Heat the oil in a heavy skillet over medium heat. Sauté the fatback and prosciutto for 2 minutes.

3. Add the artichokes, salt, pepper, and mint, cover, and cook for 10 minutes. Add the lettuce and continue to cook, covered, for another 10 minutes.

4. Add the broth, cover, and cook for 20 minutes or until the artichokes are soft and all flavors blended.

5. Divide the croutons among 4 bowls. Pour the soup over and serve hot, garnished with the parsley.

ZUPPA DI CARCIOFI O
Artichoke Soup

Artichokes originated in the Mediterranean area and were cultivated first in southern Italy and Sicily, where they were considered a delicacy and served in vinegar or brine. Centuries later, when Catherine de' Medici left Florence to become queen of France, she took her own cooks as well as numerous crates of this wonderful vegetable, which she subsequently introduced to the French. The following soup depends for its flavor on what the Garfagnini consider a "natural marriage"—that of artichokes and tomatoes. Unlike the previous soup, which also uses artichokes, this one is richer due to the sausage and meat broth and its pungent flavor is further accentuated by the addition of Parmigiano cheese.

> 3 tablespoons extra-virgin olive oil
> 1 chunk (2 ounces) smoked pancetta or bacon, diced
> 3 links fennel sausage, removed from casings and crumbled
> 1 medium onion, minced
> 8 artichokes, cleaned and cut into small chunks (see page 49)
> Salt and freshly ground black pepper to taste
> 4 ounces very ripe Italian plum tomatoes, peeled and roughly
>   chopped
> ¼ teaspoon dried thyme
> ¼ teaspoon dried sage
> 8 cups Basic Meat Broth (see page 11)

1. Heat the oil in a soup pot over medium heat. Sauté the pancetta or bacon, sausage, and onion for 5 minutes or until the onion is soft. Add the artichokes, salt, and pepper and cook, covered, for 10 minutes.

2. Add the tomatoes and herbs and cook, covered, for another 15 minutes.

3. Add the broth and heat to boiling, stirring with a wooden spoon until all the ingredients are well mixed. Cover and cook over medium heat for 30 minutes. Serve hot.

ZUPPA DI CIPOLLE AL LATTE
ALLA GARFAGNANA
Onion Soup with Milk, Garfagnana Style

Onions have long been used extensively as both a food and a medicine. In the time of the Romans, it was thought that onions made soldiers brave. The Egyptians also considered them a symbol of the universe and eternity because of their spherical shape. But the Garfagnini, like their counterparts in the rest of Tuscany, look at an onion and see merely what they call quei francesi mascalsoni—*those French rogues who, they say, stole the concept of onion soup and have now convinced the world it was theirs. "It was not," says the mother of La Locanda's proprietor, Graciela Corsaro, who visited the restaurant one day while I was there. "If you listen to the French, they invented everything. Ma che . . . !"*

        2 tablespoons unsalted butter
        2 medium onions, thinly sliced
        ¼ teaspoon sugar
        ¼ teaspoon salt
        1 cup Basic Chicken Broth (see page 12)
        4 cups milk
        16 croutons fried in butter (see page 66)
        8 sprigs fresh watercress, cleaned and with stems removed

1. Heat the butter in a soup pot over medium heat. Sauté the onions for 5 minutes or until soft. Add the sugar, salt, and chicken broth and stir until the liquid has been reduced by half.

2. Reduce the heat to low and cook for 20 minutes, stirring frequently.

3. Add the milk and heat to simmering. Cook over low heat for another 20 minutes, stirring occasionally. Do not allow the soup to boil.

4. Place the soup in a food processor and pulse once or twice until the soup is creamy and homogeneous.

5. Divide the croutons among 4 bowls. Pour the soup over and serve hot, garnished with the watercress.

MINESTRA DI VERDURE PRIMAVERILE

Spring Vegetable Soup

According to Barga's Mario Venuti, the arrival of spring means a complete change in both diet and way of life. "After a long winter of bundling into wool sweaters and eating heavy soups and stews—wonderful as they are—spring means we can throw off our caps, walk with bare feet through the grass, and eat bowl after bowl of fresh light soups." Like the following!

8 ounces fresh shell beans (any type)
1 ounce dried porcini mushrooms
8 cups Basic Chicken Broth (see page 12)
8 ounces baby green beans, stems removed, and cut into 2-inch pieces
2 new red potatoes, peeled and cut into small chunks
4 baby zucchini, scraped and cut into thin rounds
½ cup fresh or frozen peas
4 very ripe Italian plum tomatoes, coarsely chopped
3 tablespoons extra-virgin olive oil
8 ounces bow-tie pasta
1 tablespoon basil pesto (see page 10)
Salt and freshly ground black pepper to taste

1. Place the shell beans in a large pot, cover with water, and heat to boiling over medium heat. Cook, covered, for 45 minutes.

2. Meanwhile, soak the mushrooms in warm water for 30 minutes. Drain, rinse, and dice.

3. Drain the beans. Add the broth to the pot and heat to boiling over medium heat. Add both the green beans and shell beans and cook, covered, for 15 minutes.

4. Add the potatoes, zucchini, peas, tomatoes, mushrooms, and oil. Cover and cook over low heat for 25 minutes.

5. Stir the pasta into the soup and cook for 10 minutes or until tender. Blend the pesto into the soup, add salt and pepper, and remove from the stove. Let sit for 2 to 3 minutes before serving.

ZUPPA DI BASILICO FRESCO

Fresh Basil Soup

Basilico. *Just the word, says La Locanda's Graciela Corsaro, and one immediately thinks of summer and sun and crisp fresh flavors. The following soup does not disappoint, blending as it does the freshness of basil with the sharpness of pecorino and the sweet crunchy texture of pine nuts.*

      6 cups Basic Meat Broth (see page 11)
      4 red new potatoes, peeled and grated
      2 medium carrots, scraped and grated
      Salt and freshly ground black pepper to taste
      ½ cup freshly grated pecorino
      12 fresh basil leaves, finely minced
      4 tablespoons extra-virgin olive oil
      1 ounce pine nuts, crushed
      4 ¾-inch-thick slices peasant-style bread
      1 clove garlic, sliced in half

1. Place the broth in a soup pot, cover, and heat to boiling over medium heat.

2. Add the potatoes, carrots, salt, and pepper and cook for 10 minutes.

3. Using a fork, beat the cheese, basil, oil, and pine nuts into a thick paste in a bowl.

4. Rub both sides of the bread with the cut garlic, 2 slices per garlic half. Divide the bread among 4 bowls. Drizzle the basil mixture onto the bread, pour the soup over, and serve hot, dusted lightly with black pepper.

MINESTRA VERDISSIMA
Very Green Soup

O

Throughout the Garfagnana, this soup is used when someone is suffering from mal al fegato—kidney pains. I'm not sure how someone deduces pain in the kidney or why this particular soup is used, but there it is.

6 cups Basic Chicken Broth (see page 12)
1 cup fresh or frozen peas
⅔ cup Arborio rice
1 small bunch fresh parsley, chopped
4 ounces fresh spinach, washed and chopped
4 ounces fresh mustard greens, washed and chopped
4 ounces fresh dandelion greens, washed and chopped
1 tablespoon unsalted butter
2 tablespoons extra-virgin olive oil
Salt and freshly ground black pepper to taste
½ cup freshly grated Parmigiano-Reggiano
4 sprigs fresh rosemary
4 sprigs fresh thyme

1. Heat the broth to boiling in a soup pot over medium heat. Add the peas and rice and cook for 10 minutes, stirring frequently.

2. Add the parsley, spinach, mustard greens, dandelion, butter, and oil. Cook uncovered for 10 to 12 minutes, stirring frequently until the rice is tender. Add salt and pepper.

3. Serve hot, dusted with the grated cheese and garnished with the fresh herbs.

MINESTRA DI PASTA
ALL'UOVO E PISELLI
Noodle Soup with Fresh Peas

Fresh peas are rivaled only by asparagus in their ability to drive perfectly sober people wild with delirium at their arrival. In the Garfagnana, peas are sown in February, which means they are already on the table in May. "And believe me," says Graciela Corsaro of La Locanda, "in May they are on everyone's table." Like the preceding recipe, this one also uses fresh peas but its flavor-base comes from an initial vegetable sauté rather than from meat broth.

8 tablespoons unsalted butter
½ medium carrot, scraped and diced
½ medium onion, diced
½ stalk celery, diced
3 tablespoons chopped fresh parsley
1 tablespoon tomato paste diluted in 2 tablespoons hot water
Salt and freshly ground black pepper to taste
8 cups Basic Vegetable Broth (see page 14)
1 cup fresh or frozen peas
4 ounces thin egg noodles

1. Melt the butter in a soup pot over medium heat. Sauté the carrot, onion, celery, and parsley until the onion is lightly browned.

2. Stir the diluted tomato paste into the vegetable mixture and cook for 10 minutes over low heat. Add salt and pepper.

3. Add the broth and heat to boiling over medium heat. Add the peas and cook for 20 minutes, stirring occasionally.

4. Stir the egg noodles into the soup. Cover and cook for 5 minutes or until the noodles are tender. Serve immediately.

MINESTRONE ESTIVO   O

Summer Minestrone

When it is finally summer and the Garfagnini have moved their flatware and cutlery to wooden chests beneath their outdoor pergolas, summer minestrones become the rule. Thicker in consistency than the previous two recipes using fresh peas, this minestrone is meant to be eaten as a one-course meal, possibly served with a large bowl of arugula and radicchio, a dish of sliced tomatoes with pecorino cheese, a terra-cotta carafe of white wine, and beautifully resplendent sunshine.

    1 tablespoon unsalted butter
    2 tablespoons extra-virgin olive oil
    3 medium onions, diced
    1 pound new red potatoes, peeled and cubed
    1 pound baby zucchini, diced
    1 cup fresh or frozen peas
    1 head *lattuga* (Boston-type lettuce), roughly chopped
    8 ounces mustard greens, washed and chopped
    Salt and freshly ground black pepper to taste
    6 cups Basic Chicken Broth (see page 12)
    4 teaspoons herb *battuto* (see page 10)

1. Heat the butter and oil in a soup pot over medium heat. Sauté the onion until lightly browned.

2. Add the potatoes, zucchini, and peas and continue to sauté for 5 more minutes, stirring constantly.

3. Add the lettuce and mustard greens and stir to mix well. Add salt and pepper.

4. Add broth, cover, and heat to boiling over medium heat. Cook for 30 minutes. Pour into 4 bowls, stir 1 teaspoon of herb *battuto* into each and serve immediately.

MINESTRA DI PUNTE D'ASPARAGI O

Asparagus Tip Soup

The word "asparagus" comes from an old Greek term meaning stalk or shoot. The plant is a member of the lily of the valley family that originated in the Eastern Mediterranean where it still grows wild. Before it was used for food, asparagus was considered a cure for heart trouble, dropsy, and toothaches. It was even supposed to prevent bee stings. Early Roman records give detailed instructions on how to cultivate it, cook it, and even how to dry it. The following soup is generally prepared in springtime, when the first spears of asparagus begin sprouting from the ground.

1 tablespoon unsalted butter
1 medium onion, diced
1 medium potato, peeled and cut into tiny chunks
24 asparagus tips
¼ cup minced fresh parsley
Salt to taste
6 cups Basic Meat Broth (see page 11)
⅔ cup Arborio rice
4 ounces fontina cheese, cut into tiny cubes

1. Heat the butter in a soup pot over medium heat. Sauté the onion for 3 minutes or until translucent. Add the potatoes and cook for 5 minutes, stirring frequently.

2. Reduce the heat to low. Add the asparagus tips and cook for 4 minutes, stirring constantly. Add the parsley and stir to mix well. Add salt.

3. Add the broth and heat to boiling over medium heat. Add the rice and fontina cheese, cover, and cook, stirring frequently, for 10 minutes or until the rice is tender. Serve hot.

Chapter Three

A SENSE OF
COMMUNITY

Castiglione Di Garfagnana

PANCOTTE, PASSATE, E CREME
Bread Soups, Purees, and Cream Soups

*J*anuary 6 is a national holiday here, one whose importance equals that of Christmas. Officially known as the Epiphany, the event commemorates the day the three wise men arrived in Bethlehem bearing gifts of gold, frankincense, and myrrh.

Traditionally, however, the celebration takes place the night before and is called *Befana* in honor of the grizzled old woman who brings gifts to good boys and girls. Dressed in rags, with a kerchief on her head and carrying a broom, the legendary *Befana* rewards children by throwing a few candies down the chimney (for those who have chimneys) or by knocking at the door and flinging them into the house when someone answers. To children, this is the most important day of the year, one that is eagerly awaited despite the constant admonishments from parents and relatives: *Stai buono o la Befana non ti porta niente.* Be good or the *Befana* will bring you nothing.

Children who ignore the warning receive *carbone*—coal. In the old days, *carbone* was exactly that, a lump of coal. But today's *carbone* has evolved into a lustrous confection of black crystallized sugar sold in specialty stores and given to every child, good or bad, as a charming accompaniment to their real presents.

The problem, says Fulvia Bertolani, an old friend of my mother's who lives in a cozy *villetta* just inside Castiglione's eleventh-century walls, is that today's presents might as well *really* be gold, frankincense, and myrrh, what with how much they cost.

"When I was a child, our stockings contained very little," she says. "An orange, an apple, maybe a few chestnuts. If you received a piece of candy, you went to bed that night thinking you were very lucky."

Fulvia and I are sitting in the offices of La Misericordia, a lay organization that gives aid to Castiglione's residents in times of sickness and death. Most villages have their own Misericordias which are generally located near the main piazzas and serve as community health centers, with on-staff doctors and a complete schedule of health-related services.

Older residents make a point of sauntering past their Misericordia every morning to see if anybody failed to make it through the night; when someone does, his or her name is printed in large black letters on tagboard and posted out front along with the date on which services will be held. There are no funeral parlors, either in Castiglione itself or elsewhere in the Garfagnana. When someone dies, the Misericordia prepares the body for home viewing while arranging for church services and burial in the village cemetery.

The word misericordia means "mercy"; to some people—especially older ones—it also means "ambulance," since it is always the Misericordia's ambulance that transports people when they need to go to the hospital. "There goes the Misericordia," they say whenever an ambulance screeches through the town.

In Castiglione, except for the three ambulance drivers, who work on eight-hour shifts, and a staff doctor, all the Misericordia's workers are volunteers. Today being the eve of *Befana,* however, volunteers were somewhat harder to come by. So when Fulvia, who is head of the volunteer committee, mentioned that she needed someone to answer the phone, I offered to help out.

I know from previous experience with the Misericordia where my mother lives that answering the phone in a town the size of Castiglione can be a fairly easy task. After only twenty minutes, however, I receive a heartbreaking call from Viareggio, from a certain Dr. Mario Pucci, who was calling on behalf of Giuseppina Bellotti, known to most people here as Beppina.

The Bellottis, Giuseppina and her husband, Davide, always spend the holidays in Viareggio with their daughter and her children. This year, as they were on their way out to view the final preparations for the

Carnival floats that were to parade down the city's streets in just a few short weeks, a car hit Davide as he was crossing the street. He died on route to the hospital.

I hand the phone to Fulvia, who starts crying as soon as she hears the news. "Tell him we will send the ambulance immediately," she manages to get out. "Tell him also to assure Beppina that I will call everyone who needs to be called."

The first person she calls is the head of the Misericordia, whom she reaches at home where he is wrapping presents for his grandchildren. *O Dio!* he says as soon as he hears the problem. *Allora, c'è da partire subito.* Then we will have to leave immediately. He is in the office ten minutes later, calling the ambulance drivers to see which one can go.

Fulvia herself begins calling friends and relatives of the Bellottis to give them the dreadful news. As the minutes go by, plans begin crystallizing. Gianfranco, whose wife had planned a big *Befana* gathering complete with the roasting of a suckling pig, will drive the ambulance. Paolo, the butcher, and his wife, who is Beppina Bellotti's sister, will follow in their car, bearing hot minestrone and prosciutto sandwiches. Don Andrea and Don Fausto, the two village priests, will ride with them.

Then the Fruzzettis say they would also go—Bonaria and Roberto, the Bellottis' neighbors. Then the Stefanis—Laura, Francesco, and Laura's mother, Adorna, who are Davide's cousins. The Sebastianis— Pietro, Anna Maria, their son Walter and his own wife and children—say they will bring some bread, cheese, and their own just-marinated olives. Beppina likes those olives, Anna Maria says. And it will be a long drive from Viareggio to Castiglione, what with the snow on the roads.

Within an hour, the entire contingent is out in front of the Misericordia and ready to leave. As they climb into their cars, they are bid a safe journey by dozens of the Bellottis' other friends and relatives who, for one reason or another, cannot go, as well as by people who only knew Davide and Beppina in passing but have been told of the terrible occurrence and want to show their support. As the procession snakes through the narrow streets and exits Castiglione's walls, you can hear the sounds of women saying their rosaries. *Ave Maria, piena di grazie, Il Signora e con te . . .*

Certo, stasera sara una misera Befana, Fulvia says as we go back inside. Tonight will certainly be a pathetic *Befana.* Her words returned me to thoughts of the colorful event that is scheduled to begin at eight—the band, the procession, the old women dressed in rags and carrying brooms. I wonder how it will unfold.

In general, *la Befana* delivers her gifts at night, around 9 P.M. Hence the traditional verse:

> *La Befana vien di notte,*
> *Con le scarpe tutte rotte,*
> *Con la gonna, con le toppe,*
> *La Befana vien di notte.*
>
> *The Befana comes by night,*
> *With broken shoes,*
> *And a dirty patched dress,*
> *The Befana comes by night.*

The legend is an ancient one, and there are varying stories as to where and why it originated. To some, *Befana* was created as an antidote to the three sumptuously dressed wise men—as a modest symbol of common people everywhere. To others, her purpose is to teach children to make judgments based on things other than appearance. To yet others, she represents the eternal paradox between the beautiful and the repulsive elements of the world in which we live—a dirty, hideous woman delivering glorious gifts.

"Beh," Fulvia says when I ask for her opinion. "Somebody must know where the idea started, but it is most certainly not me."

She begins to reminisce about her own childhood experiences, about how she and her sisters and brothers would sit around the hearth, waiting for the first sound of rustling in the chimney. "We would sit there singing songs that were supposed to make her come sooner: *O Befana, sei la mi sposa, sei la mia dama, tirami giù QUALCHE cosa.* Oh *Befana,* you are my bride, you are my Lady, throw me down a little something. She smiles. "Our voices always rose to a high-pitched squeal when we came to the word *qualche.*

"Later," she says, "I found out that it was all a hoax and that the candies thrown down the chimney were the ones Papa had saved up from his card-playing victories.

"In my family, I found out first, being the oldest. I remember hearing a song at school one day—*La Befana è mi pa e mi ma, l'hanno nel banco è non me la voglian da. Befana* is my mother and father. They have my present in the closet and they won't give it to me. And suddenly I realized what had been going on all those years."

Then, she says, came the first *Befana* in which she was actually included in the deception by her mother and father. "Papa worried for weeks that he didn't have enough candies, especially in view of my brother Paolo's assertions that he had been especially good that year and thus expected a windfall. 'I only have these few candies,' Papa would groan again and again as the event approached. So Mamma and I ripped apart an old blouse and made beautiful wrappers for each of the candies, and when they finally made their way down the chimney, everyone, including Paolo, was delighted."

Paolo figures prominently in yet another of Fulvia's childhood memories, this one having to do with *torte coi becchi*—chocolate cakes with scalloped edges—which are a regional holiday tradition.

"Mamma generally made nine or ten cakes," she says, "each filled with a rich combination of dark chocolate, rice, and candied fruits. An enormous luxury, especially in those days when it was hard to get either chocolate or sugar, the cakes took two or three days to prepare and were expected to last the entire holiday season.

"Now Paolo was not known to be a big fan of the cakes. At least that's what he led our parents to believe. We, his brothers and sisters, knew otherwise; that he actually loved the filling—the chocolate part—but since he would never have been allowed to eat just the filling and leave the crust on his plate, he would always choose to wave away his share rather than allow Papa the satisfaction of determining what he could and could not do.

"On this particular day Paolo had, as usual, waved away his share. Later, however, when the house was empty, he slithered out to the pantry, climbed up to the top of the closet where the cakes were kept, and devoured the insides of the three largest ones. When Papa realized what had happened, he spanked all of us except Paolo. 'It was obviously not Paolo,' he said. 'Paolo doesn't like *torte coi becchi!*'"

She continues with a few more stories of long ago *Befana* celebrations, and then we leave the Misericordia together, promising to be back after dinner for tonight's event.

We are not yet finished with our espresso when we hear the band coming down the street toward the piazza. I look out the window and, sure enough, there they are: Roberto with his trumpet, Agnese with a clarinet, Ignazio with the cymbals, and Santi with the big drum. Behind them are two *Befanas,* one young, one old. Both are wearing old clothes and have kerchiefs on their heads. Both carry brooms and have their faces painted in order to give the appearance of being dirty.

A group of people march behind them, mostly teenagers, although they will soon be joined by a number of the town's middle-aged residents who have yet to finish their dessert and wash and dry the dishes.

For the next few hours, this little procession will move from house to house, stopping in front of those whose inhabitants have already indicated they would like to participate. What "participating" means is that the band will play in front of their window while the *Befanas* and the rest of the group engage in a spirited traditional dance. At the end of the dance, the band will stop playing and the group will chant in unison

> *Stiamo giunti in questa corte,*
> *O Padron se vuoi volete.*
> *Dunque, Signora se potete,*
> *Vien, apritici le porte.*

Which, liberally translated, means: We have come together in this courtyard, by your wishes, oh master of the house. And now, mistress, if you can, please come down and open the door.

At that, the *Befanas* and the band members hasten inside to collect a contribution to the Misericordia and have a glass of *vin santo.* So as not to completely subvert the tradition, however, the *Befanas* will also *hand out* a few candies.

They will not be the only *Befanas* in Castiglione's streets. A host of others are also making their rounds. In fact, in most houses with young children, the parents will have arranged with someone—the old woman down the street, the young teenaged girl who lives next door, even the boy who works for the butcher (as a last resort, a male can also play the part, in which case he is called a *Befanotto*)—to make an appearance for the sake of maintaining the tradition. Last year, Castiglione's streets *teemed* with *Befanas,* each carrying baskets filled with nougats, chocolates, oranges, caramels, apples, and cookies—*befanini*—baked in the shape of nativity characters.

Since Fulvia and I had said we would be back at the Misericordia by nine, we don our coats and hurry across the piazza. When the band is finished touring, they and their following will join us here for coffee and cake.

They finally arrive at eleven-fifteen, a group of 150 or so revelers who range in age from eleven to ninety. There are parents carrying babies, teenagers enfolded in their own small groups, elderly people walking on the arms of fifteen year olds, middle-aged couples with their arms around each other.

I am, as usual, amazed at the outpouring of people, at the camaraderie between old and young, at the guileless joy evident on their faces, at the absence of pretension. I felt the same way last time I was here, in June for the feast of Corpus Domine, which is a religious holiday commemorating the sacred body of Christ. For that tradition, residents engineer a continuous carpet of flowers spanning many blocks along the town's established processional route. They labor for hours, arranging thousands of beautiful blossoms in patterns that vary according to which group of volunteers created which particular stretch.

Work on the carpet actually begins at two the morning before. Men, women, and children fill the streets along the processional route, laying flowers and commenting on which color group should go where. By nine A.M. the entire town is out with their brooms and watering cans, making final adjustments before rushing home to change into their Sunday clothes.

At 11 A.M. residents begin processing alongside the carpet in two rows, singing hymns and praying. The town's priests lead the group, followed by a number of lay attendants dressed in white and that year's first communicants—small children also dressed in white and wearing gold crowns.

The *Befana* celebration breaks up around twelve-thirty. It has been a good night, and the Misericordia's coffers have swelled from the contributions. "Perhaps people felt more generous tonight," says Fulvia. "In view of poor Davide, may he rest in peace."

We leave together, and as we make our way down the street towards her house, we see two teenagers kissing on the low stone wall next to the hardware store. Fulvia recognizes them immediately and acquaints me with the background details: The girl is the daughter of the jeweler, and his mother and father are both teachers at the elementary school. Neither set of parents is very happy over the liaison; for one thing, the teenagers are too young.

"This is not the first time I have seen them here," Fulvia says. "Obviously it is a good place, since the streetlight has been broken for over a month." She taps her cane on the ground. *Andate a casa!* she tells them. Go home.

But they are too involved in each other to notice. *Dai, ragazzi,* she says again, this time with more volume. *Andate a casa!* Nothing.

Aspetta, she says. *L'accomodo io,*—I'll fix them—and she strides away from me with a vitality that makes me sorry for what is to rain upon these two star-crossed lovers.

Avanti! She cuffs them with her cane. *A casa! Non vi vergonate a farvi vedere dalle persone che passano?* Aren't you ashamed to be seen here by all who pass by?

The two are obviously startled, but they jump up immediately. *O scusa,* they stammer. *Per favore, scusateci!* We're sorry, please forgive us. And they amble away, continuing to excuse themselves until they have turned the corner and are out of sight.

"They will not be back," Fulvia says with obvious satisfaction. And then she rethinks her conduct. "I should have taken care of this the first time," she says plaintively. "Anyone else in town would have already gone and talked to their parents."

ABOUT PANCOTTE, PASSATE, AND CREME

Pancotto means "cooked bread," and *passate* means "pureed soups." Both, at one time, were used in feeding convalescents as well as children reluctant to eat foods with coarser textures. *Creme,* or creamed soups on the other hand, have always been considered refined foods for refined occasions, such as holidays or celebrations. Made with either milk and/or cream and eggs, creamed soups are thick, rich concoctions that are often served in small porcelain bowls. In many cases, *creme* and *passate* are served over croutons.

Making Croutons

There are two types of croutons: those fried in oil, which lend themselves to more rustic types of soups, such as bean, chickpea, and lentil; and those fried in butter, which are reserved for cream soups and broths. Croutons are best if the bread used is slightly stale. For four servings, 16 large croutons are needed.

To make croutons, cut 4 ¾-inch slices of peasant-style bread into 4 wedges each and divide into two batches of 8. Those fried in oil will require 4 tablespoons of extra-virgin olive oil. Heat half the oil in a heavy skillet over medium-high heat. Add the first batch of croutons and toss continuously until all sides are toasted. Drain on paper towels and repeat with the second batch.

Those fried in butter will require 2 tablespoons unsalted butter. Melt half the butter in a heavy skillet, add the first batch of croutons, and toss continuously until all sides are browned. Drain on paper towels and repeat with the second batch.

The Befana. *A dirty, hideous woman delivering glorious gifts to the children upstairs.*

PANCOTTO ◖

Pancotto, *which literally means "cooked bread," is a thick, farinaceous soup that at one time was prepared mainly for children and old people. Today this delightful concoction is once again popular with restaurateurs dedicated to keeping alive the hearty and succulent dishes of the old tradition. In summer* pancotto *changes its name to* panzanella, *which uses the same ingredients but assembles them raw. Its consistency resembles that of porridge.*

The undying popularity of pancotto, *alternately called* pappa al pomodoro, *is attested to by a song that was once—and to a large degree, still remains—one of Italy's most popular songs:* Viva la Pappa al Pomodoro—*Long Live Pappa al Pomodoro—sung by Rita Pavone.*

>   7 tablespoons extra-virgin olive oil
>   4 cloves garlic, roughly chopped
>   8 ounces very ripe Italian plum tomatoes, peeled, seeded, and
>   chopped
>   ½ cup chopped fresh basil
>   Salt and freshly ground black pepper to taste
>   1 lb. stale (or toasted) peasant-style bread, cut roughly into ½-inch
>   cubes
>   2 cups Basic Meat Broth (see page 11)

1. Heat 3 tablespoons of the oil in a soup pot over medium heat. Sauté the garlic for 1 to 2 minutes; do not allow it to brown.

2. Add the tomatoes and basil, salt, and pepper and cook for 10 minutes, stirring frequently.

3. Add the bread and the broth and continue to cook, stirring until the soup is dense and porridge-like. Serve hot, drizzled with the remaining oil.

MINESTRA DI PANE
DI TUTTI I GIORNI
Everyday Bread Soup

Says Fulvia Bertolani: "Without bread, Italians would die. During the war, you could only get it if you belonged to the Fascist Party, and believe it or not, people would make false identification cards and risk being killed in order to get one small loaf. A zuppa *without bread furthermore is like standing in front of a beautiful panorama and not having the eyes with which to view it."*

1 pound dried kidney beans, soaked according to directions on
    page 169
1 teaspoon dried crumbled sage
½ cup extra-virgin olive oil
2 small carrots, scraped and chopped
1 stalk celery, chopped
1 medium onion, diced
2 medium potatoes, peeled and cubed
8 ounces kale, washed, dried, and chopped
4 very ripe plum tomatoes, roughly chopped
2 small zucchini, scraped and sliced into rounds
12 leaves fresh basil, chopped
1 tablespoon chopped fresh mint
Salt and freshly ground black pepper to taste
1 pound peasant-style whole-wheat bread, slightly stale and cut
    into ½-inch chunks

1. Place the beans in a soup pot along with the sage and enough water to cover by 2 inches. Heat to boiling over medium heat. Cover and cook for 1 hour. Add more water if necessary.

2. Drain the beans, reserving the liquid, and pass through a food mill. Stir the mashed beans into the liquid and reserve.

3. Heat 4 tablespoons of the oil in the soup pot over medium heat and sauté the carrots, celery, and onion for 5 minutes or until tender. Add the potatoes, kale, tomatoes, and zucchini and sauté for another 5 minutes, stirring constantly.

4. Pour the bean broth over the vegetables, one ladleful at a time, stirring to mix. When all the broth has been used up, add half the basil and mint, cover and cook for 1 hour over low heat, adding more water if necessary to maintain a dense, soupy texture. Add salt and pepper.

5. Assemble the *minestra* by spreading 2 ladlefuls of the soup on the bottom of a soup terrine. Cover this with a layer of bread slices, laid end to end. Drizzle liberally with olive oil and add another layer of soup, then bread and oil, until all the ingredients have been used up. Let sit for 5 minutes, and then serve sprinkled with the remaining basil.

Remembering Davide:

Gianfranco: Era cosi gentile.
                  (*He was such a gentle soul.*)

Francesco: Si manchera molto.
                  (*We'll miss him very much.*)

PASSATO DI BORLOTTI CON VERZA

Fresh Cranberry Bean Puree with Savoy Cabbage

A passata achieves its dense texture by pureeing the ingredients after they have been cooked. The Garfagnini generally use a food mill, which leaves behind both the bean and vegetable skins. Another good reason for using a food mill is to experience the pleasure of what the proprietor of Castiglione's finest restaurant, Il Castello calls il mangiare fatto tutto a mano, *completely handmade food.*

1¼ pounds fresh shelled *borlotti* (cranberry beans)
1 teaspoon dried crumbled sage
2 cloves garlic, halved
3 tablespoons extra-virgin olive oil
4 ounce chunk prosciutto, diced
1 medium onion, diced
2 teaspoons chopped fresh parsley
6 leaves fresh basil, minced
2 tablespoons tomato paste diluted in ½ cup hot water
Salt and freshly ground black pepper to taste
½ medium head savoy cabbage, cored and chopped
3 cups Basic Meat Broth (see page 11)

1. Place the beans in a soup pot along with the sage, garlic, and enough water to cover by 2 inches. Cover and heat to boiling over medium heat. Reduce the heat to low and cook for 45 minutes.

2. Meanwhile heat the oil in another soup pot over medium heat. Sauté the prosciutto, onion, parsley, and basil for 7 minutes or until the onion is light browned. Add the diluted tomato paste to the prosciutto mixture, stirring to mix well. Add salt and pepper and cook for 10 minutes, stirring constantly.

3. Add the chopped cabbage, cover, and cook for 10 more minutes.

4. Pass both the beans and liquid through a food mill. Add the mash to the vegetables in the soup pot. Cook for 15 minutes, adding the broth, ladleful by ladleful to create a thick creamy soup.

5. Serve hot.

PASSATO DI POMODORO ALLA PANNA

O

Chilled Tomato Soup

Although sugar is used in this refreshing summer recipe, it is also important to use the very finest quality fresh Italian plum tomatoes available. Italian plum tomatoes are far sweeter than their American counterparts, and according to Il Castello's proprietor Paolo Pieroni, should be used exclusively.

8 very ripe Italian plum tomatoes, peeled and seeded
1 teaspoon sugar
1 medium onion
4 cups Basic Meat Broth (see page 11)
Juice of ½ lemon
1 teaspoon lemon zest
¼ cup heavy cream
1 chunk (4 ounces) prosciutto, diced
½ medium cucumber, peeled and seeded
Salt and freshly ground black pepper
5 fresh basil leaves, minced
16 triangles rosemary focaccia★

1. Puree the tomatoes in a food processor. Transfer to a bowl. Stir the sugar into the tomatoes, cover, and refrigerate for 20 minutes.

2. Cut the onion into thin slices. Place the onion slices in a piece of cheesecloth and press the onion liquid through the cloth into the pureed tomatoes.

3. Add the broth to the soup along with the lemon juice and lemon zest. Stir to mix well and refrigerate for another 20 minutes.

4. Stir the cream into the soup. Add the diced prosciutto and cucumber and stir until thoroughly mixed. Add salt and pepper. Serve cold, sprinkled with the basil. Garnish with the focaccia triangles.

★ Focaccia can be purchased in Italian specialty stores or bakeries. Flavored bread such as onion or prosciutto can be substituted.

LA MASCHERATA DELLA
SIGNORA BERTOLANI

Signora Bertolani's Vegetable Masquerade

*Fulvia Bertolani remembers that when she was young, she disliked vegetables of
any kind. "And so my mother, God bless her, pureed all my vegetables so that I
would not miss out on the nutrients they possessed. She would tell me it was una
crema—a cream—and somehow those were magic words, because I ate it, thinking I had never before eaten anything quite so delicious."*

    2 tablespoons extra-virgin olive oil
    1 chunk (1 ounce) Italian salami, diced
    1 clove garlic, chopped
    1 bay leaf
    1 medium onion, diced
    2 small red potatoes, peeled and diced
    2 small zucchini, diced
    2 small carrots, scraped and diced
    8 very ripe Italian plum tomatoes, peeled, seeded, and diced
    1 stalk celery, diced
    2 small red bell peppers, cored, seeded, and diced
    1 teaspoon chopped fresh thyme
    1 teaspoon chopped fresh marjoram
    1 tablespoon chopped fresh sage
    ½ teaspoon lemon zest
    8 cups Basic Chicken Broth (see page 12)
    Salt and freshly ground black pepper to taste
    8 fresh basil leaves, chopped
    2 tablespoons chopped fresh parsley

1. Heat the oil in a soup pot over medium heat. Sauté the salami, garlic, bay leaf, and onion for 5 minutes or until the onion is lightly
browned.

2. Add the potatoes, zucchini, carrots, tomatoes, celery, red peppers,
thyme, marjoram, sage, and lemon zest. Sauté for another 5 minutes,
stirring to mix well.

3. Pour the broth over the vegetables and heat to boiling. Reduce the heat to low. Add salt and pepper, cover, and cook for 30 minutes.

4. Puree the vegetable mixture and its cooking liquid, in batches, in a food processor. Return the puree to the pot and heat to boiling.

5. Stir the basil and parsley into the puree and remove from the heat. Let sit for 1 minute and serve.

An informal game of marbles outside the cafe.

IL PASSATO DEL PESCE
DEL CASTELLO

Il Castello's Fresh Fish and Tomato Soup

On Christmas Day, says Paolo Pieroni, this is one of the most requested menu items at Il Castello. "I think because many of our customers want the delicious flavor of fresh fish without having to worry about bones. I think also, however, that when you puree a fish soup, you have taken what is already a delicate food— fish—and rendered it even more delicate, and people appreciate the sheer artistry of the finished dish."

> 6 tablespoons extra-virgin olive oil
> 1 medium onion, thinly sliced
> 1 cup chopped fresh parsley
> 2 pounds assorted white fish fillets (such as haddock, Chilean sea
>   bass, monkfish, etc.), skinned and cut into small chunks
> 4 cups Basic Fish Broth (see page 13)
> 1 cup dry white wine
> 1 cup canned tomato puree
> Salt and freshly ground black pepper to taste
> 16 croutons fried in oil (see page 66)

1. Heat the oil in a heavy skillet over medium heat. Sauté the onion and chopped parsley for 3 minutes or until the onion is translucent. Reduce the heat to low, add the fish and simmer over medium heat for 10 minutes, stirring occasionally. Do not boil.

2. Pour the fish broth into a soup pot and bring to a boil. Reduce to a simmer.

3. Pour the wine over the fish and allow to evaporate. Stir in the tomato puree and simmer for 10 minutes, adding a ladleful of hot broth if necessary to keep the fish from sticking.

4. Pass the fish mixture through a food mill and return to the pot. Add the remaining fish broth, salt, and pepper and cook for 5 more minutes.

5. Divide the croutons among 4 bowls, pour the fish puree over, and serve hot.

PASSATO CON VERDURA GRIGLIATA ●

Vegetable Puree Served over Roasted Vegetables

The Garfagnini are very fond of grilled vegetables and serve them often as side dishes or as appetizers drizzled with oil. This particular recipe uses them as the base upon which sits a rich vegetable puree that makes wonderful use of summer's bounty. Try varying the vegetables to experiment with different flavors; the only fixed entity here is the concept of grilled vegetables topped by a creamy vegetable puree.

The Roasted Vegetables

4 baby zucchini, sliced in half
2 medium onions, thickly sliced
2 red peppers, seeded, cored, and cut into quarters
¼ cup extra-virgin olive oil
Salt and freshly ground black pepper

The Puree

8 cups Basic Mushroom Broth (see page 15)
2 small carrots, scraped and cut into chunks
2 stalks celery, cut in half
2 small red potatoes, peeled and cubed
2 ripe Italian plum tomatoes, chopped
2 small zucchini, chopped
½ cup chopped fresh parsley
5 leaves fresh basil, chopped
8 ounces butternut squash, peeled, seeded, and cut into chunks
5 stalks Swiss chard, stems removed, and roughly chopped
1 head *lattuga* (Boston-type lettuce), chopped
Salt and freshly ground black pepper
8 sprigs fresh watercress, thick stems removed

1. First grill the vegetables by brushing both sides of the zucchini, onion slices, and pepper quarters with olive oil, dusting with salt and pepper, and grilling over coals or in an oven-broiler.

2. Make the soup by placing the broth in a soup pot and heating to boiling over medium heat. Add salt, pepper, and all the herbs and vegetables except for the watercress. Reduce the heat to low, cover, and cook for ½ hour.

3. Puree the cooked vegetables and liquid in batches in a food processor and return to the pot. Cook until just heated through.

4. Divide the roasted vegetables among 4 bowls, top with the puree, dust with pepper, garnish with the watercress and serve.

Castiglione, a well preserved hill-top town nestled behind eleventh century walls.

PASSATO DEL PASTORE
Sheepherder's Sunday Soup

A rich semi-dense soup, this puree dates back hundreds of years, to the days when poor sheepherders wanted to serve something special for the holidays but had nothing except the regular everyday ingredients—vegetables and cheese. In this way, they managed to convince themselves that it was, in fact, a holiday without any belaboring of their resources.

> 4 new red potatoes, peeled and cubed
> 3 small carrots, scraped and cut into chunks
> 2 leeks (white part only), washed and chopped
> 4 stalks celery, chopped
> 8 cups Basic Chicken Broth (see page 12)
> 4 ounces soft creamy sheep's milk cheese
> Salt and freshly ground black pepper to taste
> ½ cup freshly grated Parmigiano-Reggiano
> 16 croutons fried in butter (see page 66)
> 1 small carrot, peeled and julienned, for garnish

1. Place the potatoes, chunked carrots, leeks, and celery in a soup pot. Add the broth, cover, and cook over medium heat for 30 minutes.

2. Puree the vegetables, in batches, along with the cheese in a food processor. Return the puree to the pot. Add salt and pepper and cook until just heated.

3. Blanch the julienned carrot in salted water for 3 minutes or until al dente. Drain.

4. Remove the soup from the heat and stir in the grated cheese.

5. Divide the croutons among 4 bowls. Pour the soup over the croutons and serve hot, topped with the julienned carrot.

PASSATO DI FESTA REALE ◖

Royal Festival Soup

Like rosemary and sage, asparagus has its origins in the Mediterranean, where it grows wild in both the sandy soil found along the banks of creeks and on mountainsides up to 1,500 feet in altitude. It also grows well in extremely dry climates and in rocky soil. Introduced to Italy during the time of the Romans, asparagus quickly became the favorite of kings, who requested it on feast days and at royal banquets. The following is a variation on the asparagus soup listed on page 57. Creamier and richer in flavor by virtue of the prosciutto, this royal soup serves as a perfect first course for the holiday table.

    1 head garlic
    2 tablespoons extra-virgin olive oil
    6 tablespoons unsalted butter
    1 chunk (2 ounces) prosciutto, diced
    1 medium onion, sliced
    1¼ pounds fresh asparagus
    6 cups Basic Chicken Broth (see page 12)
    Salt and freshly ground black pepper

1. Cut ¼-inch slice off the top of the garlic bulb so that the pointy ends of each clove are exposed. Brush with olive oil and roast in a 350-degree oven for 45 minutes. Cool.

2. Divide the bulb into individual cloves. Squeeze each clove to release the roasted garlic meat. Place in a bowl and set aside.

3. Heat 3 tablespoons of the butter in a skillet over low heat. Sauté the prosciutto and onion 3 minutes or until the onion is translucent.

4. Remove the tips from the asparagus. Blanch in a saucepan of boiling salted water for 3 minutes. Drain and reserve.

5. Cut off and discard the tough ends of the asparagus stalks. Peel the remaining stems.

6. Place the broth in a soup pot and heat to boiling over medium heat. Add the asparagus stems to the boiling broth, cover, and cook for 30 minutes.

7. Drain the asparagus stems, reserving the broth, and puree along with the roasted garlic in a food processor. Return the puree and the broth to the pot. Add the sautéed prosciutto and onion, and heat to boiling over medium heat. Add salt and pepper.

8. Just before serving, stir the remaining butter into the soup. Divide the soup among 4 bowls and serve topped with the asparagus tips.

Fulvia Bertolani and her husband Giuseppe.

ZUPPA FRULLATA PER CONVALESCENTI

Pureed Soup for the Convalescing

At Castiglione's market one day, I overheard one woman complain to another that it was the second or third time that month that her husband and children had come down with the flu. Zelmira, as she was called by the other woman, was very upset over both the situation and its accompanying reality. "The only thing we eat is pureed soup—I feel like my house is a hospital!" To which the other woman responded, "Excuse me, but when people are sick, what do you expect to make—tortellini with four cheeses?"

6 cups Basic Chicken Broth (see page 12)
8 ¾-inch-thick slices peasant-style bread
4 tablespoons unsalted butter
¼ cup freshly grated Parmigiano-Reggiano
Salt to taste

1. Place the broth in a soup pot. Heat to boiling over medium heat. Add the bread, cover, and cook for 15 minutes.

2. Remove from the heat and stir until the soup has become like a thick porridge. Stir the butter and cheese into the soup, add salt, and serve hot.

CREMA DI FINOCCHIO
Cream of Fennel Soup

⬤

Even today, with the area's newfound prosperity, the Garfagnini look upon cream soups as a bit of a luxury. Adele Palmiri, who lives on the Via Pozzole, offers her explanation for why this is so: "I suspect it is the color. That velvety white circle in your bowl that makes you think of angels and brides and the white dresses we never could have because they would get dirtier faster than gray. White is the color of rich people. Even now, when we see someone wearing a white coat or a white pair of shoes, there is a feeling that such a person must be well off."

2 large fennel bulbs, stalks and fronds removed, cleaned, halved, cored, and chopped
1 pound butternut squash, peeled, seeded, and cubed
6 cups Basic Meat Broth (see page 11)
2 egg yolks
½ cup milk
½ cup shredded Emmental cheese
Salt
16 croutons fried in butter (see page 66)
Freshly ground black pepper to taste

1. Boil the fennel and butternut squash in the broth for 15 minutes. Remove from heat and puree in a food processor.

2. Beat the egg yolks in a bowl with the milk. Add the shredded cheese and continue to beat until well blended.

3. Stir the cheese and egg mixture into the soup. Cook over low heat for 10 minutes (do not allow the soup to boil or the eggs will curdle). Add salt.

4. Divide the croutons among 4 bowls. Pour the soup over and serve hot, dusted liberally with freshly ground black pepper.

LA FINE DI AGOSTO

End of Season Tomato Soup

Paolo Pieroni, Il Castello's proprietor, calls this his "August savior." "When it comes to the middle of August, I suddenly find myself with too many bushels of tomatoes. By then I have already canned enough sauce to last a good long time, and recently I even started drying some of my tomatoes for use in the winter. This recipe came to me from a local woman who, I think, got it from someone in Castelnuovo. My customers love it. I do too."

Emboldened by the soup's already delectable flavor, I have dared to attempt an even further heightening of fragrance by adding sugar to sweeten the tomatoes a bit more and the meat broth, which I think gives a fuller, richer body.

1¼ pounds very ripe Italian plum tomatoes, chopped
2 medium onions, chopped
¼ teaspoon sugar
3 cloves garlic
Salt and freshly ground black pepper to taste
4 tablespoons unsalted butter
1 tablespoon unbleached white flour
4 cups Basic Meat Broth (see page 11)
4 ¾-inch-thick slices Italian-style whole-wheat bread
2 fresh basil leaves, chopped

1. Place the tomatoes, onions, sugar, and one whole garlic clove in a soup pot. Add salt and pepper, cover, and cook over low heat for 30 minutes, stirring occasionally. Puree in a food processor and reserve.

2. In the soup pot melt the butter over low heat. Sir the flour into the butter until a thick paste has formed. Pour the broth into the butter-flour mixture, ½ ladleful at a time, whisking constantly.

3. Stir the tomato puree into the soup and cook over low heat for 10 minutes.

4. Heat the broiler. Rub both sides of the bread with the remaining garlic, halved, 2 slices per garlic half. Cut each slice into 4 wedges and toast in the broiler.

5. Divide the wedges among 4 bowls. Pour the soup over and serve hot, sprinkled with the basil.

CREMA DI PATATE E BARBE

Cream of Potato and Rutabaga Soup

⬤

Castiglione's Adele Palmiri says this about potatoes: "In wartime, we would have given anything to have even one potato. There were times when we would go for days with no food at all because the Germans had come through and taken every-thing—poor fellows, they were starving too. Fortunately, every now and then we would go out into the fields and find one potato left out among the dried stalks. These we would treat with a respect near veneration and divide among sometimes four people." Similar to the potato soup on page 41, this version's richer and creamier texture makes it more appropriate as a Sunday soup rather than one for everyday. My personal variation is to serve the finished soup over a base of sautéed leeks.

> 1 garlic bulb
> 5 tablespoons extra-virgin olive oil
> 3 tablespoons unsalted butter
> 6 leeks (white part only), washed, dried, and chopped
> 1 pound medium potatoes, cubed
> 8 ounces rutabagas, cleaned and cubed
> 4 cups Basic Meat Broth (see page 11)
> 1 egg yolk
> ½ cup freshly grated Parmigiano-Reggiano
> Salt and freshly ground black pepper to taste

1. Cut ¼-inch slice off the top of the garlic bulb so that the pointy ends of each clove are exposed. Brush with 2 tablespoons of the olive oil and roast in a 350-degree oven for 45 minutes.

2. Divide the bulb into individual cloves. Squeeze each clove to release the roasted garlic meat. Place in a bowl and set aside.

3. Heat the butter and remaining oil in a soup pot over low heat. Sauté the leeks for 10 minutes. Remove half and keep warm in a covered bowl.

4. Add the potatoes and rutabagas to the remaining leeks as well as salt and pepper. Cover, and cook for 15 minutes.

5. Add broth and stir to mix well. Increase the heat to medium, cover, and cook for another ½ hour.

6. Puree the soup in a food processor along with the roasted garlic and return it to the soup pot.

7. Beat the egg yolk with the cheese in a bowl until a thick paste has formed. Whisk the egg and cheese mixture into the puree. Add salt and pepper and cook for 2 more minutes or until the soup is heated (do not allow the soup to boil or the egg will curdle).

8. Divide the reserved leeks into 4 bowls, cover with soup, and serve hot.

Watching four Garfagnini play Briscola is the very best way to understand everything you need to know about the way of life in this region.

VELLUTATA DI PESCE
Creamy White Fish Soup

◖

In many restaurants, creamy white fish soup is served as an appetizer, possibly because it gives the appearance of being so light. "I'm not sure you can adequately use the word 'light' when talking about a soup that contains cream and butter," says Fulvia Bertolani. "But what are we here for if not to occasionally and delightfully delude ourselves in this manner?" The following soup differs from the Fresh Fish and Tomato Soup on page 75—that one derives its flavor from a blending of white wine and tomatoes; this one, from a béchamel-like blend of eggs, butter, milk, and cream.

2 tablespoons extra-virgin olive oil

1 large onion, diced

1½ pounds assorted white fish fillets, skinned and cut into chunks

½ cup canned Italian plum tomatoes, squeezed until shredded and with liquid reserved

Salt and freshly ground black pepper to taste

1 cup milk

2 tablespoons unsalted butter

1 tablespoon unbleached white flour

4 cups Basic Fish Broth (see page 13)

2 eggs

¼ cup heavy cream

1 cup chopped fresh parsley

1. Heat the oil in a skillet over medium heat. Sauté the onion for 3 minutes or until translucent. Reduce the heat to low. Add the fish, crushed tomatoes, salt, and pepper, and simmer for 20 minutes, adding water if necessary to keep the fish from sticking.

2. Remove the fish and vegetables from the skillet and pass through a food mill. Place the puree in a bowl and add the milk, stirring with a wooden spoon until the mixture is a dense, souplike consistency.

3. Melt the butter in a soup pot over medium heat, add the flour, and stir until a thick paste has formed. Pour the fish and milk mixture into the pot a little at a time, whisking constantly. Add the broth, adjust for salt and pepper and heat through over low heat. Do not allow it to boil. Immediately remove from the heat and let sit for 3 minutes.

4. Beat the eggs with the cream in a bowl and stir the mixture into the soup along with the chopped parsley. Stir to blend. Heat through and serve.

VELLUTATA DI CARCIOFI ◖

Artichoke Velouté

"If your artichokes are not fresh," says Signora Adele Palmiri, "you might as well not even begin the soup." The Signora tests for freshness by rubbing the artichokes together. "If they squeak, they are fresh. Likewise, if they are closed tightly like a new rose. If the petals have even slightly begun to open, put it back and choose another." The following recipe uses only the stems of artichokes whose flavor is smoother and sweeter than that of the leaves. This, however, is much easier to do in Tuscany, which grows only the long-stemmed mazzeferate *artichokes. Try to compensate by choosing the longest-stemmed artichokes available. A good use for the remaining sections is to stuff them since cooking stuffed artichokes requires first removing the stems.*

> 18 large artichokes, stems attached
> 5 tablespoons unsalted butter
> 1 tablespoon unbleached white flour
> 6 cups Basic Meat Broth (see page 11)
> ¼ cup heavy cream
> 1 tablespoon herb *battuto* (see page 10)
> Salt and freshly ground black pepper to taste

1. Peel the stems of each of the artichokes and then slice them away from the body at the point at which the leaves begin to sprout. Slice the stems into short thin slivers and boil in a saucepan of salted water for 5 minutes. Drain. Reserve the artichokes for another use.

2. Heat 2 tablespoons of the butter in a skillet over low heat. Add the drained artichoke stems and sauté for 5 minutes, stirring constantly.

3. Melt the remaining butter in a soup pot over medium heat. Stir the flour into the butter until it has formed a thick paste. Pour 4 cups of the broth over the flour-butter roux, whisking constantly until thickened and smooth. Add the sautéed artichoke stems and cook over low heat for 10 minutes, adding a few tablespoons of the remaining boiling broth if necessary to maintain the desired fluidity.

4. Puree the soup in a food processor and return to the pot. Add the remaining broth and heat to boiling over medium heat.

5. Remove from the heat and let sit for 3 minutes. Stir the cream into the soup, add the herb *battuto*, salt, and pepper and serve immediately.

CREMA CON PESTO DI PEPPERONI
Cream Soup with Red and Yellow Pepper Pesto

This is a fairly new recipe invention that comes from Il Castello's Paolo Pieroni who says the original idea came from the peperonata *his grandmother used to make. "Nonna would chop red peppers very fine, sauté them in garlic and oil, and serve them as a spread on freshly made bread. I remember not only the flavor but the color—that brilliant red."*

My variation adds a few other colors. I have also toned down the flavor by adding the peppers to a velvety soup base. Paolo's nonna would, I hope, love it.

2 tablespoons unsalted butter
1 medium onion, chopped
2 medium red potatoes, peeled and diced
6 cups Basic Chicken Broth (see page 12)
½ cup heavy cream
1 red pepper, seeded, cored, and quartered
1 yellow pepper, seeded, cored, and quartered
1 green pepper, seeded, cored, and quartered
8 leaves fresh basil, slivered

1. Heat the oil in a soup pot over medium heat. Sauté the onion for 5 minutes or until soft. Add the potatoes and the broth, cover, and cook for 15 minutes.

2. Meanwhile puree the red pepper in a food processor. Remove and set aside.

3. Puree the yellow pepper and set aside, and then the green.

4. Stir the cream into the soup and heat through. Do not allow to boil.

5. Pour the soup into 4 bowls. Top with a tablespoon each of red, yellow, and green pepper purees. Sprinkle with the slivered basil and serve.

Top: Il Castello's *proprietor, Paulo Pieroni.*
Bottom: *Graciela Corsaro and Allesandro Manfredini, proprietors
and chefs of the* Locanda Fuori Porta.

Chapter Four

TWO POINTS OF VIEW

Castelnuovo Di Garfagnana

ZUPPE DI GRANO—RISO, FRUMENTO, POLENTA, E CASTAGNE
Grain Soups—Rice, Pasta, Polenta, and Chestnuts

Signora Rosa Puliti is eighty-one years old and lives with her sister, Lidia, in a lovely apartment overlooking the Porta Miccia, an eleventh-century portal through which one enters the walled city of Castelnuovo. A sprightly woman for any age, Signora Puliti presides over an empire of eponymously named small shops located on Castelnuovo's main street, Via Garibaldi. The shops sell everything from stockings and embroidery thread to dresses and leather jackets.

I have come today to visit the Signora because she has long wanted to show me the pictures taken by her father during the war, pictures that bear testimony to the tremendous damage inflicted on the town of Castelnuovo. *Era tutta una rovina,* she says. The entire city was in ruins.

When we have previously talked about this subject, I am not sure what I imagined. Tuscans of a certain age love to wax about the war, and their stories generally revolve around fear and poverty and what they did to survive. To the people of Castelnuovo, however, "war" meant all those things and more.

The city was under siege for nine months beginning on September 8, 1943, when Italy broke with the Axis powers and entered into partnership with the Allies. As a result, Mussolini fled to Lombardy, where he established his final government, the Republic of Saló! By then, of course, King Vittorio Emanuele of Savoy had already gone into exile, leaving Italy virtually without leadership.

From then on, the Signora says, the country was involved in both a war with the Germans and a civil war that pitted those still loyal to Mussolini against the partisans who had always fought on behalf of the Allies. To complicate matters even further, Hitler's strategists drew a defensive demarcation, much like France's Maginot Line, that was called the Linea Gottica. The boundary ran from the Adriatic at Rimini to the Mediterranean at Massa-Carrara and, unfortunately, right through the center of Castelnuovo. The city became a pawn in the battle between the Germans, the partisans, and the Americans.

"Nobody knew who was who anymore," says Signora Puliti. "The Germans and Mussolini's Italians were here fighting the Italian partisans and the Americans, and everybody was dressed in outfits designed to fool the other side, but, essentially, everyone looked the same. The Americans were bombing the city to liberate us, the Germans were on the ground fighting to reclaim us, the partisans were blowing up bridges and roads to secure the city for our safety, and all we knew was that people were dying by the hundreds."

There was much praying in Castelnuovo that year, the Signora says. "When we could, we went to church, and when we couldn't, we would meet in small groups and say the rosary. And in the end, our prayers produced *something,* because we had a better harvest in 1944 than we have ever had before or since. Chestnuts by the bushel. Mushrooms, berries, wild greens. Even what pigs we had were fatter."

The worst day of her life, she says, came in February of 1945, when the Germans were nearing the end of their ability to wage war. "The Allies were close to controlling the area, and one day six or seven American planes flew overhead, dropping supplies down to their ground soldiers. Well, naturally, the Germans launched an attack that night, hoping to steal the supplies, which by then, of course, we had retrieved and hidden in our homes.

"I was at home with my aunt; we were alone in the house because the men had gone to hide up in the hills and the women had gone with them to act as a front."

The Germans arrived with a fury, she says, breaking down all the doors in town. "They barged into the houses and told us that if the men were not there in five minutes, they would burn down our homes.

Having delivered their ultimatum, they stormed out. We were terrified, my aunt and I, wondering what we could do to save ourselves when, suddenly, I looked out the window and saw one of my family's servants blithely walking down the street accompanied by four or five soldiers. She had come to tell me not to worry, that my family was all right.

"The poor girl thought her escorts were partisans, but my aunt knew better. 'They're Germans,' she told her in what she hoped was an unintelligible dialect. But the soldiers understood and hastened to convince my aunt that it was not true, that they were, in fact, partisans.

"Just at that moment, however, the other Germans came back, and there was a faint flicker of recognition between them and the girl's companions. But it was enough. Well, the poor girl fainted and I fainted and my aunt was reduced to tears, begging them to spare her life."

Ultimately the girl was spared, the Signora says, adding that some Germans were better than others. "But after that, I was sent away to the mountains, to the home of another aunt whose town was not located directly in the crossfire."

Since it is time for lunch, the Signora and I don our coats and walk up the street toward Da Carlino, Castelnuovo's finest restaurant and one of the most famous in Garfagnana, if not in all of Tuscany. We are going to have lunch with Carlino himself, who is a friend of Signora Puliti's.

But then she remembers that she wanted to stop off at the market to pick up some polenta for tonight's dinner. She also has to see about buying a new pair of gloves, since the weather has recently turned somewhat colder than usual and, despite her best efforts, the buyer for her stores is chronically unable to find her a pair that fits. "Carlino is always late anyway," she tells me by way of explanation, "and it would be a shame if you left without seeing our market."

Thursday is market day in Castelnuovo, she tells me excitedly. The day when hundreds of people come from as far as thirty kilometers in every direction to buy and sell wares ranging from cardoons to live roosters to silk negligees. "On Thursdays the city is transformed," she says, "into an even livelier place than it is on the other six days." Her voice takes on a certain air of authority. "We *are,* after all, the provincial capital of the Garfagnana."

We hurry along the narrow street until we arrive in the main piazza, which is located in the shadow of the fourteenth-century *rocca* castle—

which once housed poet Ludovico Ariosto, author of *Orlando Furioso,* the great Renaissance epic of chivalry and fantasy.

The piazza itself is filled, but only with men. Hundreds of men. Men of every age, of every shape and size. Men in suits, men dressed as laborers, men smoking pipes, men eating *focaccia,* men filling out lotto forms. All are standing, some in groups of eight or nine, some involved in conversation with another person, some alone. There is a great din in the enclosed square, a din fueled by conversations ranging from the mundane (*e un po freddino oggi*—It's a little chilly today) to the important (*allora se ci vuole un permesso, si dovra andare in commune*—If we need to have a permit, we will have to go down to City Hall) to the passionate (*Ma che sei, cretino? Tutti lo sano che la prossima volta Juventus gli fara i capelli a la Parma*—What are you, an idiot? Everyone knows that next time Juventus will beat the pants off Parma). The last is a discussion of two extremely popular soccer squads.

"What's going on here?" I ask when it becomes clear Signora Puliti does not see this situation as warranting an explanation.

She glares at me as if to say, what are you talking about?

"The men. Why is the piazza filled with only men?"

Her answer is accompanied by the kind of shoulder shrugging one uses when stating the incredibly obvious. *E, le donne sono a far la spessa, no?* Eh, the women are off doing the shopping, no?

We—true to the Signora's prediction—arrive at the restaurant before our host. According to the maître d', Carlino is on his way back from Lucca, where he journeyed yesterday to inventory the antique furniture emporiums he owns in that city. We should make ourselves at home, he says, and seats us in the private dining hall.

The room is beautifully decorated in a rustic style approximating that of a seventeenth-century country mansion, filled with antiques ranging from a huge old copper chestnut masher to a sixteenth-century breakfront filled with Majolica dishes.

We have barely finished our aperitif—a bracing snifter of Cynar—when Carlino arrives, sweeping across the room with the baronial flair of someone used to making grand entrances. He flings his cape into the hands of the waiter behind him and bows low before us, kissing Signora Puliti's outstretched hand. *Ciao, Carlino, come va,* she says nonchalantly.

"Ah," he says facetiously, eyeing me to gauge my reaction. "Just look at the state to which I have been reduced. Three times I have broken my knee in the past ten years. Finally the doctor counseled me, *Tieni duro, Carlino*—Hold hard, Carlino—and so, what other choice did I have—I bought myself a cane!" He laughs a grandiose laugh and holds up the cane for our viewing. It is obviously not just *any* cane, with its polished ebony staff and elaborate silver crown.

Carlino, it is clear from his opening words, is very different from the Signora, despite the proximity in both their ages (he is eighty-four) and upbringing. Like her, he was born in Castelnuovo and has lived here all his life. Unlike her, however, he laughs at the past and calls it "his schooling."

"I have never been one to crumble in the face of adversity," he says firmly. "To lie down and admit defeat. If I can't use the experience as a stepping-stone to something better, I forget about it. Why clutter my mind?"

He asks if I have seen his Maccaris and I say yes, having noticed them clustered on the walls as we came in. Maccari is one of Italy's most famous painters, and Carlino's collection contains more than a few, many with personal dedications. The ones I like best are both quirky pen-and-ink sketches; one of a fat man lying on his back that says, *Quanto o mangiato!* I've eaten far too much!; and the other, of Sylvia Koscina, a famous Italian actress, portrayed with pursed lips and a bubble over her head that says, *Sai di baccalà. Sei stato da Carlino.* You smell like *baccalà.* You must have been to Carlino's.

The one of the fat man is inscribed with dozens of signatures, and I ask about its significance. Carlino explains that every year, on his birthday, which is November 4, he gives an enormous dinner and invites many of his closest friends. "I was, coincidentally, born on the feast day of Saint Carlo," he says facetiously, "and at one point early in my career as a restaurateur, someone suggested that I give a dinner to celebrate this amazing synchronicity. So I did. The first dinner was for six, the second for twelve, then fifty, then a hundred, and this year, there were a hundred fifty-two people here."

I amble over to the frame and glance at the signatories. Quite a few are names I recognize—government figures, local celebrities, film personalities. He tells me the story of one who is now a member of the Senate. "Our friendship goes back many years," he says. "From the days when *quel fanciullo*—that young lad—was just starting out and went to Sardinia to work as a teacher. It was there, actually, that he made the decision to run for office.

"And when he was finally elected, he returned to Castelnuovo and gave a fabulous dinner, with twenty-four lobsters flown in live from Sardinia. At one point, he rose to toast his guests. 'I want to thank you all for your loyalty,' he said. 'In Garfagnana, even the chestnuts on the trees voted for me.'"

I ask about his life back when and he laughs. "You probably think I was *born* on a white horse," he says. "But you are wrong. I have had many jobs in my life, from being a butcher to raising silk worms to earning a diploma as an antiquarian and opening a shop."

He opened this restaurant, he says, on August 28, 1939. "I knew that, with the market here on Thursday, I couldn't go wrong. From the very first week, I was serving fifty dinners on Thursday and selling twenty-four liters of wine.

"During the war, the Germans bombed this site and I had to temporarily move the restaurant to another location—to down there"—he points down the street to where his daughter-in-law, Loredanna Gai-Andreucci, now runs an antique furniture store. "The day after the bombs fell, I put white linen cloths on the tables in the new location and planted a big sign out front: *Da Carlino, oggi trote!* At Carlino's today, freshwater trout! No German was going to stop me from serving my customers."

I ask if he was ever in the army, and he says that he was a partisan, that he was captured at one point by the Germans and taken to a prison in Lucca, where he spent fifteen days. "But then I escaped, and as I was walking along the road, I was stopped by a German commander. He began questioning me—'Where are your papers? Where are you going?'—and then realized suddenly who I was; that he knew me from the days when he was assigned to one of the platoons building the road to Arni and I had loaned him my storeroom to house his supplies."

He gives me a sly wink. "The road to Arni was going to benefit *us* too, you know."

So the German told him to get in the car, that he would take him home. "When we got to Borgo a Mozzano," he says, "the SS guard stopped us and wanted to know who I was. For me, it could easily have been the end. But, the German commander merely said that I was one of his workers, and after a few more questions they finally let us pass."

The soup we have for lunch is a specialty of this restaurant, a dish that was created by Carlino's wife, Virginia, who was one of the original cooks. "In the old days we kept everything in its own specific bin," he says, "The *farro* in one, the *cannellini* beans in another, the *borlotti* in yet another. We threw away nothing, but when we got to the end of the bins, there was never enough of any ingredient to make a complete dish. So Virginia created this soup, *mescola alla garfagnana* ("Garfagnana blend"), using a small quantity of many different things—lentils, favas, chickpeas, *fascistini* (small black beans). Each of course requires its own soaking and cooking, but the result is well worth the effort."

Because we are dining with Carlino, we eat far more than either of us would otherwise consider. After the soup course we move on to *linguine coi frutti di mare* (linguine with fruits from the sea), which is followed by *arrosto di maiale con patatine fritte e rape soffritte* (roast pork with fried potatoes and sautéed turnip greens), and finally, some fruit, a few wedges of cheese, a slice of *torta di cioccolata* (chocolate cake), a snifter of *grappa* (brandy), and coffee.

We also drink more—everything from a 1994 Vernaccia to a wonderful 1989 Brunello di Montalcino to a 1994 Vino del Cardinale— Cardinal's wine—which is a wine made in the Versilia region of western Tuscany by a vintner who produces less than one thousand cases of it annually. "He chooses the grapes individually," Carlino explains, "discarding any that are less than perfect."

Signora Puliti has said very little during lunch. She plainly likes Carlino very much, however, and obviously he returns the feeling. And yet it is clear they speak two different languages and travel in two different worlds.

To him, the world is a delightful place; to her, a scary one. To him, one moves forward regardless of the obstacle; to her, you sit and wait to see if someone takes the obstacle away. He laughs constantly; she, only occasionally, and even then it is more of a grin than an outright laugh. He loves autumn and sees it as a time of renewal; she becomes melancholy at the first sign of autumn—to her, it is a time of death.

I have spent a large part of this lunch assessing and comparing these two Castelnuovo elders, sometimes moving closer to her, sometimes to him. They are both delightful people, and yet they are as different as chestnut flour and *farro*.

As the waiter arrives to clear the table, I realize finally that, of all their differences, the most pronounced is in the way they embody the dual character of the Garfagnino. The Signora, with her war memories and photo archives, represents the past, while Carlino—aggressive, successful, and energetic—points unquestionably to the region's rich and vibrant future.

ABOUT RICE, PASTA, POLENTA, AND CHESTNUTS

Grain soups are very popular in the Garfagnana, unquestionably because they once filled the stomach and thus allowed the mind a brief respite from thoughts of poverty. For the most part, they are eaten as one-dish meals and without the addition of either bread or croutons.

Rice

Although there are many types of rice in the Garfagnana, Arborio is the type used exclusively for soups. One reason has to do with its superior quality, to the fact that its polished kernels are all the same size and therefore produce a more evenly cooked dish. Another is that the kernels are larger than other rices and thus can withstand a longer cooking time without dissolving. Arborio rice can be purchased in most specialty food shops.

Pasta

Italian pastas are, by law, made of durum wheat, which is a harder grain than that used by American pasta makers. Only Italian pasta should be used in making soups, since it remains in the liquid even after its allotted cooking time, and softer varieties will most likely turn into mush.

Polenta

Polenta is ground corn. In the Garfagnana, when the corn harvest is over, every *alimentari*—grocery store—carries a sign announcing *polenta nuova,* new polenta. Freshness is so important, in fact, that stores rarely carry polenta in summer, when, obviously, it would be almost one year old. The Garfagnini buy their polenta directly from the miller and then pass it through a sieve before using to remove any remaining bits of corn casing. While Americans are not lucky enough to have that option, those who buy it in bulk from an Italian specialty shop can choose between fine and coarse grinds. The recipes that follow stipulate coarse grind; fine grinds can also be used, although cooking time will be reduced by approximately 30 percent.

The Garfagnini have a saying: "The only reason for going into the forest is to take from its bounty." Rarely has there been a greater truth. In addition to dozens of varieties of mushrooms and berries, the region's forests offer an abundance of the sweet, meaty chestnuts that have served as a regional food staple for almost five hundred years. Originally thick with many varieties of firs and oaks, the forests of the Garfagnana were, by the sixteenth century, almost completely taken over by the more aggressive chestnut.

Since then, chestnuts have been used for an infinite variety of dishes including *ballocciori* (chestnuts boiled with bay leaves), *tullore* (dried chestnuts boiled in milk), *mondine* (roasted chestnuts), *necci* (pancakes made from chestnut flour and wrapped around fresh sheep's milk ricotta), *castagnaccio* (a sweetbread made from chestnut flour, water, and nuts), *incaciata* (chestnut polenta sliced and served with newly pressed oil and pecorino cheese), and a number of extraordinary soups whose recipes are included in this chapter.

"In all my childhood memories, there is always the smell of chestnuts," said an old woman who was selling *necci* outside Castelnuovo's walls during one of my visits. "We would gather around the fire and wait for them to cook and eat them with a glass of red wine, and, for a minute, everything was happiness."

Chestnut flour can be purchased in most Italian specialty shops.

MESCOLA ALLA GARFAGNANA

Many Ingredients Soup

When Signora Virginia Andreucci, Carlino's wife, was the cook at Da Carlino, she often found herself with small quantities of many types of things left over. And so at one point she created this wonderful soup, a delicious blend of lentils, beans, chickpeas, and rice that is cooked over low heat for a long enough time to meld the flavors together. Use only the very best oil, she advises: "This soup deserves it."

9 tablespoons extra-virgin olive oil
1 medium carrot, scraped and diced
1 medium onion, diced
1 stalk celery, diced
3 cloves garlic, minced
1 chunk (2 ounces) pork fatback, minced
1 tablespoon chopped fresh rosemary
1 teaspoon dried crumbled sage
1 cup canned Italian plum tomatoes, squeezed until shredded and
    with liquid reserved
⅔ cup lentils, soaked according to directions on page 148
⅓ cup each of dried cranberry beans, fava beans, black beans, and
    chickpeas, each soaked according to directions on pages 148 and
    169
Salt and freshly ground black pepper to taste
1 cup Arborio rice

1. Heat 5 tablespoons of the oil in a large soup pot over medium heat. Sauté the carrot, onion, celery, and garlic 5 minutes or until the onion is soft. Add the fatback, rosemary, and sage and continue to sauté for another 3 minutes.

2. Add the tomatoes and stir to mix well.

3. Add the lentils, beans, chickpeas, and enough water to cover by 4 inches. Heat to boiling over medium heat. Reduce the heat to low, cover, and cook for 3 hours, adding more water if necessary to maintain a rather thick broth.

4. Add the rice, cover, and cook for another 15 minutes or until the rice is tender. Add salt and pepper.

5. Remove from the heat and let sit, covered, for 1 hour. Serve luke-warm, drizzled with the remaining oil.

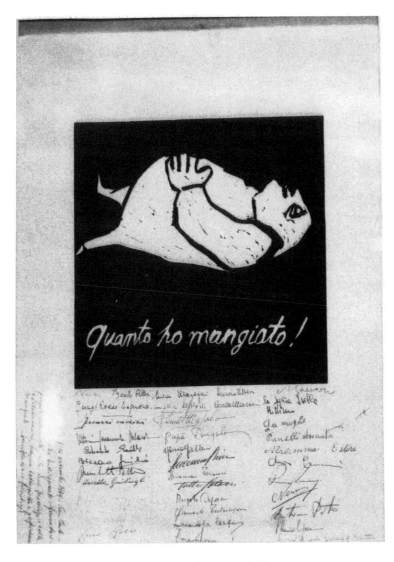

"I've eaten far too much!"

INTRUGLIA

Polenta, Savoy Cabbage, and Red Bean Soup ●

Intruglia originated in Versilia, in the beachfront areas of the Lucchesía, where it was made simply with vegetables and polenta flour. In the Garfagnana the recipe has taken on a mountain flavor with the addition of sausage. Generally served as a hearty first course, leftover intruglia can also be sliced and fried in olive oil and served the following day as a wonderful second course accompanied by sautéed spinach.

> 1 pound dried kidney beans, soaked according to directions on
>   page 169
> 1 tablespoon dried crumbled sage
> 2 medium onions, one halved and one diced
> 1 medium carrot, scraped and cut into 3 sections
> 2 stalks celery, one cut into 3 sections and one diced
> ½ cup extra-virgin olive oil
> 3 tablespoons chopped fresh parsley
> 3 cloves garlic, minced
> 1 small carrot, scraped and diced
> 3 links fennel sausage, removed from casings and crumbled
> 2 tablespoons tomato paste
> 2 cups Basic Meat Broth (see page 11)
> 1 small head savoy cabbage, cored and roughly chopped
> 3 medium potatoes, peeled and cut into small chunks
> Salt and freshly ground black pepper to taste
> 3 cups coarse-ground polenta

1. Drain the beans. Place them in a soup pot along with the sage, the onion halves, and the carrot and celery chunks and enough water to cover by 2 inches. Heat to boiling over medium heat. Cover, and cook for 1 hour, adding more water if necessary. Salt at the halfway mark.

2. Heat ¼ cup of the oil in another soup pot over medium heat. Sauté the parsley, garlic, diced onion, carrot, celery, and sausage for 3 minutes or until the onion is translucent. Dilute the tomato paste in the broth and add to the vegetable mixture. Cook for 5 minutes, stirring constantly.

3. Drain the beans, reserving the liquid, and pass half through a food mill. Add the mashed beans to the soup pot with the vegetables and the reserved bean liquid. Reserve the whole beans. Heat the soup to simmering over low heat, stirring frequently.

4. Add the cabbage and potatoes, cover, and cook over low heat for 30 minutes. When the cabbage is cooked, add salt and pepper and the whole beans and stir to mix well.

5. Pour the polenta into the soup in a steady stream, stirring constantly with a wooden spoon. Add water if necessary to maintain a thick, soup-like consistency.

6. Serve hot, drizzled with the remaining olive oil.

Note: Any leftover soup can be sliced and reheated the next day. Simply place 2 tablespoons extra-virgin olive oil in a skillet and fry the slices for a few minutes on each side.

*Thursday, and Castelnuovo's piazza is filled, but only with men.
"Eh, the women are doing the shopping, no?"*

MINESTRA DI RISO E LIMONE ◖

Rice and Lemon Soup

A very simple recipe served at Castelnuovo's Da Carlino. Says Carlino: "I can often be quite lazy when I am home alone and making myself something to eat. A few years ago, I had only rice, a few eggs, and a lemon. So I pulled some chicken broth out of the freezer and experimented with making a paste of the eggs, lemon, and cheese, which I then stirred into the heated broth. I was extremely surprised with the light, lemony results and added the soup to the restaurant menu where it quickly became a favorite first course."

    8 cups Basic Chicken Broth (see page 12)
    1 cup Arborio rice
    3 medium egg yolks
    ¼ cup freshly grated Parmigiano-Reggiano
    1 teaspoon freshly grated lemon zest
    1 teaspoon lemon juice

1. Place the broth in a soup pot. Heat to boiling over medium heat. Add the rice, cover, and cook for 20 minutes.

2. Meanwhile, beat the egg yolks in a bowl. Add the cheese, lemon zest, and lemon juice.

3. When the rice is tender, stir the egg yolk and cheese mixture into the soup. Heat through and serve.

FARINATA DI FARINA DI RISO
Rice Flour Soup

●

According to Paolo Almonti, a local cook (and, as they say in Tuscany, un buon gustaio—a hearty eater), the recipe for this dish dates back to 1839, when it was easy to find rice flour. He notes, however, that with the advent of health-food stores ("sì," he says, "even we in the Garfagnina are now plagued with stores proclaiming their food healthy. *As if there were something unhealthy about our day-to-day cooking!"), rice flour is much easier to find. I have added a slight variation to Signor Almonti's preparation and that is to dust the bottom of the bowl with freshly ground black pepper before adding the soup. It is a technique I learned years ago from another Garfagnina culinarian and one that adds a welcome zest.*

8 cups Basic Meat Broth (see page 11)
2⅓ cups rice flour
8 tablespoons unsalted butter
2 tablespoons chopped fresh parsley
½ cup freshly grated Parmigiano-Reggiano cheese
2 tablespoons freshly ground black pepper

1. Heat 2 cups of the broth to a slightly lukewarm temperature. Place the rice flour in a bowl and whisk the broth, ½ cup at a time, into the flour until the consistency is thick and pastelike.

2. Heat the remaining broth to boiling in a soup pot over medium heat. Whisk the rice paste into the broth and reduce the heat to low. Cook, stirring until the texture is smooth and dense.

3. Stir the butter and parsley into the soup. Sprinkle the pepper over the bottoms of 4 bowls. Top with soup and serve dusted with the grated cheese.

MINESTRONE RUSTICO

Country-Style Minestrone

●

This is Rosa Puliti's favorite soup, one made with what she calls every gift we have ever received from God—meat, vegetables, rice, and cheese. "I make it whenever I entertain my favorite people, and I will not reveal who they are or aren't, so don't even bother to ask." As we stand in the kitchen, side by side, cooking, however, she reveals to me that I have quickly become part of that group.

12 ounces fresh shelled *borlotti* (cranberry beans)

5 medium potatoes, peeled and cut into small chunks

1 stalk celery, halved

1 medium onion, peeled

5 small carrots, scraped and cut into thick rounds

2 medium red apples, peeled, cored, and cubed

6 very ripe plum tomatoes, peeled, seeded, and quartered

8 ounces rutabagas, cleaned and cubed

¼ pound chunk smoked pancetta or bacon, diced

12 cups Basic Meat Broth (see page 11)

1 chunk (1 ounce) pork fatback, diced

3 tablespoons chopped fresh parsley

1 tablespoon chopped fresh sage

2 cloves garlic, minced

½ small head savoy cabbage, cored and cut into rough chunks

¼ cup freshly grated Parmigiano-Reggiano

2 cups Arborio rice

Salt and freshly ground black pepper to taste

1. Place the beans, potatoes, celery, onion, carrots, apples, tomatoes, rutabagas, pancetta or bacon, and meat broth in a large soup pot. Heat to boiling over medium heat. Reduce the heat to low, cover, and cook for 1 hour.

2. Meanwhile, heat the fatback in a heavy skillet until the fat is rendered. Sauté the parsley, sage, and garlic over low heat for 5 minutes or until the garlic is lightly browned.

3. When the soup has cooked for 30 minutes, stir in the parsley-sage mixture, cabbage, cheese, and rice. Stir to mix well. Add salt and pepper. Cover, and cook for the remaining 30 minutes or until the rice is tender. Serve lukewarm.

LA MINESTRA DELLA SIGNORA VIRGINIA (SENSA PESCE)

Virginia's Soup (Without Fish)

"For a long time," says Da Carlino's owner, "I thought my wife Virginia [the restaurant's original cook] was making this soup with fish. After eating it a few hundred times, I finally one day saw her make it. 'Where is the fish?' I asked her. To which she replied that I should leave the kitchen and attend to the books. I finally realized that since parsley is so tied to soups made with fish, whenever I taste a soup with parsley, I assume it contains fish." Following is Virginia's own recipe for this rice and parsley soup modified only by my addition of Emmental cheese, which furthers the already creamy texture.

3 tablespoons unsalted butter
2 potatoes, peeled and grated
4 cups Basic Chicken Broth (see page 12)
3 cups milk
Salt and freshly ground black pepper to taste
4 ounces Emmental cheese, cubed
1⅓ cups Arborio rice
¼ cup chopped fresh parsley

1. Melt the butter in a soup pot over low heat. Add the potatoes and sauté for 5 minutes.

2. Pour both the broth and milk into the pot, add salt, pepper, and heat through.

3. Add the rice and cheese and reduce the heat to low. Cover, and cook for 20 minutes, stirring frequently.

4. Stir the parsley into the soup, remove from the heat, and serve hot.

MINESTRA ESSENZIALE

Essential Soup ◖

The expression chosen by Garfagnini when they want to say "mind your own business" is fatti i cavoli tuoi, *which, literally translated, means "grow your own cabbages." The only rationale I can come up with by way of background is that every garden in the Garfagnana contains at least one row of cabbages and that telling someone to grow their own is tantamount to saying "Tend to your own garden." The following soup is like many of those prepared by the Garfagnini, a variation on a theme. But it serves to show the genius of these people who could derive a strikingly different flavor from a simple change of ingredient or technique, in this case by adding a final dollop of basil pesto.*

3 tablespoons unsalted butter
2 tablespoons extra-virgin olive oil
1 chunk (2 ounces) prosciutto, diced
1 small onion, minced
1 medium head white cabbage, cored and cut into thin slivers
8 cups Basic Meat Broth (see page 11)
Salt and freshly ground black pepper to taste
1⅓ cups Arborio rice
2 tablespoons chopped fresh parsley
4 tablespoons basil pesto (see page 10)

1. Heat the butter and oil in a soup pot over medium heat. Sauté the prosciutto and onion for 5 minutes or until the onion is soft.

2. Add the cabbage, broth, salt, and pepper, cover, and heat to boiling. Simmer over low heat for 10 minutes.

3. Stir in the rice, cover again, and cook for another 20 minutes. Remove from heat.

4. Stir the parsley and basil pesto into the soup and serve.

LA MINESTRA DI RAPE
DELLA SIGNORA ROSA   ○

Signora Rosa's Broccoli Raab Soup

Says Signora Rosa: "Whenever I eat broccoli raab, I know the next day I am go-
ing to have stomach pains. But I have made do without many things in my long
life, and a wonderful soup prepared with those bitter little greens is one luxury I
absolutely will not renounce."

1¼ pounds broccoli raab, thick stems removed, washed and
   roughly chopped
Salt to taste
2 tablespoons unsalted butter
3 cloves garlic, crushed
2 tablespoons extra-virgin olive oil
1 chunk (4 ounces) prosciutto, diced
1 small onion, diced
8 cups Basic Meat Broth (see page 11)
1⅓ cups Arborio rice
2 tablespoons chopped fresh parsley
Freshly ground black pepper to taste

1. In a skillet melt the butter over medium heat. Sauté the garlic until
golden. Add broccoli raab and sauté for 5 minutes, stirring constantly.

2. Heat the oil in a soup pot over medium heat. Sauté the prosciutto
and onion for 7 minutes, or until the onion is lightly browned.

3. Add the broth to the soup pot and heat to boiling. Stir in the rice
and reduce the heat to low. Cover and cook for 15 minutes.

4. Add the sautéed broccoli raab, parsley, and pepper. Adjust for salt and
cook for another 3 minutes, stirring constantly. Serve hot.

ZUPPA DI FRUMENTO
Wheat Berry Soup

My voyage through the Garfagnana in search of traditional soup recipes would not have been complete without the following, a dish born from the most abject poverty and yet flavored with a genius so ingrained as to pass unnoticed. The recipe itself comes from the kitchen of Vincenzina Da Prato, who made it for me one particularly cold day as we sat in her kitchen by the woodstove. Wheat berries, she explained, are like farro and pasta: quintessential grains used by the Garfagnini on a regular basis. "At one time we also made regular use of walnuts, when our forests contained many of those beautiful trees. Today, due to logging and blight, walnuts have become a luxury."

> 1¼ cups whole wheat berries,★ rinsed and soaked in cold water for
>   2 to 3 hours
> 1 medium onion, diced
> 1 clove garlic, minced
> 4 cups water
> Salt and freshly ground black pepper to taste
> 1 cup walnut halves, roughly chopped
> ¼ cup extra-virgin olive oil

1. Drain the wheat berries and place in a soup pot along with the onion, garlic, and water. Add salt and pepper and heat to boiling over medium heat. Reduce the heat to low, cover, and cook for 2 hours.

2. Stir the walnuts into the soup and cook for another 15 minutes.

3. Add the oil, stir to mix well, and serve hot.

★Wheat berries are a barley-like grain that can be purchased in specialty or health-food stores.

MINESTRA DI UOUA
E PANGRATTATO

Soup Made with Eggs, Cheese, and Bread Crumbs

At one time selling eggs was a way of making a living, albeit a hard and uncertain one. In his poem "Valentino," Giovanni Pascoli tells the story of a poor poultry farmer who, because he was without a coat in the dead of winter, warmed himself by sitting in the henhouse, where the hens would console him with their song, Un cocco, ecco, ecco un cocco, un cocco per te. *An egg, here, here is an egg, an egg just for you.*

> 3 eggs
> ¼ cup unflavored bread crumbs
> ¼ cup freshly grated Parmigiano-Reggiano
> ⅛ teaspoon grated nutmeg
> 8 cups Basic Chicken Broth (see page 12)
> 1 pound escarole, cleaned and chopped
> Salt and freshly ground black pepper to taste
> 8 sprigs fresh watercress, cleaned and with stems removed

1. Beat the eggs in a bowl until they are well blended. Add the bread crumbs, grated cheese, and nutmeg. Continue to beat with a fork until a thick paste has formed.

2. Heat the broth to boiling in a soup pot. Add the escarole and cook covered for 5 minutes over medium heat. Remove from the heat.

3. Whisk the egg mixture into the hot soup until the egg has cooked. Add salt and pepper and serve hot, garnished with the watercress.

MINESTRA CON PANE GRATTATO ALLA POVERA

Poor People's Dumpling Soup

⬤

Says Vincenzina Da Prato: "Thank God I always had hens. I had no meat, and fish was something I could only dream of eating. But eggs were something I could use to create a meal. And then on Christmas or Easter, I could kill a hen and make a broth and, for a second course, we could have boiled hen with potatoes. Those were the days!"

> 3 eggs, separated
> ¾ cup unflavored bread crumbs
> ⅛ teaspoon grated nutmeg
> Salt
> 6 cups Basic Chicken Broth (see page 12)

1. Beat the egg whites until they form stiff peaks.

2. In a separate bowl, beat the egg yolks. Carefully fold the yolks into the whites, adding them a little at a time to maintain the stiffness of the peaks.

3. Fold in the bread crumbs and nutmeg, taking care not to disturb the texture of the eggs. The final mixture should be solid and soft. If it is too liquidy, correct by blending in a small additional quantity of bread crumbs.

4. Heat the broth to boiling over medium heat. Drop the egg mixture into the broth, 1 tablespoon at a time. After all the dumplings are added, add salt and cook for 10 minutes or until the dumplings are cooked. Serve hot.

BRODETTO CON DITALINI

Fish Broth with Ditalini

Says Quinta Cestoil, a Castelnuovo native: "If we Garfagnini don't eat pasta at least once a day, it is as if we are dying." The following recipe combines the delicacy of a fine fish broth with the consistency of ditalini (little thimbles), which, as Angelina says, "fills your stomach day and night." I have made just one alteration in the version created for me by Signora Cestoli, and that is the addition of saffron, which gives the flavor added richness.

> ¼ cup extra-virgin olive oil
> 1 small onion, diced
> 1 clove garlic, minced
> 1 cup drained canned Italian tomatoes, squeezed until shredded
> 1 dried red chili pepper, crushed
> ¼ teaspoon dried oregano
> 8 cups Basic Fish Broth (see page 13)
> ¼ teaspoon saffron
> 8 ounces ditalini or other small-cut pasta

1. Heat the oil in a soup pot over medium heat. Sauté the onion and garlic until lightly browned. Add the tomatoes, chili pepper, and oregano. Cook for 3 minutes, stirring constantly.

2. Add the fish broth and cook over medium heat for 5 minutes, stirring occasionally. Stir the saffron into the broth and continue cooking for another 3 minutes.

3. Drop the pasta into the simmering broth and cook for 8 to 10 minutes or until the pasta is done. Serve hot.

MINESTRA DI PASTA GRATTATA
Grated Pasta Soup

⬤

This ancient recipe speaks both to the region's historic poverty and to its ingenious ability to create culinary wonders out of virtually no ingredients. The pasta can be made several hours before using or even the night before. Says Signora Rosa: "This is a wonderful soup to serve guests. Wait until they have arrived before grating the pasta into the hot broth and do it while they are watching. In most cases, they will be amazed that such bonta'—*goodness—can be created in just a few minutes."*

¼ cup unbleached flour
½ cup freshly grated Parmigiano-Reggiano
½ cup unflavored bread crumbs
½ teaspoon lemon zest
⅛ teaspoon freshly grated nutmeg
Salt
1 large egg, lightly beaten
8 cups Basic Chicken Broth (see page 12)
Freshly ground black pepper

1. Place the flour, cheese, bread crumbs, lemon zest, nutmeg, and salt in a large bowl. Mix well. Add the egg and mix by hand until a dense, semi-hard ball has formed. Wrap in plastic and refrigerate for 4–6 hours or overnight.

2. Heat the broth to boiling in a soup pot over medium heat. Remove the refrigerated pasta, unwrap and place in a ricer. Using a ricer grate the pasta over the soup, keeping the ricer as far from the steaming broth as is possible.

3. Serve immediately, dusted with black pepper.

VINATA ALLA POVERA
Poor People's Wine Soup

When most of the Garfagnana's men worked in local caves extracting marble for the likes of Michelangelo, they ate sparingly, and each meal had to thoroughly fill the stomach. Vinata, *a hearty blend of chestnut flour and diluted wine, was a frequent part of their diets along with* necci *(chestnut-flour pancakes) and thick sturdy* focaccia *made either from wheat flour or polenta. . . .* O una ciotola di vinata, o una pila di necci, o un tozzo di pane inagliato e . . . via al lavoro! *Or a crock of* vinata, *or a pile of* necci, *or a big wedge of bread rubbed with garlic and . . . off to work! In the old days, the wine used for this dish was called* picciolo *and consisted mainly of the lightly colored water that was pressed through the grapes after several vats of wine had already been extracted. So mild was* picciolo *that it was consumed by small children as a breakfast beverage.*

    4 cups chestnut flour
    1 cup red wine, or more as needed
    8 cups water, or more as needed

1. Place the chestnut flour in a soup pot. Blend together the wine and water and whisk the liquid into the chestnut flour, one ladleful at a time, until the texture is liquidy and pastelike.

2. Heat the soup over medium heat, stirring constantly until boiling. Continue to cook for 5 minutes, adding more wine/water mixture if necessary to maintain a very dense consistency. Serve immediately.

DOLCE DI CASTAGNE
Sweet Chestnut Soup

Since the forests of the Garfagnana are blanketed largely with chestnut trees, this soup made from the fruit of those trees has long been a regional favorite. Generally served as a first course on winter holidays such as Christmas Eve, chestnut soup tastes best when accompanied by a robust red wine.

1 pound dried chestnuts, rinsed and soaked in cold water for 12
   hours
1 fennel frond, chopped
Salt and freshly ground black pepper to taste
8 cups Basic Chicken Broth (see page 12)

Heat the broth to boiling in a soup pot over medium heat. Drain the chestnuts and add to the pot. Add the fennel frond, salt, and pepper and cook, covered, for 3 hours over low heat, stirring occasionally and adding more water by the ladleful when necessary. The soup is done when it has achieved a dense, creamy consistency. Serve lukewarm.

For Rosa Puliti, the world is a scary place. She clearly remembers the war and what had to be done to survive.

MANAFREGOLI
Sheepherder's Chestnut Soup

●

"On the one hand," says Carlino, "this area has always been very poor. On the other hand, we have always had plenty to eat, what with the sheep that grazed in our mountains and the meats of the forests—chestnuts—that were free for the taking." The following recipe is one of the oldest from this area, a wonderful blend of sweet chestnut flour and heavy cream. Unfortunately, sheep's milk ricotta is not always available in this country and so goat's milk ricotta can be substituted.

8 cups water
3½ cups chestnut flour
2 cups heavy cream
4 ounces fresh sheep's milk ricotta★

1. Heat the water to boiling. Using a whisk, slowly stir the chestnut flour into the water, adding more water if necessary to maintain a slightly thick consistency. Cook for 30 minutes over low heat, stirring frequently.

2. Remove from the heat and stir in the heavy cream. Serve hot, each serving topped with a few tablespoons of ricotta.

★Sheep's milk ricotta can be found in a limited number of specialty cheese shops.

MINESTRONE DI CASTAGNE
E FAGIOLI SECCHI
Chestnut and White Bean Soup

Signora Rosa recites this poem about chestnuts:

> *Son riccio spinoso*
> *Dal cuor generoso*
> *Mi mangiano cotta*
> *Bruciata e ballotta*
> *Son natta in montagna*
> *Mi chiamo castagna.*

> *I am prickly and spiny*
> *And of generous heart*
> *They eat me cooked*
> *Burned and boiled*
> *I am born of the mountains*
> *And am called chestnut.*

8 ounces dried chestnuts, rinsed and soaked in cold water for 12
    hours
¾ cup dried *cannellini* beans, soaked according to directions on
    page 169
Salt and freshly ground black pepper to taste
2 tablespoons extra-virgin olive oil
1 chunk (3 ounces) smoked pancetta or bacon, diced
1 medium onion, diced
1 small carrot, scraped and diced
½ stalk celery, diced
⅔ cup Arborio rice
⅛ teaspoon grated nutmeg

1. Drain the chestnuts and beans. Place in a large soup pot with
enough water to cover by 2 inches. Heat to boiling over medium heat
and add salt and pepper. Reduce the heat to low, cover, and cook for 2
hours. Add more water if necessary.

2. Heat the oil in a skillet over medium heat. Sauté the pancetta or bacon, the onion, carrot, and celery for 7 minutes or until the onion is lightly browned. Add to the soup pot and stir to mix well.

3. Add the rice and nutmeg, cover, and cook for 20 minutes or until the rice is tender. Serve hot.

Carlino at the fireplace of Da Carlino, *Castelnuovo's finest restaurant and one of the most famous in Tuscany.*

Chapter Five

DRAWN TO THE LAND

Piazza Al Serchio

ZUPPE DI FARRO
Farro *Soups*

*I*n the early 1980s, Italy relaxed its laws with respect to foreign ownership of land, and as a result the Garfagnana is now home to large numbers of foreigners from Germany, Britain, and the United States—in that order. Tales are told of that *americana* who goes running every day, even in the rain; of the *inglese* who had to obtain special permission to bring over twenty of his own roses; of the *tedesco*—the German—who gave $5,000 to each of the sixty-seven inhabitants of the village where he had been stationed during the war and in which his troop massacred a hundred fourteen partisans.

A somewhat different war-related story involves a former Nazi officer who commanded a battalion stationed in a small village, this time on the eastern end of the province, near Emilia-Romagna. This man so loved the area, it seems, that, when the war was over, he bought the village and now employs many of the same people who were terrorized by his rule.

"Can you believe it?" asks my friend Beth, an American photographer who recently bought an old stone house on the outskirts of Piazza al Serchio, one of the Garfagnana's northernmost villages. "I'm not sure which bothers me more. The German commander, who should have been more sensitive, or the Italian peasants, who were so mercenary as to sell their souls for money and jobs? It's probably a tie."

Beth's own story is not nearly as dramatic. She came to Piazza al Serchio to photograph an olive oil cooperative four years ago, fell immediately in love with the terraced hillsides that surround the village, bought an old stone house on a large tract of land, and now—except for job-related travel—lives here year-round. When I ask what she likes most about her new home, she singles out the land, the connection she feels to that particular blend of mountains, forests, rivers, and fields that is unique to the Garfagnana.

She tells a funny story about the time she decided she needed a tool shed on the far side of her property. Advised by many in the town that she should first consult a surveyor, she went to City Hall and asked if there were any ordinances preventing the construction of a building on that particular site. "I was told that, unfortunately, the site carried a variance allowing the passage of bullock carts from surrounding farms," she says. "When I asked if anyone still used bullock carts in this day and age, they said no, but that it would still be illegal for me to block the route."

For a while, she says, she put her plans on hold. "But then my neighbor, Duilio, told me I should go ahead and build the shed anyway and that, eventually, the structure would be *condonata* which means 'made legal upon payment of an assigned penalty.' I thought about it for another six months, talked to a few more people and then simply called the contractors."

"And?" I prompt.

"And it happened exactly as Duilio said. Approximately four months after the shed was finished, I received a letter saying that it was in violation of the building code. If I wanted, the letter said, I could apply for a *condono*, which I did. I paid the penalty last year. Eight hundred dollars. Duilio says that *condoni* are the staff of life here, that without them no one would ever get anything built, whether a tiny tool shed or a new balcony."

The *condono* method serves everybody, he believes. "The government ministers who turn to it whenever they need a new influx of lire. And the Italian people who need regularly to feel the magnificent flush that comes from thwarting the law."

I ask Beth how she gets along with the people here. She says that, after the land, Piazza al Serchio's people are the main reason she was able to so easily settle in. "They make me feel as if, together, we are living out a centuries-old tradition. It took a while, however. At first, everyone was naturally reticent. But then they began stopping by with bags of chestnut flour, offering to show me how to make *necci* (chestnut-flour pancakes).

And before long they were inviting me to their homes for dinner and offering to show me how to trim my olive trees.

"Rarely do they ask about me, my friends, what I do for a living," she continues. "More often they talk about their own way of life, about how to do this or do that. Some people might resent the exclusivity of their focus, but I feel strangely liberated by it."

How different, she notes wryly, from her experience in other European countries where she has lived and worked. "In Switzerland and Germany, for example, outsiders can buy houses, make friends, work and pay taxes sometimes for as long as twenty years. But they will never be truly taken in by the community, never be granted residency."

I have come to her house to help with the preparations for tonight's dinner—a very special dinner, since she is playing host to four friends of ours from New York who are traveling through the Garfagnana. As a tribute to me, all the food is to come from recipes included in my previous book, *From the Tables of Tuscan Women.* When I walk through the door, she is working on *farro con pesce,* a wonderful dish combining the barley-like *farro* with shrimp and squid.

"Try it," she says when she sees me sniffing around the big pot on the stove. "It is my first time cooking this particular *farro* dish."

The dish is good, very good if one were to be completely truthful. I tell her as much, and add that it is hard to go wrong when cooking with *farro,* that every *farro* dish I ever tasted has been exceptional.

She asks if I have ever tasted *torta di farro* (farro cake). I shake my head no. How about *polpettone di farro* (farro meatloaf)?

"No."

"*Focaccia di farro?*"

"No."

"Well, what *have* you tasted?" she asks, laughing at my chagrin.

"I guess not much," I admit. "I really had no idea *farro* was used in so many different ways."

"Every day brings a dozen new recipes," she says in a not altogether pleased tone of voice. "In fact, *farro* is now to Tuscany what avocados were once to California."

She recovers from her momentary pique over *farro's* newfound chic. "It is a hard thing to explain to people of this area that the foods they once consumed because they were too poor to afford anything else now command twenty dollars per plate at even the tiny local restaurants."

"I'll tell you what!" She brightens suddenly. "Tomorrow, I have to photograph a few people for an article on the use of traditional tools. One of my subjects is a man who mills *farro* using a five-hundred-year-old wooden machine. Why don't you come along, and when I'm done, we'll go to a wonderful restaurant in town and I'll introduce you to a bevy of new *farro* dishes."

We leave at eleven-thirty, after Beth returns from Piazza al Serchio's weekly market. My preference would have been to leave earlier, to see the area with the morning fog still hugging the gorgeously terraced slopes of the surrounding hillsides. But priorities are priorities, and Beth would rather eat stale bread than miss the weekly market, enmeshed as she has become with local food producers, who gladly fill her orders for just-picked vegetables, ricotta made that morning, and freshly killed pheasant. Naturally we cannot leave without sampling the *farro,* so two wedges of fresh pecorino cheese, a few dozen olives, and two glasses of *novello* wine later, we are on our way.

The first stop on the tour is San Romano, four kilometers outside Piazza al Serchio. Here, Beth says, she is going to photograph two weavers who work on looms that are over seventy years old. We climb a long series of steps, wind our way through a lovely vegetable garden, and finally arrive at the door to the *telaio,* only to find a note saying that the studio is closed. It is Thursday, and as someone later tells us, weavers do not work on Thursday. I make a mental note to add that to my list. Clothing stores closed on Monday mornings, butchers closed on Tuesday afternoons, pizzerias closed on Wednesdays, libraries closed whenever they feel like popping out for an espresso.

Che volete? a voice calls down from the third-story window. What do you want? Beth tells the woman she is looking for Marilena and Giorgina Salotti, the two weavers from the studio. *Non lavorano oggi,* the woman says. *E giovedi.* "Ah," says Beth. "I had been hoping to photograph the girls for a book to be published in America."

The reaction is immediate. *Aspetta! Le mando subito giù!* And in the next moment Marilena and Giorgina are down in the studio and the looms are humming. Beth shoots her pictures as I stand in the doorway, ruminating about people who accept what you tell them without even asking for the most basic of proofs. We are strangers to these people, complete and total strangers, and yet they have interrupted their one day of rest in order to pose for someone who has not even offered a full explanation of why she needs the pictures or what she will use them for. In fact, like the typical Garfagnina she has become, Beth hadn't even thought to make an appointment.

Perhaps these people don't care, I speculate; perhaps the mere vanity of being photographed makes up for whatever inconvenience results. More likely it is the character of the Garfagnini, on the one hand introverted and suspicious, on the other (especially if no money changes hands), generous and exceptionally giving.

Marilena is now yelling upstairs to her mother. She wants her to come and move the bolts of thread to one side so that Beth can get a better view of the antique looms. I smile at the old woman when she walks through the door and drift into wondering what she might think we are doing. Stop analyzing, I eventually tell myself. Just accept the fact that this is the way mountain people are. We leave with hugs and kisses all around and Beth thanks them again for being so gracious.

We circle back to the road leading to Piazza al Serchio's outskirts, on route to the miller. Along the way, we pass dozens of gently undulating hills and green terraced panoramas, and just before reaching the town, we see an unusual church whose back and sides are built directly into the surrounding slopes. A few seconds later, we see another, almost just like it. Beth laughs. "I wonder whether they were designed that way or whether they simply lost the battle against the forces of nature."

We finally come to the hairpin curve that indicates we have arrived at Il Mulino di Colognola, the Colognola *farro* mill. Alessio Corsi, the son of the owner, is sitting at an outdoor table with a group of older men drinking wine. *Ola!* he says with great surprise. It has apparently been two years since Beth's last visit.

During the drive she had filled me in on the details, on the fact that Alessio's father, Guido, had taken over the mill twenty-two years ago from his own father, one of the original large-scale *farro* millers in the region. Beth herself had first met the two in 1992, which is the year she first discovered *farro*. Since then, she says, she has been back more than a dozen times both to buy some freshly milled *farro* and to introduce new people to this marvelous grain.

Papá e in arrivo, Alessio says. Pappa is on his way. He pulls over two additional chairs, and we chat for a few minutes about life and the weather and work. Business is fine, Alessio says in answer to Beth's questions.

But his words are waved away by the oldest of the three men. *E io sono il Papa,* the man huffs. And I am the Pope. When Alessio laughs and shrugs away the comment, the man becomes enraged. "With the new taxes thrown at us by Dini and his group of so-called moderates, no one is doing fine!" he shouts.

It is an opinion with which I am familiar, one that curries much favor in a week that has seen acting president Lamberto Dini vote in favor of increased tariffs on everything from telephone rates to gasoline. Before anything further can be said on the subject, a car pulls up and it is Guido himself. *O Dio!* he says, and gives Beth a firm, surprised hug.

She explains why she has come and asks if she can take a few pictures. *Allora dami un momento,* he says and hurries off. Two seconds later, he is back, preening in his miller's hat and coat.

Beth asks to see the milling machines, and he walks us into a dusty room containing three large wooden structures. I notice an antique-looking poster on the wall. On closer inspection, I see that it is a reproduction of a recipe from a book written in 1648 by Jesuit priest and noted culinarian Francesco Gaudenzio. The name of the book is *Il Panunto Toscano* (Tuscan Bread Soaked in Oil), and the recipe is for, in Gaudenzio's words, "a recipe from my mother illustrating a simple method for cooking modern foods at little expense." It tells how to make *minestra di farro,* a *farro* soup that, in this particular incarnation, is cooked for three hours in almond milk and then sweetened with "a few heaping tablespoons of sugar."

The recipe concludes with this little adage: "I have eaten well in famous restaurants and taverns, in the houses of friends and in a thousand public houses, but the dishes made by my mother were simply another thing altogether!"

By now, Guido has gotten a bag of *farro* kernels—*chicchi*—from the back and is tossing it into the uppermost spout, churning manually until a grainy white powder begins pouring out the bottom chute. As she photographs, Beth asks about his life in order to relax him for the camera. Why, she wonders, does he restrict himself to milling *farro*—to buying his grain from growers instead of growing it himself.

"My dream has always been to own a large field of my own," he answers wistfully. "But I never had enough money, and so, for me—a person involved in a lifelong love affair with the land—milling *farro* is a way to be close to my *innamorata.*"

Thirty minutes later, Beth has finished her shoot and we say our *arrivederci,* each of us holding a "gift" sack of *farro* kernels.

"Stay here and eat here with us," Guido pleads as we climb into the car. But Beth says she has promised to take me to Il Pisanino. *Buonissimo,* he says with raised eyebrows and a slow shaking of the head. Excellent. "Make sure you order the *farro con ceci e fagioli*"—the *farro* with chickpeas and beans.

Il Pisanino means "little Pisan," and nobody—not even Rita Asti, the owner—can tell us why. "My husband opened the restaurant and hotel in 1965, after returning from Australia, where he lived for fourteen years. No, he is not from Pisa, and nobody in either of our families have ever lived there or wanted to live there. I think it happened one afternoon after a good bottle of wine and before we could stop the printer from stamping out the business cards."

We order an "all *farro* meal" and leave the rest of the details to Rita and her daughter-in-law, Valeria, who soon begin arriving at the table with a series of dishes, each more extraordinary than the last. There is *farrotto di zucca gialla* (dense *farro* soup made with butternut squash), *polpettone di farro* (*farro* meatloaf), *farro e pomodori al forno* (oven-baked *farro* and tomato casserole), and *budino di farro e ballotte* (*farro* and chestnut custard). After each course we are asked for an opinion by people at the surrounding tables—all of whom had chuckled upon overhearing the initial order. Beth responds by turning her ecstatic face in their direction, eyes closed and murmuring an enthusiastic "Hmmmmmm!"

On our way home, we talk about her life in the Garfagnana, about how the mountains and the greenery have had a positive effect on her art, about how she has come to love the customs and traditions of the area, about how she feels a part of things here in a way that was never before possible. "I feel as if I have been drawn here by some force that always operated just under the surface of my desires," she says. "I'm not sure what will happen next, but I do know that the Garfagnana is one of the few places where I have ever really thrived."

It is clear as I watch her easily navigating the mountain curves that, like the area's natives, Beth has fallen under the powerful spell of this magnificent region called the Garfagnana.

ABOUT "FARRO"

Barley-like in appearance and light brown in color, *farro* has recently been rediscovered by trendy Italians, who are as enamored of its taste and nutritional value as of the memory it evokes of a time long since past.

Because it grows almost exclusively in the Garfagnana, its use has come to connote Tuscan cooking in general and, specifically, that of this rugged mountainous region.

Cooking with *farro* requires patience: the patience required by a twenty-four-hour soaking period and the patience required by the two hours or longer it takes to cook. As such, it brings to mind a way of life that once was standard throughout these mountain villages—a way of life that made it possible for the Garfagnana's women to spend all day making a delicious soup for their husbands returning from the fields or the marble mines.

It is said that *farro* was first cultivated and consumed by the Assyrians as well as by other Middle Eastern peoples and those of North Africa. The Egyptians must have valued it very highly, since kernels of the grain were found in many of the ancient pyramids.

In Italy, its use dates back to the Roman Empire. In fact, without *farro,* the Romans would never have become the powerful rulers they turned out to be. It was their primary food, both in the form of kernels, which they boiled into a stew, and as ground flour, which they used to make the polenta-like *puls* that was the mainstay of their diet. They also used it for *mola salsa,* a type of porridge made with toasted *farro* flour and salt, and *labum,* a *farro* cake that was offered to the gods.

While the ancient Romans used *farro* as an offering to *all* the gods, they were especially careful to reserve a sizable portion for Demeter, wife of Pluto and goddess of earthly fertility, in hopes that she would remember them come harvest time.

Farro is planted in October or November on graduated terraces that can be seen throughout the Garfagnana's hill towns. It likes water, but not standing water, which is why it does so well in mountain settings.

The grain itself is almost totally resistant to disease and therefore needs no fungicide or insecticide. It is harvested in June, when the stalks are cut from the fields and allowed to dry for a few months before being beaten to remove the kernels. The kernels are then placed in a *spogliatoio*—an "undressing" machine—which separates them from their outer shells and divides them into those that will be sold whole, as *farro,* and those that will be ground into flour.

There are two types of *farro: Gran farro,* known botanically as *Triticum dicoccum,* is basically a dense, hard grain that maintains its kernel-like consistency even after both its required 12-hour soaking period and

2- to 3-hour cooking period. *Triticum spelta,* also called *farricello,* or spelt, is a considerably softer grain that can be cooked without soaking. Each has its own use, but it is important to know which is which, since they produce very different results. In the United States both kinds of *farro* can be found at specialty shops and health-food stores or they can be mail-ordered from the following sources:

Pasta Shop Delicatessen
5655 College Avenue
Oakland, CA 94618
510-547-4005
Fax: 510-601-8251
Carries whole-grain *farro* in 500-gram packages for $6.99, also *farro* spaghetti in 250-gram packages for $4.99, and *penne di farro* in 250-gram packages for $4.99.

Dean & DeLuca
560 Broadway
NY, NY 10012
1-800-221-7714
Fax: 1-800-781-4050
Carries whole-grain *farro* in 500-gram packages for $8.95, also *farro* spaghetti in 250-gram packages for $5.50, and *penne di farro* in 250-gram packages for $5.50.

Zingerman's
422 Detroit Street
Ann Arbor, MI 48104
313-769-1625
Fax: 313-769-1235
Carries whole-grain *farro* in 250-gram bags for $5.00, also both *farro* spaghetti and *farro penne* in 250-gram quantities for $5.00 each.

Agribosco USA
6203 24th Avenue
Brooklyn, NY 11204
718-645-6898
Fax: 718-382-9219

Carries various types of organic *farro* in vacuum-packed bags sold six to a case. Six 14-ounce bags of whole-grain *farro* cost $24.90. Six 14-ounce bags of half-peeled *farro* cost $25.80. Six 15-ounce bags of crushed *farro* cost $29.40. Six 14-ounce bags of stone-ground *farro* flour cost $27.00. Six 8-ounce bags of *farro* pasta cost $24.90.

Preparing "Farro"

Farro should be rinsed in cold running water before soaking. To soak, place in enough water to cover by 4 inches and let sit for 24 hours. Rinse and drain before using.

Farro, *an ancient grain with newfound chic.*

ZUPPA DI FARRO E FRUTTI DI MARE
Farro *and* Shellfish Soup

No one knows who invented this miraculous soup. What is known is that it is now one of the Lucchesía's most popular recipes, one that unites its two most precious resources: fish from the Tyrhennian Sea and farro from the Garfagnana.

1¼ cups *farro,* soaked according to directions on page 128
Salt to taste
3 tablespoons extra-virgin olive oil
3 cloves garlic, minced
1 fresh chili pepper, seeded and diced
4 ounces baby squid, cleaned and cut into thin slices
12 small shrimp, cleaned and deveined
1 pound mussels, scrubbed and debearded
1 pound Manila clams, scrubbed
1 cup dry white wine
8 cups Basic Fish Broth (see page 13)
¼ cup chopped fresh parsley
Freshly ground black pepper to taste

1. Drain the *farro,* rinse and drain again, and place in a soup pot. Cover with cold water by 2 inches and heat to boiling over medium heat. Reduce the heat to low, cover, and cook for 1½ hours or until tender. Add more water if necessary. Add salt.

2. Heat the oil in a large deep skillet over medium heat. Sauté the garlic and chili pepper for 3 minutes. Add the squid and cook for 5 minutes. Add the shrimp, mussels, and clams and cook for another 3 minutes.

3. Drizzle the wine over the seafood and continue to cook until more than half the liquid has evaporated. Discard any mussels or clams that have not opened. Remove the meat from the remaining shells and add it along with the shrimp, squid, and broth to the *farro.* Cook for 5 more minutes, stirring to blend the grains and seafood.

4. Divide the soup among 4 bowls. Sprinkle with parsley, dust with pepper, and serve hot.

MINESTRA DI PAZIENZA E FARRO
Soup Made with Patience and Farro ●

"In the olden days, women took their time with household chores," says farro *miller Guido Corsi. "They rose at dawn and began preparing food for lunch. If that day, they were making* farro, *they cooked it for hours over a low flame, a preparation that resulted in a dense, delicious broth. In general, they made enough for two days, which, with* farro, *was a very good idea, since it is equally as good the following day."*

¾ cup dried *borlotti* (cranberry beans), picked over, rinsed, and
    soaked for 12 hours
2 cloves garlic, peeled
1 tablespoon dried crumbled sage
3 links fennel sausage, removed from casings and crumbled
1¼ cups *farro,* soaked according to directions on page 128
6 cups Basic Meat Broth (see page 11)
4 tablespoons extra-virgin olive oil
Salt to taste
8 sprigs fresh parsley, cleaned and stems removed

1. Drain the beans and place in a soup pot along with the garlic, sage, 2 tablespoons oil, the sausage, and enough water to cover by 2 inches. Heat to boiling over medium heat. Reduce the heat to low, and cook for 1 hour. Salt at the halfway mark.

2. Remove half the beans with a slotted spoon and pass through a food mill. Return to the pot.

3. Drain the *farro,* rinse and drain again, and add to the pot along with the broth and the remaining oil. Cover, and cook over low heat for 1¼ hours or until both the *farro* and beans are tender. Add more water if necessary to maintain a dense, souplike consistency. Add salt and serve hot, garnished with the parsley.

MINESTRONE COL FARRO
Minestrone with Farro

Like rice, farro *lends itself to many different preparations. In a minestrone with many ingredients such as the following, it gives its best, enhancing the flavor of the vegetables and adding texture to the broth.*

¾ cup dried *cannellini* beans, soaked according to directions on
    page 148
1 tablespoon dried crumbled sage
3 small carrots, scraped and roughly chopped
2 stalks celery, one roughly chopped and one diced
Salt to taste
3 tablespoons extra-virgin olive oil
1 medium carrot, scraped and diced
1 medium onion, diced
¼ cup chopped fresh parsley
2 cloves garlic, minced
½ teaspoon dried rosemary
3 fresh basil leaves, chopped
1 chunk (4 ounces) prosciutto, diced
⅔ cup *farro,* soaked according to directions on page 128
6 cups Basic Vegetable Broth (see page 14)

1. Drain the beans and place in a soup pot along with the sage, chopped carrots, chopped celery, and enough water to cover by 2 inches. Heat to boiling over medium heat. Reduce the heat to low, cover, and cook for 45 minutes. Salt at the halfway mark.

2. Heat the oil in another soup pot over medium heat. Sauté the diced carrot, onion, diced celery, parsley, garlic, rosemary, basil, and prosciutto for 5 minutes or until the onion is lightly browned. Add the beans and their liquid and continue cooking, covered, until the bean liquid has returned to a boil.

3. Drain the *farro,* rinse and drain again, and add to the soup pot along with the broth. Stir to mix well, cover, and cook for 1½ hours over low heat. Add more water if necessary to retain a dense, souplike consistency. Serve hot.

FARRO E CECI
Farro *and* Chickpeas

●

Farro and chickpeas—immediate poetry. Imagine it in winter when the sun sets early and thoughts turn to wool blankets and knit mufflers. A rich, dense soup perfumed with bay and served with a mixed green salad and one—or preferably more—carafes of red wine. Best when served lukewarm.

> 1 pound dried chickpeas, soaked according to directions on page 148
> ½ teaspoon dried rosemary
> 3 bay leaves
> 3 tablespoons extra-virgin olive oil
> 1 medium onion, diced
> 1¼ cups *farro*, soaked according to directions on page 128
> 8 cups Basic Chicken Broth (see page 12)
> Salt and freshly ground black pepper to taste

1. Drain the chickpeas, rinse under cold running water, and drain again.

2. Place the chickpeas in a soup pot along with the rosemary, bay leaves, and enough water to cover by 2 inches. Heat to boiling over medium heat. Reduce the heat to low, cover, and cook for 2 hours, adding more water if necessary.

3. Heat the oil in another soup pot. Sauté the onion over low heat for 7 minutes or until lightly browned.

4. Add the cooked chickpeas with their liquid to the onion. Drain the *farro*, rinse and drain again, and add to the pot along with the broth. Cover, and cook over low heat for 2 hours, stirring often and adding more water if necessary, but in doses small enough to retain a very dense texture. Add salt and pepper.

5. When both the *farro* and chickpeas are tender, remove from the heat and let sit for 45 minutes. Serve lukewarm.

IL FARRO DI GUIDO
Guido's Farro *Soup*

Farro *miller Guido Corsi talks about the many misconceptions regarding* farro: *"Some people think it is brown rice; others, that it is barley. I once heard a conversation between two women, one of whom recounted in a smug voice how she had just the day before made a soup with fish and* farro. *As she said it, she placed particular emphasis on the word* farro. *The other one listened for a while and then said, 'In my house, we make* farro *twice a week. What did you think, that you had discovered boiling water?'" The following recipe is one of Guido's own. The one he makes when his entire family comes together to celebrate a birthday or feast day. I have varied it only by adding the thyme, which I find adds a delightful pungency.*

7 tablespoons extra-virgin olive oil
1 chunk (4 ounces) smoked pancetta or bacon, diced
3 cloves garlic, minced
3 small zucchini, sliced into thin rounds
1 medium red onion, minced
1 teaspoon dried thyme
6 fresh basil leaves, chopped
¼ cup minced fresh parsley
3 cups canned Italian plum tomatoes, squeezed until shredded and
    with liquid reserved
6 cups Basic Meat Broth (see page 11)
1¼ cups *farro,* soaked according to directions on page 128
Salt and freshly ground black pepper to taste
¼ cup freshly grated Pecorino Romano

1. Heat 3 tablespoons of the oil in a soup pot over medium heat. Sauté the pancetta or bacon, garlic, zucchini, and onion for 10 minutes, stirring constantly.

2. Add the thyme, basil, parsley, and tomatoes. Cook over medium heat, stirring constantly, until the mixture has reduced somewhat. Add the broth and tomato liquid and heat to boiling.

3. Drain the *farro,* rinse and drain again, and add to the pot. Cover, and cook over low heat for 2 hours, adding more water if necessary to retain a souplike consistency. Add salt and pepper.

4. Remove from the heat and let sit, covered, for 45 minutes. Serve lukewarm, drizzled with the remaining oil and dusted with the grated cheese.

Piazza al Serchio, in the heart of farro country.

FARRO, VINO E SALSICCIA
Farro, *Sausage, and White Wine Minestrone*

When asked about the proper quantity of farro *kernels to use per person in a given recipe, many Garfagnini respond:* Un pugno—*a fist. Farro "grows," they say, and when cooked in a soup, tends to absorb as much of the liquid as it can. The following recipe is made with wine, which adds to the liquid and enhances the taste even further.*

    1 pound boneless pork loin, cut into ½-inch cubes

    12 cups Basic Meat Broth (see page 11)

    3 tablespoons extra-virgin olive oil

    4 links fennel sausage, removed from casings and crumbled

    ¼ cup chopped fresh marjoram

    2 cloves garlic, minced

    1 medium onion, diced

    1 can (32 ounces) Italian plum tomatoes, squeezed until shredded
       and with liquid reserved

    5 fresh basil leaves, chopped

    5 tablespoons chopped fresh parsley

    1¼ cups *farro,* soaked according to directions on page 128

    2 cups dry red wine

    Salt and freshly ground black pepper to taste

1. Place the pork loin in a soup pot along with the broth. Heat to boiling over medium heat. Cook, covered, for 45 minutes. Remove the pork with a slotted spoon, cool and shred. Reserve broth.

2. Heat the oil in another soup pot over low heat. Sauté the shredded pork, sausage, marjoram, and garlic for 10 minutes, stirring constantly.

3. Add the onion and continue to sauté until the onion is lightly browned. Add the tomatoes, tomato liquid, basil, and parsley and stir well.

4. Drain the *farro,* rinse and drain again, and add to the onion mixture along with the wine and the reserved broth. Stir to mix well. Cover, and cook over low heat for 2 hours, adding more water when necessary to maintain a dense consistency. Add salt and pepper. Remove from the heat and let sit, covered, for 45 minutes before serving.

MINESTRONE DI FARRO E ZUCCA ●

Farro *and* Butternut Squash Minestrone

This recipe comes from Signora Allesandra Magnoni of Piazza al Serchio, who served it to her son and daughter-in-law when they came down from Milan on her birthday. "They think they are so sophisticated," she confided in me. "But I placed this in front of them and stood there, waiting. For all their sophistication, they had never before tasted farro. *Hah!" Although the Signora made it with water, I have substituted vegetable broth for a richer flavor.*

3 tablespoons extra-virgin olive oil
1 medium onion, diced
1 pound butternut squash, peeled, seeded, and cut into ½-inch chunks
2 to 3 tablespoons water or as needed
⅔ cup *farro*, soaked according to directions on page 128
1 cup dry white wine
8 cups Basic Vegetable Broth (see page 14)
Salt and freshly ground black pepper to taste

1. Heat the oil in a soup pot over medium heat. Sauté the onion for 7 minutes or until lightly browned.

2. Add the squash and continue to sauté for 2 more minutes, stirring constantly. Add a few tablespoons water and cook for 5 minutes or until the squash is tender.

3. Drain the *farro*, rinse and drain again, and place in another soup pot. Cover with water by 2 inches, cover, and heat to boiling over medium heat. Reduce the heat to low and cook for 1 hour or until somewhat soft. Add more water if necessary. Drain and add to the squash mixture, stirring to mix well.

4. Add the wine and cook over medium heat for 15 minutes, stirring constantly.

5. Add the broth, 1 ladleful at a time. Wait until one ladleful has been absorbed before adding another. Continue in this way until most of the broth has been taken up. The consistency should be dense but souplike. Add salt.

6. Remove from the heat and let sit, covered, 45 minutes. Serve lukewarm, dusted with freshly ground black pepper.

Top: *Rita Asti, owner of* Il Pisanino, *explaining
the subtleties of* Farrotto di Zucca Gialla.
Bottom: *The church built directly into the
surrounding slopes. Did it simply lose the battle
against the forces of nature?*

Chapter Six

OF SAINTS AND SUPERSTITIONS

Isola Santa

LENTICCHIE E CECI
Lentils and Chickpeas

" . . . They entered the room, the seven most important spirits of which the first was Lucifer, Dr. Faust's true master, the one to whom he had sold his soul. Lucifer was tall, hairy and shaggy with red skin like that of a squirrel and a tail that pointed upwards and curved towards his head. Then came Beelzebub, a sorry nag with light, very hairy skin. With two horrible ears and a tail like that of a cow, his sides spouted two large bristling wings that looked like cardoons, half green and half a fiery, fulminating yellow. Next was Asteroth, the serpent. . . . "
—From *The Story of Doctor Faustus*

*I*sola Santa is a tiny, picturesque village on a spectacular mountain road leading from Massa to Castelnuovo. Surrounded by trees and situated on its own miniature turquoise lake, it once served as a hideout for medieval renegades, but is now largely abandoned, save for one-hundred three people and an insurgent herd of sheep that can generally be found nesting in a particularly tranquil nook behind the altar of the local church. Ask Isola Santa's residents for information about the origin of the village and you get a number of oddly conflicting stories.

One of the more colorful is told by two men, Antonio and Pietro, who are seated in the corner of the local bar, next to the woodstove. The two have been friends for over forty years and, for at least twenty of those forty, have been meeting here for morning coffee and a discussion of the day's events.

In their version of Isola Santa's origins, the village was founded in the 1700s by Corsicans who contracted malaria and were sent here to live in isolation. As evidence, they point to Daniela Cipollini, the proprietor of the eponymously named restaurant located just up the stairs. Daniela, who is also the proprietor of this bar, is hunched over the espresso machine, making coffee for the men; Pietro has ordered *un caffè alto*—a tall espresso, which means that more water is added; and Antonio, *un caffè basso*—a short or more concentrated one.

"Daniela is Corsican—aren't you, Daniela?" Pietro extends his open palm in her direction. She nods, obviously having had previous exposure to the twisted logic that is to come. "And if you ask her grandfather, he will tell you that not one, but quite a few of his ancestors died of malaria. *Vero?*" She nods again, and Pietro turns his gaze to me, quite content with how he has laid out his case. *Allora?* So?

Perhaps because of its isolation and the silence created by the surrounding mountains and placid lake, perhaps because fearful parents needed a reason to keep their children at home at night, perhaps just because this is the Garfagnana, where superstitions abound in *all* villages this size. For whatever reason, Isola Santa seems to be a hotbed of metaphysical traditions.

As Pietro sees it, the Devil lurks everywhere, waiting, plotting, licking his whiskers in frenzied glee over the prospect of yet another victory for his cause. I have not solicited this information; in fact, Pietro and I have barely met. I merely asked about the tenor of life in such a small village, and he launched into an explication of Satan's family tree—of the multiplicity of guises assumed by the Devil when in the throes of the eternal struggle for souls.

"There's the Buffardello, who comes from this exact region," he says. "Then there's the Linchetto and Osso in Gamba—Bone on Foot, so named because of his gaunt demeanor—who live a little north of here but are frequently seen in the nearby woods. Then of course, there are the familiar guises—cows, sheep, insects, trees—that the Devil takes on in certain cases at certain times."

"Which ones have you personally experienced?" I ask. Despite my aversion to the topic of superstitions, he has truly piqued my interest.

He settles back in his chair, lights a cigarette, and launches into what he swears is the true story of a local woman he knew who was so close to giving birth that she asked her husband to go immediately and get the midwife who lived on the other side of the woods.

"Now it was late at night in the dead of winter, and the man was, naturally, afraid to go trudging through the snow by himself." He pauses to make sure I understand the reasoning behind why this man was right to be afraid—why *anyone* would be afraid faced with the same circumstances. I clearly do not.

Ascolta, he says, sitting forward in his chair and straining for just the right words. Listen. "When you have to go and summon either a priest or a midwife, you should never go alone. The Devil waits for just those moments."

My face is evidently not signaling the proper understanding, so he moves his chair even closer and switches to speaking in a slower, more precise fashion. "If you're going to call a midwife, there is obviously, somewhere, a baby about to be born, *vero?* And since that baby will not yet have been baptized, it is in the Devil's interest to intervene and take the baby before birth, no?"

I think I'm beginning to understand, and my face must indicate as much because he is nodding his head up and down, up and down, as if to say, "Finally!"

He moves in for the kill. "And if you're going to call a priest, you obviously have a sick person on your hands." He waits, watching closely as I attempt to parlay my understanding of the newborn baby situation to one involving a sick person.

"Extreme Unction," he prods. "If the Devil can prevent you from bringing a priest and the sick person dies without Extreme Unction—*eh, e chiaro dove andrà quello, no?*—eh, it's clear where that one will wind up, no?"

He returns to the story. "*Allora,* the man came to a clearing in the forest, and suddenly he saw a calf standing in the snow. Who could have been so stupid as to have left an animal out in this kind of weather? he thought. But his mission was of greater urgency than the impending woes of a frostbitten calf and so he kept walking.

"Just as he was getting close to the home of the midwife, however, he turned to see if the calf had followed him and, sure enough, there it was. He walked even faster, and when he finally got to where he was going, he told the midwife what had happened. But the calf was gone, and she assumed it had all been a hallucination resulting from his anxiety over the impending birth.

"Bothered by her skepticism, the man determined to prove his sanity. 'Come,' he said, 'I'll show you the footprints.' By then, however, the midwife had figured out what had happened and woke her husband so that he would accompany them.

"They went to where the man had seen the calf, but there were no footprints anywhere. The midwife turned to him and said, 'Tonight you encountered the Devil, and you are very lucky to still be alive.'"

Pietro sits back in his chair. *Allora?* he says. So?

I am unsure how to respond, so I merely shake my head as if to say, "Incredible."

He takes that as a sign that he should continue. "There are many stories I could tell you that originate in this very village and with which I have had personal experience. But the most powerful one I've ever heard is the true story of one Giovanni Bernabo," who was, apparently, a young libertine from Lucca whose parents lived modestly in an old stone house on the Via Fillungo.

"Now this Giovanni played the violin very well, and on All Souls' Day, instead of going to the cemetery with his parents, he decided to go out to play in the piazzas, hoping to earn some money.

"His father begged him to change his plans. 'Come with us,' he said. 'Don't you know it is a sacrilege to play a musical instrument on All Souls' Day?' But Giovanni responded with the impudence that seems to be characteristic of most young people his age. 'Whoever is dead is dead forever,' he answered. 'I on the other hand am alive and am going to play even if it means I ultimately go to hell.'"

Pietro purses his lips. These children, his expression implies. What is a father to do?

"Giovanni met up with his friends in the Piazza San Michele," Pietro continues, "and one of his friends invited him to play at a big feast in an elegant *palazzo*. The friend handed him a great sum of money and said there would be more if he played for the entire night.

"So Giovanni went, and after playing for a few hours, he began to feel very feverish, but he kept on playing because he wanted the rest of the money. Before long, however, the heat began spreading from his face to his arms to the lining of his stomach, and it felt as if his entire body was on fire.

"When he was unable to withstand the heat any longer, he put aside his violin and ran to the nearest window. As he threw open the shutters, he saw below him a raging fire and hundreds of people writhing within its flames. People were everywhere, groaning and begging for mercy.

Quest'è l'Inferno, one person finally yelled up to him. 'This is hell. Go home now. Don't wait for any more money.'

"Giovanni closed the shutters and hurried in search of the friend who had brought him. 'Take me home,' he begged. And the man took him to the Church of San Michele, where the priest bathed him in holy water and restored him to life."

There is silence for a moment and then Pietro says: "Giovanni never again ignored his parents' wishes."

I am not quite sure I would have chosen that particular outcome as the moral of the story, but I keep my thoughts to myself.

"So, is there anything a person can do to keep these things from happening?" I ask Antonio, who has kept completely silent except to nod his head at the appropriate moments.

He thinks for a few seconds and then begins reciting a litany of preventive measures that he personally swears by:

On the feast day of Saint Lorenzo (August 10), search through the garden for pieces of coal and then place them on the windowsill to prevent bad storms.

Upon hearing that someone is sick, touch steel immediately.

On the feast day of Saint Cristina (May 10), bake two round loaves of bread, have them blessed by the priest, and then save them for display in times of trouble.

When a hearse passes, touch your testicles.

On the feast day of Saint Michael (September 29), at night, go hunting in the woods for witches, and every so often yell *Macconeccio! Macco* is polenta flour, and *neccio* is chestnut flour. The ritual is designed to drive away witches and spirits who might otherwise prevent a good corn and chestnut harvest.

Antonio also tells me about placing extra-virgin olive oil in a dish of water to find out whether a bad-tempered friend or relative is really suffering from the *malocchio.* Literally translated, *malocchio* means "evil eye," but the word is traditionally used to signify some sort of evil spirit. "You pour a few drops into the water," he says. "If the oil floats, no *malocchio.* If it sinks, *male.*" Bad.

"Actually," he continues, "many of our superstitions revolve around olive oil. It is, after all, our most precious resource." He points to a row of bottles containing this year's oil. All come from an olive grove owned by the same people who own both this bar and the restaurant upstairs, he says.

"Observe their beauty. Next to a bottle of new extra-virgin oil, even the purest gold pales."

He calls out to Daniela for another cup of espresso. "The worst thing one can do with respect to his future good fortune," he says, "is to spill some oil. Whenever that happens, you will always hear the immediate sound of an *Ave Maria* offered in hopes of resolving the situation."

For the same reason, he continues, olive oil is used when signing the cross on the forehead of both newborn babies and people receiving Extreme Unction. *E, certo,* he says. Naturally. "Those are the two most important moments in life. The first, you are coming in; the second, you are going out. What else would we use but a little new oil?"

We are interrupted by Daniela Cipollini, the owner. "Will you be joining us for lunch?" she asks. And before I can say a word, Antonio and Pietro have answered that, in fact, I will be sitting at their very table.

We go upstairs and have a perfectly delectable lunch consisting of *zuppa di ceci rustica* (rustic chickpea soup) served with fresh crusty bread, a plate of assorted meats, a mixed green salad, and a bottle of 1992 Vernaccia. On the table is also a bottle of extra-virgin olive oil so fresh that the sediment has not yet settled.

Daniela herself joins us at one point, and I ask how she came to open this restaurant. She tells me she has had it for fifteen years (which is incredible given that she appears to be no more than thirty-five) and that it is an outgrowth of the new *strada monte mare,* the road that connected this part of the mountains to the sea. Originally, she says, the restaurant was a private house and she started with just a few tables. It now seats one hundred twenty, and she is planning, soon, to expand to one hundred sixty.

When she leaves to attend to the kitchen, our conversation turns to marble, to the string of caves along the road going south, and, specifically, to working in those caves, which is what Antonio and Pietro do for a living. They tell me that when you say "marble" in Italian—*marmo*—you only mean one thing: white marble. The kind used by Michelangelo. All other kinds of marble, they say, are less valuable and therefore not worthy of sharing the same name.

I ask why there are so many marble caves situated along this particular stretch of road—there are more than three hundred quarries in the area dating back to Roman times, making this the world's oldest industrial site in continuous use, and most are, in fact, on this road. Marble quarries must be near rivers, Antonio responds, because marble can only be cut when it is wet.

After lunch we go outside and walk a little along the road. At a certain point, I notice a life-size statue of the Madonna perched on a hillside opposite the village. The statue faces the forest, which, according to Pietro and Antonio, is the residence of choice for most of the demons plaguing the village of Isola Santa.

"She does what She can, our beautiful Madonna," says Pietro when he notices me staring at the statue. "In some cases, however, even *with* Her help, we still lose the battle."

ABOUT LENTILS AND CHICKPEAS

. . . One day, after Jacob had cooked a soup thick with lentils, his brother, Esau, arrived from a day of working in the fields. When Esau saw what Jacob had made, he begged his brother to give it to him. "I have used all my strength and will not last until tomorrow unless you give me that soup. In exchange, I will give you my first-born son." So Jacob gave him the soup and although Esau went away renewed he was sad because he had given away his primogeniture.
—Genesis 25:29–34

As this passage from the Bible demonstrates, lentils have always been considered a very important food. In Middle Eastern countries they form an essential part of the diet and are served at almost every meal. Likewise in Milan and other areas of Northern Italy where the people also view it as a dish for every day. Most Milanese restaurants in fact have at least one lentil entrée on the menu—*arrosto di maiale con lenticchie* (roast pork with lentils) or *maiale in umido con lenticchie* (stewed pork with lentils) or even *sformato di lenticchie* (a type of molded lentil quiche).

In the Garfagnana, however, lentils are reserved for use in soups and on holidays, when they are generally served with a type of bulbous pork sausage called *zampone*. Because of their round flat shape, which is suggestive of money, they are a quintessential part of every Garfagnino's New Year's Eve menu in hopes that they will bring good luck in the form of a financial windfall.

While lentil recipes are few and far between, chickpeas are quite another story. As much a part of the diet as *borlotti*—cranberry beans—

chickpeas are prepared in a nearly infinite number of ways, including marinated in a garlic and parsley pesto, as a side dish for grilled *baccalà,* or simply drizzled with oil and eaten with bread and wine. The number of chickpea soups alone confounds the mind, as the following selection of recipes will demonstrate.

Chickpeas

Soaking Lentils

There is wide discrepancy of thought on the need for soaking lentils. Some say it is not necessary, that lentils will cook just as easily in the soup. Others say that cooking lentils without their first having been soaked causes the skin to harden around the pulp, which then remains dense and chewy after cooking. To this way of thinking, presoaking serves to tenderize lentils by puffing out the insides and enabling all parts of the lentil to cook equally.

The following recipes adhere to the latter school of thought, and as such the lentils should be placed in a bowl with enough water to cover by 4 inches, and soaked for 2 hours. In any case, prior to soaking (or not), lentils should be picked over to remove bits of stone or dirt and rinsed.

Soaking Chickpeas

Dried chickpeas are among the hardest of the legumes and thus require 2 full days of soaking. Initially, they should be placed in a bowl with enough water to cover by 4 inches and let sit for 5 or 6 hours until the water has been absorbed. Additional water should then be added, and after another 10 to 12 hours, that water should be changed.

Many Garfagnini remove the skins from chickpeas after cooking and before eating because they say the skins are too tough to digest. Whether you do or not is purely a matter of taste; the recipes included in this section do not require peeling.

If you ever spill olive oil, offer an immediate Ave Maria
and pray you haven't cursed your future.

MINESTRONE DI LENTICCHIE AL POMODORO

Minestrone with Lentils and Tomatoes

"Lentils are a more-than-worthy alternative to beans," said Pellegrino Artusi in his classic nineteenth-century text, The Science of the Kitchen and the Art of Eating Well. *In this recipe, they are indeed a worthy alternative, blended as they are with tomatoes, prosciutto, rice, and a hefty sprinkling of Parmesan cheese.*

1⅓ cups lentils, soaked according to directions on page 149
4 quarts Basic Chicken Broth (see page 12)
3 tablespoons extra-virgin olive oil
1 small onion, diced
1 clove garlic, minced
1 dried chili pepper, crushed
1 chunk (2 ounces) prosciutto, diced
¼ cup canned Italian plum tomatoes, squeezed until shredded and
     with liquid reserved
Salt and freshly ground black pepper to taste
1⅓ cups Arborio rice
½ cup chopped fresh parsley

1. Drain the lentils and place in a soup pot along with half the broth. Heat to boiling over medium heat. Reduce the heat to low, cover, and cook for ½ hour, adding more broth if necessary.

2. Heat the oil in another soup pot over medium heat. Sauté the onion, garlic, chili, and prosciutto for 5 minutes or until the onion has lightly browned.

3. Add the tomatoes and the remaining broth and stir well to mix. Add salt and pepper, cover, and heat to boiling.

4. Add rice to the soup and cook covered for 15 minutes over low heat, stirring frequently. Add the lentils and their broth to the soup. Cook for another 5 minutes, stirring to mix well. Serve hot, sprinkled with the parsley.

ZUPPA DI LENTICCHIE AL POMODORO E PROSCIUTTO
Lentil Soup with Tomatoes and Prosciutto

Lentils seem like a poor people's dish, says chef Daniela of Isola Santa's Ristorante Daniela, but they are rich in the carbohydrates that were important during the war when the name of the game was to fill one's stomach in a way that lasted until the next day.

This and the following recipe are for very different types of lentil soups, one a rather delicate combination of lentils, tomatoes, and prosciutto; the other a richer blend achieved by the addition of anchovies and fish broth. "Both wonderful," Daniela says, "both worthy of gracing the tables of kings!"

2 cups lentils, soaked according to directions on page 149
¼ cup extra-virgin olive oil
5 cloves garlic, 3 cloves minced, remainder halved
1 stalk celery, diced
8 ounces Swiss chard, stems removed, cleaned and chopped
1 chunk (8 ounces) prosciutto, diced
2 tablespoons canned tomato paste
4 cups Basic Vegetable Broth (see page 14)
Salt and freshly ground black pepper to taste
8 ¾-inch-thick slices peasant-style bread, stale or toasted

1. Drain the lentils and place in a soup pot along with enough water to cover by 2 inches. Heat to boiling over medium heat. Reduce the heat to low, cover, and cook for ½ hour, adding more water if necessary.

2. Heat the oil in a skillet over low heat. Sauté the minced garlic, celery, chard, and prosciutto for 10 minutes, stirring constantly. Add the tomato paste, broth, salt, and pepper and cook for 3 more minutes.

3. Add the sautéed vegetables to the soup pot with the cooked lentils, stirring to mix well. Cover, and cook for 30 minutes over low heat.

4. Rub both sides of the bread with the garlic halves, 2 slices per garlic half. Divide the slices among 4 bowls. Pour the soup over the bread and serve hot.

ZUPPA DI LENTICCHIE
CON LE ACCIUGHE
Lentil Soup with Anchovies

⬤

> 1 pound lentils, soaked according to directions on page 149
> 2 tablespoons extra-virgin olive oil
> 2 cloves garlic, crushed
> 4 anchovy fillets, drained and mashed
> 1 cup canned Italian plum tomatoes, squeezed until shredded and
>   with liquid reserved
> Salt and freshly ground black pepper to taste
> 8 cups Basic Fish Broth (see page 13)
> 3 tablespoons chopped fresh parsley

1. Drain the lentils and place in a soup pot along with enough water to cover by 2 inches. Heat to boiling over medium heat. Reduce the heat to low, cover, and cook for ½ hour, adding more water if necessary. Drain, reserving the cooking liquid. Return the liquid to the pot and keep hot.

2. Heat the oil in a soup pot over medium heat. Sauté the garlic until lightly browned. Remove with a slotted spoon and discard.

3. Add the mashed anchovies, crushed tomatoes and liquid, and drained lentils to the oil in the pot. Cook for 3 minutes over low heat, stirring to mix well. Add salt, pepper, and the reserved lentil cooking liquid as well as the fish broth. Cook for 10 more minutes.

4. Serve hot, sprinkled with the chopped parsley.

CREMA DI LENTICCHIE
Thick Lentil Cream

At one time cream of lentil soup was reserved for children and old people because of both its texture and digestibility. Later people began adding other ingredients— like pepper and prosciutto—and eventually it evolved into a popular soup for the simpler, lighter evening meal that characterizes this area's culinary tradition.

> 2 pounds lentils, soaked according to directions on page 149
> 1 small carrot, scraped
> 1 stalk celery
> 6 tablespoons extra-virgin olive oil
> 2 medium onions, chopped
> 2 cloves garlic, minced
> 1 chunk (4 ounces) prosciutto, diced
> 6 cups Basic Chicken Broth (see page 12)
> 1 cup half-and-half
> Salt and freshly ground black pepper to taste
> 16 croutons fried in oil (see page 66)

1. Drain the lentils and place in a soup pot along with the carrot, celery, and enough water to cover by 2 inches. Heat to boiling over medium heat. Reduce the heat to low, cover, and cook for ½ hour.

2. Remove the carrot and celery and discard. Pass the lentils and their liquid through a food mill.

3. Heat 2 tablespoons of the oil in another soup pot over medium heat. Sauté the onion and garlic for 7 minutes or until lightly browned. Add the diced prosciutto and cook over low heat for 10 minutes, stirring constantly.

4. Add the mashed lentils to the pot along with the broth, stirring to mix well. Add salt and pepper and cook, covered, over very low heat for 15 minutes. Add the half-and-half and stir to blend.

5. Divide the croutons among 4 bowls. Pour the soup over and serve hot, drizzled with the remaining oil.

ZUPPA DI LENTICCHIE CON BATTUTO DI NOCE

Lentil Soup with Fresh Walnut Paste

The Garfagnini eat lentils for good luck, hoping to receive as much good fortune as there are lentils in the bowl. But restaurateur Daniela Cipollini suspects that any good luck comes not from magical powers, but from the fact that lentils are an excellent source of nutrition. "They have almost no fat, no cholesterol, and many many vitamins as well as protein," she says. "I never, however, speak of such things to my clients who I know want to hear only that lentils taste good and will bring them an immediate windfall of riches." This is a recipe devised by Daniela and me on one of many wonderful days spent cooking together in her enormous kitchen.

> 1 pound lentils, soaked according to directions on page 149
> 4 cups Basic Chicken Broth (see page 12)
> 2 cloves garlic, peeled
> ¼ cup shelled walnuts
> ½ cup heavy cream
> Salt and freshly ground black pepper

1. Drain the lentils and place in a soup pot along with enough water to cover by 2 inches. Heat to boiling over medium heat. Reduce the heat to low, cover, and cook for ½ hour, adding more water if necessary.

2. Add the broth to the pot and heat through.

3. Crush the garlic in a mortar and pestle. Add the salt and walnuts and crush to a paste. Add the cream, 1 teaspoon at a time, crushing with the pestle until a thick paste has formed.

4. Ladle the lentil soup into 4 bowls. Stir one tablespoon of walnut cream into each bowl, dust with pepper, and serve.

ZUPPA DI CECI RUSTICA
Country-Style Chickpea Soup

Signora Angelina Benedetti is a self-described ninety-year-old "youngster" who lives in Isola Santa proper. When I talk to her of chickpeas, she sighs and says, "Write, write, but about cenerata you know nothing." And she laughs to herself. "You are right," I tell her. "What is it?" My question satisfies her need to have one up on me. She settles back in her chair and says, "In my day, we placed the chickpeas in a bowl, covered them with a clean white cloth, dusted it with cenere—chimney ashes—and poured lukewarm water over the top. We soaked the chickpeas overnight in this solution and then, in the morning, rinsed and cooked them. Ah, those were chickpeas!" While Signora Angelina's soaking method certainly bears trying, the following recipe results in a perfectly good soup using the more traditional method described.

⅔ cup dried chickpeas, soaked according to directions on page 149
3 medium potatoes, peeled and cubed
2 small carrots, scraped and chopped
1 stalk celery, diced
1 tablespoon canned tomato paste
1 cup chopped fresh parsley
Salt and freshly ground black pepper to taste
8 ¾-inch-thick slices peasant-style bread, toasted
¼ cup extra-virgin olive oil
¼ cup freshly grated Parmigiano-Reggiano

1. Drain the chickpeas, rinse them under cold running water, and drain again.

2. Place the chickpeas in a soup pot along with the potatoes, carrots, celery, tomato paste, parsley, and enough water to cover by 2 inches. Heat to boiling over medium heat. Reduce heat to low, cover, and cook for 3 hours, adding more water if necessary.

3. Pass the soup through a food mill and return to the pot. Add salt and pepper and cook until heated.

4. Divide the bread among 4 bowls. Pour the soup over and serve, drizzled with oil and dusted with the grated cheese.

CACCIUCCO DI CECI

Chickpea Stew

⬤

Says Isola Santa's Signora Angelina: "If you think this cacciucco was a dish for poor people, you are wrong. Its origins are very old, dating back, in fact, to the 1890s. And believe me, those who ate it were anything but poor!"

> 1 pound dried chickpeas, soaked according to directions on page 149
> ¼ cup extra-virgin olive oil
> 1 medium onion, diced
> 3 cloves garlic, crushed
> 4 canned anchovy fillets, rinsed, drained, and mashed
> Salt and freshly ground black pepper to taste
> 10 leaves Swiss chard, cleaned and chopped
> 4 very ripe plum tomatoes, roughly chopped
> 2 tablespoons basil pesto (see page 10)

1. Drain the chickpeas, rinse under cold running water, and drain again.

2. Place the chickpeas in a soup pot along with enough water to cover by 2 inches. Heat to boiling over medium heat. Reduce the heat to low, cover, and cook for 2 hours or until tender. Add more water if necessary.

3. Heat the oil in another soup pot over medium heat. Sauté the onion, garlic, and anchovies for 5 minutes, stirring constantly. Add salt, pepper, and the chickpeas along with their liquid.

4. Add the Swiss chard to the soup pot along with the tomatoes. Continue to cook, covered, for 20 minutes over low heat.

5. Pour into 4 bowls, stir 1 tablespoon basil pesto into each and serve hot.

CECI, MELE, SALSICCIA E PATATE ALLA GARFAGNANA

Chickpeas, Apples, Sausage, and Potatoes Garfagnana-Style

Like beans, chickpeas are often paired in soups with potatoes for reasons having to do with both texture and taste. Generally, the preparations call for long cooking times over low heat in order to completely dissolve the potatoes and allow them to create a dense, creamy broth. This particular recipe dates back to the 1800s but is still prepared in many of the Garfagnana's finest restaurants. I have substituted sausage for the pork skin used originally.

⅔ cup dried chickpeas, soaked according to directions on page 149
2 tablespoons extra-virgin olive oil
2 cloves garlic, minced
1 dried chili, crushed
1 medium onion, diced
4 links fennel sausage, removed from casings and crumbled
1½ pounds potatoes, peeled and cubed
2 medium red apples, peeled, cored, and cubed
8 cups Basic Meat Broth (see page 11)
Salt and freshly ground black pepper to taste
1 tablespoon chopped fresh sage
4 tablespoons chopped fresh parsley
½ cup freshly grated Pecorino Romano

1. Drain the chickpeas, rinse under cold running water, and drain again.

2. Heat the oil in a soup pot over medium heat. Sauté the garlic, chili, onion, and sausage for 7 minutes or until the onion is lightly browned. Add the drained chickpeas, potatoes, apples, and broth. Heat to boiling over medium heat. Reduce the heat to low, cover, and cook for 3 hours, adding more water if necessary.

3. When the chickpeas are tender, add the sage and parsley, stirring to blend. Serve immediately, dusted with the grated cheese.

CECI E FUNGHI ALLA DANIELA ●

Daniela's Chickpea and Mushroom Soup

In winter the Garfagnini rely on chickpeas almost as often as they do beans. Like beans, chickpeas are used as an accompaniment for baccalà*; as a salad with minced garlic, parsley, oil, and lemon; boiled and served with bread and oil, and, of course, in a wonderful variety of soups. One thing is certain, says chef Daniela. "If meat was the food of the rich and beans and chickpeas that of the poor, at least the poor can console themselves in knowing that their rustic cuisine saved them from problems with both cholesterol and gout." The following recipe pairs the pungency of dried porcinis with the delicate flavor of chickpeas to create a rich, dense soup appropriately served as a one-dish meal. I have added the sausage to create an even richer flavor.*

⅔ cup dried chickpeas, soaked according to directions on page 149
3 tablespoons extra-virgin olive oil
1 medium onion, chopped
1 chunk (2 ounces) smoked pancetta or bacon, diced
4 links hot pork sausage, removed from casings and crumbled
3 ounces dried porcini mushrooms, soaked in lukewarm water for
   30 minutes
6 tablespoons chopped fresh parsley
2 tablespoons canned tomato puree
8 ounces potatoes, peeled
8 cups Basic Mushroom Broth (see page 15)
Salt and freshly ground black pepper to taste

1. Drain the chickpeas, rinse under cold running water, and drain again.

2. Place the chickpeas in a soup pot with enough water to cover by 2 inches. Heat to boiling over medium heat. Reduce the heat to low, cover, and cook for 1½ hours, adding more water if necessary. Drain and reserve one cup of the cooking liquid.

3. Heat the oil in the soup pot over medium heat. Sauté the onion, pancetta or bacon, and sausage for 7 minutes or until the onion is lightly browned. Drain the mushrooms and cut them into slivers. Add to the pot along with half the parsley. Stir to mix well.

4. Stir the tomato puree and 1 cup of the reserved cooking liquid into the mixture in the pot.

5. Boil the potatoes in salted water until soft. Pass through a food mill and add to the pot along with the chickpeas and broth. Stir to blend, add salt and pepper, cover, and cook for 30 minutes over low heat.

6. Serve hot, sprinkled with the remaining parsley.

The tiny picturesque village of Isola Santa was once a hideout for medieval renegades.

MINESTRA DI CECI CON PENNE E GORGONZOLA

Chickpea Soup with Penne and Gorgonzola

●

"No one else knows how to make this soup," says chef Daniela. "Not even the best chefs in the Garfagnini." She tells me that, despite how her clients love her regular chickpea soups, she tires of always making the same ones. "So I invented this new recipe," she says. "And of course my clients now love it even more than the others. How could they not? It has penne and gorgonzola in it. And everyone knows how the Garfagnini feel about their pasta and cheese." In re-creating Daniela's recipe, I improvised even further with the addition of spinach and rutabagas, which give the soup added complexity.

> 1 pound dried chickpeas, soaked according to directions on page 149
> 3 cloves garlic, crushed
> 1 small (2-inch square) piece pork skin
> 3 medium carrots, scraped and sliced into ¼-inch rounds
> 8 ounces rutabagas, cleaned and cut into ½-inch chunks
> 2 tablespoons tomato paste
> 4 cups Basic Chicken Broth (see page 12)
> Salt and freshly ground black pepper to taste
> 8 ounces fresh spinach, washed and roughly chopped
> 8 ounces penne pasta
> 4 ounces gorgonzola cheese, crumbled

1. Drain the chickpeas, rinse under cold running water, and drain again.

2. Place the chickpeas in a soup pot along with the garlic, pork skin, and enough water to cover by 2 inches. Heat to boiling over medium heat. Reduce the heat to low, cover, and cook for 2 hours, adding more water if necessary.

3. Pass the chickpeas and their cooking liquid through a food mill. Return the mash to the pot along with the reserved liquid. Add the carrots, rutabagas, tomato paste, broth, salt, and pepper. Heat to boiling over medium heat. Reduce the heat to low, cover, and cook for 20 minutes.

4. Add the spinach and cook for another 5 minutes.

5. Add the penne and gorgonzola and cook for 8 minutes or until the pasta is tender, stirring occasionally. Serve hot.

Top: *Angelina Benedetti, "About chickpeas you know nothing."*
Bottom: *Piero, an expert on the devil's tricks, and Antonio, who knows
how to thwart them.*

Chapter Seven

THE FRUITS OF ISOLATION

Sasso Rosso

ZUPPE DI FAGIOLI
Bean Soups

*F*our times a year, Italian teenagers turn away from their motor scooters and CD players in favor of a quiet room, a stack of books, and an endless pot of good strong espresso. The transformation is the result of end-of-term exams, a quadrennial ordeal that calls for sobriety; in Italian high schools, these exams—both their oral and written components— must be passed in order to continue to the next level.

Ordinarily, my cousin Elena is an excellent student. But somehow this term she is lagging behind. Perhaps, as her mother so wryly points out, the blame belongs to the new boyfriend—*quello con l'anello nel naso;* the one with the ring in his nose. Whatever.

At any rate, her father Mariano and I are now on route to retrieve Elena and her two also-lagging-behind friends from the rustic wood hut in Garfagnana where they went three days ago to study in isolation. Perched on a precipice four kilometers outside the village of Sasso Rosso, the hut has feather beds, a woodstove, four chairs, a table, and nothing else. It belongs to Mariano's cousin, Ivano, who lives in Sasso Rosso itself and agreed to both keep an eye on the girls and make daily deliveries of food.

The road to Sasso Rosso snakes through the verdant forests of the Garfagnana, rising higher and higher until, in the distance, one spots the humplike red boulder for which the village is named. With sixty-four inhabitants (twenty of whom are currently over eighty) and a location that precludes outside contact, Sasso Rosso's charms depend on how one views isolation. To my cousin Santi, a big-city fashion designer, it reeks of death. "If I had to live here," he says, "I would stay in bed all day. What reason would there ever be to get up?"

But to Mariano, who becomes lighter and more amiable the closer we get to Sasso Rosso, isolation is merely a pseudonym for *essere libero*— being free. "The mind sees farther," he explains. "When you are in a small space with many people, you are always reacting. To what people say, to what they do, to all that you see, to that which you do not see but resolve to see as soon as possible. Here everything has a rhythm of its own, and the rhythms vibrate in spaces so far from each other that you eventually give up reacting and move instead to reflecting. And at that point, you discover a sustenance that was never before possible."

Sasso Rosso is indeed isolated. The closest town of any stature (which means one that has a grocery store and restaurant) is ten kilometers away. But it is not so much the distance as the view; wherever you look, all you see are mountains, valleys, and trees. *Che altro ci dovrebbe essere?* Mariano asks. What else should there be?

We park the car at the bottom of the hill and walk up a stone pathway dating back to the eleventh century, past the church tower, which was rebuilt in 1845 after a ferocious brawl between village residents and an impoverished municipal administration. Underlying the brawl were what villagers saw as two unmistakably related facts: (1) The church tower had begun leaning three years earlier when, for some reason, there was a shift in the earth beneath the church; (2) during those same three years, villagers experienced particularly bad chestnut harvests (historically chestnuts have been a food staple in the Garfagnana).

Have it as you will, but as any of Sasso Rosso's residents will tell you, the autumn after the church tower was rebuilt brought the greatest chestnut harvest of the century, and there has never been a problem since.

We continue up the steep path to Ivano's house, which, like everything else in the town, is made of stones—red ones, of course. When we finally—and breathlessly—stand before his ornate wooden door, we see that it sports a handwritten message informing us that he has gone to help the girls carry down their belongings. He left, the message says, at four. It is now five, which means we have approximately an hour and a half to wait.

Just at that moment, we hear the sound of bells. A glance in the distance reveals the source—a herd of sheep moving from a distant pasture to one closer to town. *Ciao, Alduino,* Mariano shouts out.

Alduino is the shepherd, who lives two houses away from Ivano. He is on his way home, carrying two large metal buckets filled with sheep's milk. For the next two hours, he and his wife, Elda, will be making cheese. "Do you want to watch?" Mariano asks. I nod my head.

The cheese they make is a type of pecorino. Which type exactly depends on how much the cheese is allowed to age. Alduino begins by pouring the milk into an iron pot, which is then hung on a metal hook suspended over the coals in the fireplace. When the milk has boiled, he removes the pot and sets it in the middle of the kitchen to cool. As her husband sinks into his chair, Elda pulls out the coffeepot and turns on the nineteen-inch color television that seems so strikingly out of place in this sparse, meager kitchen.

The news blares forth, a grainy video montage showing the first contingent of Italian soldiers leaving for Bosnia. We watch for a few minutes in silence and then Alduino tells us how he spent World War II in Mostar, very close to where the NATO forces are now encamped.

"Italy was still on the side of the Axis then," he says. "Our companies fought many battles together, but at one point a German commander ordered the execution of three hundred Yugoslav partisans. They were lined up against the wall in a small mountain village, and when the sergeant gave the signal, we were all supposed to shoot. *Io no, ho detto.* Not me, I told myself. I stayed in the back and when no one was looking, ran away across the mountains. It took me twelve days to reach safety, walking through ice and snow with bare feet because my shoes had worn through."

The news anchor moves on to a story about flooding in Liguria and after a few minutes' silence, Alduino also moves on, to the story of how he came to be a shepherd. It was his father's occupation, he says, and after the war he just naturally took it up.

"But I was already married"—he pats Elda's hand—"and the money was not enough." So he went to work as a miner in the marble caves above Vagli.

The marble there was red, he explains, and then poses the possibility of a connection between Vagli's red marble and nearby Sasso Rosso's red rocks. Mariano shakes his head and laughs. It is obvious he has heard this theory before.

"The pay was good, but by the early 1960s there was no more marble," Alduino continues, "and so I returned to sheepherding. I had over a hundred sheep then. In the mornings I would take the flock up on the hill, up behind the village where the land levels off. At one point I realized I could plant potatoes up there too, so I did, and when it came time to harvest them, I would bring the flock back down with almost two hundred pounds of potatoes on my back. I bartered them for other food."

One day, he says, a man with whom he had bartered marveled at the vast quantities of potatoes he was able to deliver. You must have a strong donkey, he told him, and asked to see the animal. Here Alduino laughs. " 'I AM the donkey,' I told him!"

Another time, he purchased two pigs to use for food. "At night I kept the pigs in the back room. But in the morning, I would bring them up the hill to graze with the sheep. *Quei maledetti!* Those cursed animals! They always refused to walk up by themselves. I had to tie their feet and carry them up. Down, of course, they came with no problem."

His story contains elements of the familiar—long hours, little pay, a meager existence. It also contains a few oddities. One has to do with salt, which was so scarce that he had to barter prosciutto in order to get it, a pound for a pound. Another involves the animosities that are possible even in a village of sixty-four people—in this case, the animosity between Alduino and his neighbor, who is also a shepherd.

"My son came to visit last week," Alduino says, "and he drove his motor scooter up the dirt road past the man's herd. The way that *vigliacco* bellowed, you would have thought my son had slaughtered a few of his sheep! I don't know why he keeps his sheep so close to the road in the first place. Everybody knows the closer sheep are to the road, the less milk they produce."

By now the milk has cooled, and it is time to make the cheese. Elda hands Alduino a bottle marked CAGLIO—rennet—which he sprinkles over the milk, and then begins to swish his hands through the liquid. After a fair amount of swishing, a ball begins to form. More swishing and the ball grows larger. When the ball is as large as a cantaloupe, he removes it from the milk and places it in a round, perforated form.

For the next ten minutes, Alduino kneads the ball into the form, squeezing and smoothing to remove as much liquid as possible. When satisfied with both the shape and the texture, he removes the hardened ball and places it in a solid form, where it will stay until ready. In twelve hours he will salt the top of the cheese; in twenty-four hours he will salt the other side. In one month the cheese will turn yellow, which signifies the beginning of the aging process. How long after that it is eaten depends on taste.

"If you want soft creamy pecorino, eat it right away. If you want a harder type, let it sit for a few weeks longer."

The remainder of the milk will turn into ricotta, he tells us. It will happen overnight, like magic, the liquid condensing into the soft creamy curds around which one will then roll *necchi*—a type of thin crepe made from chestnut flour and water.

The door opens and Ivano comes in, followed by Elena and her friends, Lorenza and Liliana. "I knew you would be here," Ivano says, pointing to me and laughing. My tendency always to be in places having to do with food is well known.

I have not seen him in two years, during which time he became engaged to a woman from Lucca. But it didn't work out because they could not agree on geography. She, a fashion stylist, wanted to live in Lucca, both for her work and her social life; he, naturally, wished to remain in the mountains. "In a big city, walls and ceilings are used to create private oases. Here, they are the structures within which people socialize; outside is where you go for privacy. That, to me, seems a more logical arrangement."

We say good-bye to Alduino and Elda, who send us off with a form of three-week-old pecorino and a warning to the girls to maintain a proper balance with respect to their studies, quoting a local proverb: *Chi troppo studia, matto diventa, e chi non studia, mangia polenta.* Who studies too much becomes mad and who doesn't study enough eats polenta. Ivano gives each of the girls a bundle of herbs tied with a yellow ribbon. *Buona fortuna,* he says. "I hope you pass your exams with perfect scores."

Back on the road Mariano questions the girls about their studies. When he ascertains that they have, in fact, truly grasped the subject matter, he tells them he will take them out to dinner as a reward.

We go to Il Casone, an old posthouse built in 1845 by the Duke of Modena, Francesco IV d'Este. The hotel and restaurant takes its name from the town in which it is located: Casone di Profecchia, and has twenty-nine sleeping rooms upstairs from the three main dining halls, many decorated with furniture dating back five hundred years. The owner, Agostino Regoli ("Regolino" to his friends) is a short, talkative man who exudes pride in his accomplishments. Two years ago, he tells us, Il Casone was given the Gold Spoon award for culinary excellence.

Signore Regoli has also expanded the hotel and installed new bathrooms in each of the rooms. He takes us to see room number 9, clearly the most beautiful of all; the bishop of the region slept here whenever he passed through this part of the province, he tells us with pride.

He also resolves the mystery of the peculiar photographs hanging on the wall over the front desk. Upon first glance I thought they portrayed local discus-throwing contests. When I look closer, however, I see that where the camera recorded the actual landing of the so-called disks, the objects seemed to shatter upon impact. Furthermore, the participants seemed afterwards to be *eating* the fragments.

"The Throwing of the Pecorino," says Signore Regoli, smiling at my confusion. "It is an annual event held even now in January. A holdover from the days of poverty, when cheeses were all we had."

As a *primo piatto,* I order *minestra di fave e cardoni*—a soup of fresh fava beans and cardoons. The taste is sublime, and I ask for the specifics of how it was prepared. *Vai in cucina,* Signore Regoli tells me. Go in the kitchen and talk to the chef. I do and am rewarded with not only that particular recipe but a few others as well. In the ensuing exchange, I let slip that I sometimes add a little red wine to my tomato sauce. Clearly astonished, the chef asks for a demonstration. *Buono,* he says of the result, but his expression is not convincing.

Three courses later we are on our way, the girls chattering in the backseat about school and boys and whether or not they should put green streaks in their hair.

Mariano's face is serene, his relaxed body swaying from side to side with each of the mountain curves. "If you like it so much up here in Garfagnana, why don't you move or at least buy a vacation home," I tease him. His response lets me know that, if not physically, spiritually, he has long been a resident. "If I moved here," he explains, "what would I have left to dream about?"

ABOUT BEAN SOUPS

In the Garfagnana, beans have always been known as the beefsteak of poor people, and bean soups, the quintessence of survival. Giovanni

Venturi, a butcher in Massa di Sasso Rosso, which is a somewhat larger town just down the road, remembers the rationalizations made by his father on days when the old man would rummage through his pockets and come up with only a few measly coins. "Papa would then begin to tout the nutritional value of beans and especially bean soups, the vitamins, the minerals, the blood-building qualities. All the time we knew that the real reason had more to do with how they both filled your stomach and gave him twenty-four more hours to come up with some money."

Types of Beans

There are over ten types of beans used by the people of the Garfagnana. Among the reds are: *stregoni,* which means "warlocks," *dall'occhio, scritti, rossi,* which are like kidney beans, and—the cream of the crop—*borlotti,* which are equivalent to cranberry beans.

The whites include *cannellini, piatelle, corone,* and *fagiolane,* which is a larger bean, more like a lima. There is also a type of small black bean known, tellingly, as *fascistini.* Used fresh, as shell beans, they generally require an hour of cooking time and can be cooked as part of the soup.

Soaking

Dried beans should all be soaked before using. First, however, they should be picked over to remove any small stones or discolored pellets, then rinsed thoroughly in cold water. They should be soaked in three to four times as much water as there are beans, and any that float or appear moldy should be discarded. Although many people cook beans in the actual water in which they were soaked, Garfagnini generally drain them first, a process they claim reduces flatulence.

Soaking times depend on type of bean: *cannellini* and other small white beans require the least—4 to 6 hours; while red beans require 12 hours. *Fascistini,* and large white beans also 12 hours. All beans should be cooked until tender; again, this varies according to type. For the most part, 1 cup of dried beans yields 2 to 2½ cups of cooked.

Those who forget to presoak can avail themselves of this quick method of tenderizing: Cover the beans with cold water, bring to a boil, simmer for 5 minutes, and then remove from the heat. Let them sit for an hour, tightly covered, at room temperature, and then use them as you would beans that have soaked overnight.

Another, less acceptable route for those who forget to soak is to buy preprocessed beans, which are now available even in the Garfagnana, although very few people seem to actually use them. Bland in taste and virtually devoid of nutrients, their sole attraction lies in the amount of time saved. As noted culinarian Ada Boni once said, however: "If you lack the time to adequately prepare the food, eat out."

Peeling Fava Beans

Fava skins are thick and should be removed before cooking. To peel, blanch in a pot of boiling water for 2 minutes and then transfer to ice water. Drain and pinch open the thick skin of each bean. Peeled beans will slip out easily.

Il Casone, *an old posthouse built in 1845 by the Duke of Modena.*

ZUPPA DI FAGIOLI ●

Fresh Cranberry Bean Soup

Among the various types of bean soups, zuppa di fagioli *is the mother of all. The reason, according to Agostino Regoli, proprietor of Il Casone, is its perfect blend of ingredients and the slow cooking time, which allows the sage and garlic to* profumare—*perfume the soup. "A very simple recipe," he says, "but one with stupendous results!"*

1 pound fresh shelled *borlotti* (cranberry beans)
8 cups Basic Vegetable Broth (see page 14)
2 teaspoons dried crumbled sage
3 cloves garlic, minced
2 whole cloves
7 tablespoons extra-virgin olive oil
1 chunk (1 ounce) pork fatback, minced
½ medium onion, diced
1 stalk celery, diced
½ teaspoon dried thyme
8 ounces fresh mustard greens, cleaned and roughly chopped
¼ cup tomato paste diluted in ¾ cup water
1 medium fennel bulb, stalks and fronds removed, halved, cored, and roughly chopped
Salt and freshly ground black pepper to taste

1. Place the beans in a large soup pot along with the broth. Add 1 teaspoon of the sage, 1 clove garlic, and the 2 whole cloves. Heat to boiling over medium heat. Reduce the heat to low, cover, and cook for 1 hour.

2. Meanwhile, heat 3 tablespoons of the oil in another soup pot over medium heat. Sauté the fatback, onion, celery, mustard, thyme, and remaining sage and garlic for 3 minutes or until the onion is translucent.

3. Add the diluted tomato paste and the fennel. Stir to mix well and cook for 15 minutes, stirring occasionally.

4. Add the sautéed vegetables to the pot and mix well. Add salt and pepper, cover, and return to a slow boil.

5. Ladle the soup into 4 bowls, drizzle with the remaining oil, and serve hot.

ZUPPA DI TERRA E MARE

Earth and Sea Soup

●

The secret ingredient in this recipe is neither the beans nor the baccalà, *but the herb* battuto, *which gives the broth a rich, savory taste. "Nevertheless," says Il Casone's Agostino Regoli, "choose the* baccalà *carefully. What you want for this soup is one of the thickest meatiest fillets." I have also made this soup using fresh cod fillets in which case I added the chunks during the last 20 minutes of cooking.*

> 1 pound *baccalà* (dried codfish; see Note)
> ¾ cup dried kidney beans, soaked according to directions on page 169
> 8 ounces leeks (white part only), washed well, dried, and diced
> 1 stalk celery, diced
> 3 tablespoons extra-virgin olive oil
> 4 tablespoons chopped fresh parsley
> Salt and freshly ground black pepper to taste
> 4 teaspoons herb *battuto* (see page 10)

1. Soak the *baccalà* in cold water for 48 hours, changing the water 4 or 5 times during this period. Drain, rinse, and dry. Remove the skin and cut the flesh into 1-inch chunks.

2. Drain the beans and place in a soup pot along with enough water to cover by 2 inches. Heat to boiling over medium heat. Reduce the heat to low, cover, and cook for 1 hour. Add more water if necessary. Salt at the halfway mark.

3. Meanwhile, heat the oil in another soup pot. Sauté the leeks and celery for 7 minutes or until the leeks are lightly browned. Add the *baccalà* and sauté for another 5 minutes.

4. When the beans are done, drain, reserving the liquid, and pass half through a food mill.

5. Add the mashed beans, along with the whole beans, to the soup pot with the vegetables. Add enough water to the bean cooking liquid to make 8 cups and add to the pot as well. Stir to mix well, cover, and cook over low heat for 1½ hours.

6. Divide among 4 bowls, stir 1 teaspoon of herb *battuto* into each and serve.

Note: *Baccalà* can be purchased at Italian specialty shops. If unavailable, use any fresh, firm white fish, sautéed separately and added to the soup 15 minutes before serving.

"Red wine in tomato sauce? Incredible!"

INVERNALE DELLA SIGNORA ELDA ●

Signora Elda's Winter Soup

According to Alduino and Elda Cecchi, the following recipe is a perfect one for winter when it is hard to find fresh vegetables. The potatoes add flavor as well as texture, since they completely dissolve during the long slow cooking and produce a thick, creamy broth. I have tried shortening the process by mashing the potatoes in a food mill and heartily recommend sticking to the old way.

> 1 pound dried small kidney beans, soaked according to directions on page 169
> 2 teaspoons dried crumbled sage
> 2 cloves garlic, peeled
> 1 fennel bulb, stalks and fronds removed, halved, cored, and chopped
> 6 tablespoons extra-virgin olive oil
> 2 medium onions, diced
> 3 tablespoons tomato paste, diluted in 1 cup Basic Vegetable Broth (see page 14)
> 3 medium potatoes, peeled and cut into ½-inch chunks
> 2 stalks celery, diced
> 5 fresh basil leaves
> Salt and freshly ground black pepper to taste
> 16 large croutons fried in oil (see page 66)

1. Drain the beans and place in a large pot along with the sage, garlic, fennel, and enough water to cover by 2 inches. Heat over medium heat to boiling. Reduce the heat to low, cover, and cook for 1½ hours. Add more water if necessary. Salt at the halfway mark.

2. Heat the oil in a large skillet. Sauté the onion until soft. Add the diluted tomato paste to the skillet and sauté for 1 minute, stirring constantly. Add the potatoes and sauté for another 5 minutes.

3. Add the celery, basil leaves, salt, and pepper to the skillet. Stir to mix well. Continue to cook until all the ingredients are lightly browned.

4. Add the vegetable mixture to the soup pot with the beans. Cook over low heat until all the ingredients are heated.

5. Divide the croutons among 4 bowls. Pour the soup over and serve hot.

ZUPPA ALLA FRANTOIANA ●

Soup Olive Presser–Style

During olive harvest time, which is generally in November, Garfagnana's growers and pressers come together to test the oil for flavor, body, and acidity, and, above all, to toast the completion of another successful year. Because so many people are involved, the menu is simple and standard: huge vats of bean and vegetable soup, which is then poured over thick slices of crusty bread and covered with a hefty dose of newly pressed oil. The men sit at long tables set up in the frantoio—olive-pressing room—*eating, drinking, and breathing in the heady aroma of newly pressed oil.*

1 pound dried *borlotti* (cranberry beans), soaked according to directions on page 169

¾ cup dried *cannellini* beans, soaked according to directions on page 169

⅓ cup plus 4 tablespoons extra-virgin olive oil

2 leeks (white part only), washed well, dried, and diced

1 medium onion, roughly chopped

2 cloves garlic, minced

8 cups Basic Vegetable Broth (see page 14)

3 stalks celery, diced

3 carrots, scraped and diced

1 fennel bulb, stalks and fronds removed, halved, cored, and roughly chopped

8 ounces Swiss chard, washed, dried, and roughly chopped

12 ounces savoy cabbage, roughly chopped

12 ounces kale, washed, dried, and roughly chopped

1½ cups fresh or frozen peas

6 very ripe Italian plum tomatoes, chopped (or 1½ cups canned)

1 teaspoon dried crumbled sage

3 small zucchini, peeled and diced

8 ounces butternut squash, peeled, seeded, and cut into 1-inch chunks

2 medium potatoes, peeled and cut into ½-inch chunks

1 teaspoon dried thyme

½ teaspoon grated nutmeg

Salt and freshly ground black pepper to taste

4 ¾-inch-thick slices peasant-style bread, stale or toasted

1. Drain the cranberry beans and place in a soup pot along with enough water to cover by 2 inches. Heat to boiling over medium heat. Reduce the heat to low, cover, and cook for 2 hours. Add more water if necessary. Salt at the halfway mark.

2. Drain the *cannellini* beans and place in a large saucepan along with enough water to cover by 2 inches. Heat to boiling over medium heat. Reduce the heat to low, cover, and cook for 2 hours.

3. Heat ⅓ cup oil in a large soup pot over medium heat. Sauté the leeks, onion, and garlic for 5 minutes or until soft. Pour a ladleful of broth over the vegetables and stir to mix well.

4. Add the remainder of the ingredients save for the nutmeg, thyme, and bread. Stir to mix well, cover, and cook for 25 minutes.

5. Using a slotted spoon, remove 1 cup of the kidney beans and ½ cup of the *cannellini*. Pass the remainder through a food mill along with their liquids and stir the mash into the soup pot with the vegetables, adding the thyme, nutmeg, salt, and pepper. Add the whole beans, cover, and cook for 1½ hours over low heat.

6. Divide the bread among 4 bowls, pour the soup over, and drizzle with the remaining oil. Let stand for 15 minutes before eating.

Note: Although this recipe serves considerably more than 4 people, it is so very good the following day that I highly advise making it in the larger quantity.

ZUPPA SOSTANZIOSA ●

Hearty Kale and White Bean Soup

Elda Checchi of Sasso Rosso says that, in winter, she hardly ever goes out of doors. Fortunately, the grocery store is next door, milk is always available by walking into the sheep pen adjacent to the house, and her husband, Alduino, plants a fall garden from which she is able to obtain most of the vegetables she needs. "I cook very simple things during the winter season," she says, "using whatever ingredients I have. There is no other choice, being isolated up here from the rest of the world." The following soup is perfect for winter, rich and hearty and more delicate than other bean soups because of its use of white beans and milk. I have substituted the more accessible cow's milk for the milk donated by Elda and Alduino's sheep.

> ¾ cup dried *cannellini* beans, soaked according to directions on
>   page 169
> 2 teaspoons dried crumbled sage
> 8 cloves garlic, peeled
> ½ cup extra-virgin olive oil
> 1 stalk celery, diced
> 1 medium onion, roughly chopped
> ¼ cup chopped fresh parsley
> 2 tablespoons tomato paste, diluted in 1 cup water
> 12 ounces kale, washed, dried, and roughly chopped
> 8 ounces rutabagas, cleaned and cubed
> 3 medium potatoes, peeled and cut into ½-inch chunks
> 8 ounces parsnips, peeled and chopped
> Salt and freshly ground black pepper to taste
> 1 cup whole milk
> 12 ¾-inch-thick-slices peasant-style bread, stale or toasted

1. Drain the beans and place in a large soup pot along with half the sage, 2 garlic cloves, and enough water to cover by 2 inches. Heat to boiling over medium heat. Reduce the heat to low, cover, and cook for 1 hour. Add more water if necessary. Salt at the halfway mark.

2. Meanwhile, heat ¼ cup of the oil in another soup pot over medium heat. Sauté the celery, onion, remaining 1 teaspoon sage, and parsley for 7 minutes or until the onion is lightly browned. Stir in the diluted tomato paste, cover, and cook for 10 minutes.

3. When the beans are done, drain, reserving the liquid. Pass half through a food mill. Add the mashed beans, with the liquid, to the vegetables in the pot. Reserve the whole beans.

4. Add the kale, rutabagas, potatoes, and parsnips to the pot, cover, and cook over low heat for 30 minutes.

5. Add the whole beans to the soup and stir to mix well. Add salt, pepper, and the milk and heat through.

6. Cut the remaining 6 garlic cloves in half. Using half a clove for each 2 slices of bread, rub the bread with the cut sides of the garlic until each slice is perfumed with the odor.

7. Place 2 slices of the bread in the bottom of a soup terrine. Cover with soup, layer with more bread, then more soup until all the ingredients are used up. Allow to rest for a few minutes and then ladle into bowls. Drizzle with the remaining olive oil before eating.

ZUPPA DI FAGIOLI E SALAME COTTA IN FORNO ◐

Oven-Baked Bean and Salami Soup

The following soup is one of Il Casone's most popular both for the fluffier texture of oven-baked beans and for the fact that it is served piping hot in a beautiful earthenware casserole. "We bring it to the table right from the oven," says proprietor Agostino Regoli, "and when the waiter lifts the lid, the air is perfumed with a complex hearty fragrance." Before serving, Regoli advises dusting the bottoms of the soup bowls with freshly ground black pepper. "The flavor should be very pungent," he says. In recreating the recipe, I took his advice to heart and added crushed chilis to the initial sauté, which gave the finished soup a truly complex flavor.

2 tablespoons extra-virgin olive oil

1 medium onion, chopped

1 medium carrot, scraped and chopped

3 cloves garlic, crushed

1 (or more) dried chili pepper, crushed

2 small links Italian salami (*cacciatorini*)★ diced

Salt and freshly ground black pepper

4 cups Basic Vegetable Broth (see page 14)

1 cup dry white wine

1 pound *cannellini* beans, soaked according to directions on page 169

3 tablespoons chopped fresh parsley

1. Heat the oil in a soup pot. Sauté the onion, carrot, garlic, chili pepper, and salami for 7 minutes or until the onion is lightly browned. Add salt, pepper, the broth, and the wine, cover, and cook for 10 minutes over medium heat.

2. Preheat the oven to 350 degrees. Drain the beans and place in an oven-proof covered casserole (preferably terra-cotta) along with enough water to cover by 2 inches. Stir the salami and vegetable sauté into the bean pot, cover, and bake for 2 hours, stirring 2 or 3 times during that period.

3. Stir the parsley into the soup just after lifting the lid. Dust the bottoms of 4 soup bowls with freshly ground black pepper and serve.

★*Cacciatorini* are air-cured links of salami found in Italian specialty stores. A 4-ounce chunk of Genoa salami can be substituted.

ZUPPA BASTARDA

"Bastard" Soup

●

Bastard soup is so named because it uses black beans, which are called fascistini *in honor of what Elda Cecchi calls "that black-shirted bastard who brought Italy to the brink of destruction during WWII." On the positive side, it is very easy to prepare. "All you need," she says, "are good* fascistini *beans, some stale bread, and—above all—some exceptionally good extra-virgin oil. Il gioco e fatto!" The game is won.*

> 1¼ cups dried black beans, soaked according to directions on page 169
> 7 cloves garlic, peeled
> 1 medium red onion, peeled
> 2 teaspoons dried crumbled sage
> 8 ¾-inch-thick slices peasant-style bread, stale or toasted
> Salt to taste
> 4 tablespoons extra-virgin olive oil
> Freshly ground black pepper to taste
> 4 tablespoons basil pesto (see page 10)

1. Drain the beans and place in a soup pot along with 5 cloves of the garlic, the onion, sage, and enough water to cover by 2 inches. Heat to boiling over medium heat. Reduce the heat to low, cover, and cook for 1½ hours. Add more water if necessary. Salt at the halfway mark.

2. Cut the remaining garlic cloves in half. Using half a clove for each 2 slices of bread, rub the bread with the cut sides of the garlic until the bread is perfumed with the odor. Divide the slices among 4 bowls and top each with 1 tablespoon of the basil pesto.

3. Pour the bean soup into the bowls over the bread. Serve hot.

RIBOLLITA GARFAGNINA
Twice-Cooked Bean Soup, Garfagnana-Style

There are as many versions of ribollita *as there are Tuscan villages. The name means "boiled again," and refers to the fact that the underlying base is an already-cooked bean soup, which is then layered with bread and olive oil. Although many versions start with a complex recipe, the Garfagnini version uses a simple bean soup preparation and relies on the combination of newly pressed oil and herb* battuto *for its wonderful fragrance.*

> 1 pound dried kidney beans, soaked according to directions on
>   page 169
> 2 cloves garlic, peeled and halved
> 1 medium onion, halved
> 1 medium carrot, scraped and cut into three chunks
> 1 teaspoon dried crumbled sage
> Salt and freshly ground black pepper
> 1 pound stale peasant-style bread, sliced into ½-inch slices
> ½ cup herb *battuto* (see page 10)
> ¼ cup extra-virgin olive oil

1. Drain the beans and place in a soup pot along with the garlic, onion, carrot, sage, and enough water to cover by 2 inches. Heat over medium heat to boiling. Reduce the heat to low, cover, and cook for 1½ hours. Add more water if necessary. Salt at the halfway mark.

2. Drain the beans and vegetables, reserving the liquid. Pass through a food mill into a bowl. Add salt and pepper.

3. Preheat the oven to 350 degrees. Using a covered, oven-proof bowl (preferably earthenware), assemble the soup. Pour a layer of olive oil across the bottom, place the bread slices side by side on top of the oil, spread 2 or 3 tablespoons *battuto* over the bread and cover with a layer of bean mash and 2 ladlesful of bean broth. Repeat the process until all ingredients have been used up. Cover, and bake for 1 hour. Cool for 45 minutes before serving.

ZUPPA DI SCAROLA E FAGIOLI BIANCHI
White Bean and Escarole Soup

A very simple and ancient recipe given a new twist with the addition of a final dollop of herb battuto. *Can also be served with a floating wedge of toasted bread topped with the* battuto.

12 ounces dried *cannellini* beans, soaked according to directions on
   page 169
1 medium onion, halved
1 bay leaf
2 cloves garlic, peeled and halved
1 large head escarole, cleaned and roughly chopped
Salt and freshly ground black pepper
4 teaspoons herb *battuto* (see page 10)

1. Drain the beans and place in a soup pot along with the onion, bay leaf, garlic, and enough water to cover by 2 inches. Heat to boiling over medium heat. Reduce the heat to low and cook, covered, for 1 hour. Remove and discard the bay leaf. Salt at the halfway mark.

2. Add the escarole, salt, and pepper and continue to cook, covered, for 10 minutes.

3. Stir the *battuto* into the soup and serve.

SBROSCIA DELLA VECCHIA GARFAGNANA

Ancient Lima Bean Soup Made with Apples and Butternut Squash in the Old Garfagnini Style

Sbroscia *is an ancient peasant-style recipe combining the sweetness of apples and butternut squash with the pungency of onions, garlic, and red pepper. Until recently, the name was used only by those Garfagnini old enough to remember the days of extreme poverty. Today, however, it has been resuscitated by trendy restaurateurs fascinated by anything having to do with the simple ways of their grandparents. This wonderful soup is described by Rosa Da Prato, one of Sasso Rosso's elder cooks, as being "poor of ingredients but rich in appeal."*

¾ cup dried lima beans, soaked according to directions on page 169

3 tablespoons extra-virgin olive oil

1 onion, diced

1 stalk celery, diced

1 carrot, scraped and diced

¼ cup fresh parsley, minced

1 clove garlic, minced

1 dried red chili pepper, crushed

12 ounces butternut squash, peeled, seeded, and cut roughly into 1-inch chunks

4 medium red apples, peeled, cored, and cut into rough chunks

Salt and freshly ground black pepper to taste

4 wedges *focaccia*

1. Drain the beans and place in a large soup pot along with enough water to cover by 2 inches. Heat to boiling over medium heat. Reduce the heat to low, cover, and cook for 2 hours. Add more water if necessary. Salt at the halfway mark.

2. Heat the oil in a heavy skillet over medium heat. Sauté the onion, chili, celery, carrot, parsley, and garlic for 3 minutes until the onion is translucent.

3. Add the vegetables to the cooked beans, stirring to mix well. Add the apples and squash and cook, covered, for another 20 minutes. Add salt and pepper.

4. Divide the *focaccia* among 4 bowls. Pour the soup over and serve hot.

ZUPPA DI FAVE FRESCHE

Fresh Fava Bean Soup

In the Garfagnana, fava bean soup is generally made in springtime, which is when fresh fava beans are available. Some people, however, also use frozen fava beans, although, as Elda Cecchi says, the Garfagnini rarely eat foods out of season. "If you make this soup in the winter using frozen or dried beans, it will not taste the same," she says. "One reason why fava beans are used in springtime is because they carry within them the flavor of the approaching summer. If you eat them in winter, it is like wearing a flimsy white cotton dress when snow is on the ground. Even in a heated house where warmth is not a problem, it somehow has the wrong effect."

¼ cup extra-virgin olive oil
2 medium onions, sliced
1 chunk (4 ounces) smoked pancetta or bacon, diced
2 pounds fresh shelled fava beans, peeled according to directions
    on page 170
¼ cup minced fresh parsley
Salt and freshly ground black pepper to taste
16 large croutons fried in oil (see page 66)

1. Heat the oil in a soup pot over medium heat. Sauté the onions and pancetta or bacon for 3 minutes or until the onions are translucent.

2. Add the peeled fava beans and cook over medium heat for 10 minutes, stirring often.

3. Cover the beans with boiling water and cook for another 20 minutes.

4. Stir the parsley, salt, and pepper into the soup. Divide the croutons among 4 bowls. Pour the soup over and serve hot.

ZUPPA DI FAVE E PATATE ⬤

Fava Bean and Potato Soup

The following recipe comes from Sasso Rosso's Ivano who makes it in big batches "because I am basically a very lazy man and if I go to the trouble of actually cooking something for myself, I like to benefit many times from that one burst of effort." He says this secretively, in hushed tones. "If anyone hears that I eat this fresh soup as a leftover, they will be at my door instantly, offering me bowls of soup as it should be eaten."

  2 pounds fresh shelled fava beans, peeled according to directions
      on page 170
  3 tablespoons extra-virgin olive oil
  1 medium onion, chopped
  4 new red potatoes, peeled and cut into 1-inch cubes
  4 tablespoons chopped fresh parsley
  8 cups Basic Vegetable Broth (see page 14)
  ½ cup half-and-half
  Salt and freshly ground black pepper to taste
  ¼ cup freshly grated Parmigiano-Reggiano

1. Place the peeled fava beans in a soup pot with enough water to cover, cover, and cook over medium heat for 15 minutes. Drain and set aside.

2. Heat the oil in another soup pot. Sauté the onion for 5 minutes over medium heat until soft. Add the potatoes, half the parsley, and the beans and sauté for 2 more minutes, stirring constantly. Add the broth, cover, and cook for 20 minutes.

3. Reduce the heat to low. Add the cream, salt, and pepper and simmer, uncovered, for 5 minutes. Do not allow to boil. Stir in the cheese.

4. Puree the soup in batches in a blender. Return to soup pot and heat through without boiling. Serve immediately sprinkled with the remaining parsley.

MINESTRA DI FAVE E CARDI   ◖

Fresh Fava Bean and Cardoon Soup

Although cardoons are closely related to globe artichokes, their appearance is quite different. In the field, mature cardoon plants look like rangy thistles with stalks that can reach to five feet in height. In the market, they look like an oversized clip-topped celery, dusty green in color and with regular rows of little spurs on the edges of their stalks. Cardoons were once grown in Argentina by Italian immigrants, but they have since escaped their domestic setting and are now flourishing as an irritating weed on the pampas.

The flavor of cardoons is a pleasant combination of celery and globe artichoke. Their innermost shoots are sublimely tender and can be eaten raw like celery. To prepare cardoons, remove and discard the large, tough outer stalks. Rinse the inner stalks well, separate, pare off the spurs on the sides, cut into sections, and boil in a small amount of water. A little lemon juice or vinegar added to the water will prevent the white flesh from discoloring.

In addition to using cardoons in making the following recipe, they can also be boiled until tender and marinated in oil and vinegar. Tuscans prefer to parboil the cut-up stalks, dip them in egg batter, and fry them in olive oil—meravigliosi!

2 pounds fresh shelled fava beans, peeled according to directions
　　on page 170
1 pound cardoons, cleaned and with fibrous strings removed
2 tablespoons extra-virgin olive oil
1 small onion, diced
12 cups Basic Meat Broth (see page 11)
Salt and freshly ground black pepper to taste

1. Place the peeled fava beans in a soup pot with enough water to cover. Heat to boiling over medium heat. Reduce the heat, cover, and cook over low heat for ½ hour.

2. Meanwhile, cut the cardoon stalks into 1-inch pieces. Boil in a saucepan of salted water for 30 minutes.

3. When the beans are done, pass both liquids and solids through a food mill. Reserve the mash.

4. Heat the oil in the soup pot over low heat. Sauté the onion for 5 minutes. Stir in the bean mash.

5. Drain the cardoons and add to the soup pot along with the broth. Add salt and pepper and stir to mix well. Bring to a boil and serve immediately.

"Everybody knows the closer sheep are to the road, the less milk they make." Alduino's flock is ten minutes from the nearest road.

IL CASONE'S MINESTRONE RUSTICO ◗
CON TAGLIERINI ALL'UOVO
Country-Style Minestrone with Thick Egg Noodles

Agostino Regoli, proprietor of Il Casone, explains the popularity of this marriage of noodles and bean soup: "After you have spent a hard day trekking through the woods—perhaps with snow on the ground—how are you going to be able to stare in piedi—stand on your own two feet—if all you have to eat is a simple bean broth? Long ago, people were happy with what they had, but today we Garfagnini must have our pasta. If we don't eat it at least twice a day, we become crazy." Skiers who eat at Il Casone after a hard day at the slopes often choose the following soup as their primo, *he says. "It heats their insides."*

The Soup

1 pound fresh shelled *borlotti* (cranberry beans)

3 medium potatoes, peeled

3 dried sage leaves, crumbled

4 cloves garlic

3 tablespoons extra-virgin olive oil

1 chunk (2 ounces) smoked pancetta or bacon, diced

3 tablespoons chopped fresh parsley

2 very ripe Italian plum tomatoes, peeled, seeded, and chopped, or
   ½ cup canned, drained, squeezed into shreds

⅛ teaspoon ground cinnamon

Salt and freshly ground black pepper to taste

The Taglierini (see Note)

1 cup unbleached white flour, sifted

1 tablespoon extra-virgin olive oil

1 egg, lightly beaten

⅛ teaspoon salt

1. Place the beans in a soup pot along with the potatoes, sage, 2 cloves of the garlic, and enough water to cover by 2 inches. Heat over medium heat to boiling. Reduce the heat to low, cover, and cook for 45 minutes, adding more water if necessary. Salt at the halfway mark. Pass solids and liquid through a food mill and return the puree to the pot.

2. Heat the oil in another soup pot over medium heat. Sauté the pancetta or bacon, parsley, tomatoes, the remaining garlic, and the cinnamon for 5 minutes. Adjust for salt and pepper. Add to the bean puree, cover, and simmer over low heat.

3. Mix together the flour, egg, salt, and the 1 tablespoon of olive oil until a soft dough has formed. Roll into a ball and place in a bowl, covered, for 15 minutes.

4. Using a floured rolling pin, roll the dough on a floured work surface into a flat sheet, no more than ⅛-inch thick. Cut the sheet into ½-inch-thick strips and then cut the strips into 6-inch-long thick noodles.★

5. Add the noodles to the bean soup and cook for 5 minutes over medium heat. Serve hot.

Note: Purchased egg noodles can also be substituted for the homemade variety.

★A pasta machine can be used to flatten the dough into a workable sheet, which can then be sliced into noodles by hand.

*Alduino begins to swish his hands through the
warm milk. After a fair amount of swishing, a ball
of cheese begins to form.*

MINESTRONE GARFAGNINA

Minestrone Garfagnana Style ●

Minestrone means "very big soup" and the following version is a very big soup in-deed. Its combination of meats and vegetables has a definite rustic feel, especially when served with whole wheat bread and hearty red wine. I have altered the orig-inal recipe by replacing pork skin with hot sausage, which gives the final prepara-tion a more complex flavor.

4 potatoes, peeled and cut into ½-inch chunks

1 medium head savoy cabbage, cored and roughly chopped

1 pound dried *borlotti* (cranberry beans), soaked according to
   directions on page 169

2 stalks celery, roughly chopped

2 carrots, scraped and roughly chopped

2 cloves garlic, minced

6 very ripe Italian plum tomatoes, chopped

1 chunk (4 ounces) smoked pancetta or bacon, diced

12 cups Basic Meat Broth (see page 11)

1 chunk (1 ounce) pork fatback

3 tablespoons extra-virgin olive oil

4 links hot Italian sausage, removed from casings and crumbled

1 medium onion, roughly chopped

5 fresh basil leaves, chopped finely

¼ cup finely chopped fresh parsley

2 tablespoons finely chopped fennel fronds

Salt and freshly ground black pepper to taste

4 ¾-inch-thick slices peasant-style whole wheat bread, stale or
   toasted

1. Place the potatoes, cabbage, beans, celery, carrots, garlic, tomatoes, and pancetta or bacon in a large soup pot along with the broth. Cook, uncovered, over medium heat for 2 hours, adding more water if neces-sary.

2. Divide the soup into batches, pureeing each batch in a food proces-sor. Return the pureed soup to the pot.

3. Heat the fatback in a heavy skillet over medium heat until the fat renders out. Add the oil and sauté the sausage, onion, basil, parsley, and fennel fronds for 7 minutes or until the onion is lightly browned. Stir the mixture into the soup.

4. Divide the bread among 4 bowls. Pour the soup over and serve hot.

Beans

MINESTRONE DI CASTAGNE E FAGIOLI SECCHI

Chestnut and White Bean Soup

According to Elda Cecchi, the following soup dates back to a time when a good many of the Garfagnana's men worked as shepherds and needed something substantial and energizing when they returned at the end of a long, hard day. "Now," she says, "Alduino is one of only two shepherds in the entire area." But she still makes the soup because "When you combine beans and chestnuts, you get not only a particularly good flavor, but a soup that can be served as a platto unico," meaning that it does not require a second course.

> 1 pound dried peeled chestnuts, rinsed and soaked in cold water for 12 hours
> ¾ cup dried *cannellini* beans, soaked according to directions on page 169
> Salt and freshly ground black pepper to taste
> 2 tablespoons extra-virgin olive oil
> 1 chunk (3 ounces) smoked pancetta or bacon, diced
> 1 medium onion, diced
> 1 small carrot, scraped and diced
> ½ stalk celery, diced
> ⅔ cup Arborio rice
> ⅛ teaspoon grated nutmeg

1. Drain the chestnuts and beans. Place in a soup pot with enough water to cover by 2 inches. Heat to boiling over medium heat. Reduce the heat to low, cover, and cook for 2 hours. Add more water if necessary.

2. Heat the oil in a skillet over medium heat. Sauté the pancetta or bacon, onion, carrot, and celery for 7 minutes or until the onion is lightly browned. Add to the soup pot and stir to mix well.

3. Add the rice, nutmeg, salt, and pepper. Cover, and cook over low heat for 20 minutes. Serve hot.

MINESTRA DI FAGIOLI MINUTI ●

Black-Eyed Pea Soup

Despite their English name, black-eyed peas are (as their Italian name—fagioli minuti—makes clear) really beans. Although not as readily available in the Garfagnana as other types of beans, these speckled little marvels create a wonderfully subtle soup given an extra kernel of flavor by the addition of a good basic meat broth.

> 8 ounces black-eyed peas, soaked according to directions on page 169
> 1 medium onion, quartered
> 2 cloves garlic, halved
> 3 tablespoons dried crumbled sage
> 8 cups Basic Meat Broth (see page 11)
> 2 cloves garlic, minced
> 1 medium onion, diced
> 1 carrot, scraped and diced
> 9 tablespoons extra-virgin olive oil
> 5 stalks kale, washed, dried, and chopped (discard toughest parts)
> 1½ cups Arborio rice

1. Drain the peas and place in a soup pot along with the quartered onion, the garlic halves, half the sage, 2 tablespoons of the oil, half the broth, and enough water to cover by 2 inches. Heat to boiling over medium heat. Reduce the heat to low, cover, and cook for 1 hour. Add more water if necessary.

2. Drain the peas, reserving the liquid, and pass half through a food mill. Return the mashed peas to the pot along with the reserved liquid. Reserve the whole peas.

3. Heat 3 tablespoons of the oil in a skillet over medium heat. Sauté the minced garlic, diced onion, carrot, and remaining sage for 7 minutes or until the onion is lightly browned. Add the mixture to the soup pot along with the remaining broth.

4. Stir the kale into the soup and cook for another 10 minutes.

5. Add the rice, cover, and cook for 20 minutes. Just before serving, add the whole peas and cook just until heated. Pour the soup into 4 bowls and serve hot, drizzled with the remaining oil.

Chapter Eight

LIVING WITH POETRY

Castelvecchio Pascoli

ZUPPE DI PESCE
Fish Soups

It is ten o'clock on a Wednesday morning in January, the sun is shining in a widespread arc across the mountain sky, and I am wondering how it is possible for the weather to be so blessedly mild in midwinter. It is clearly winter, however; one has only to look at the mountain peaks in the distance and notice their velvety white hoods to know that soon it will be Ash Wednesday and the Carnival floats will parade like so many soldiers down the streets of the Garfagnana's villages.

I am sitting in Castelvecchio's Bar Ghini, indulging myself in a mid-morning *macchiato* as I await Alberto Borecchio, a friend who lives in an almost-reconstructed stone villa, up on the hill near Casa Pascoli. Alberto had to come to town this morning to meet with the contractor who is going to install yet another heating system in his house. This will be the third, but Alberto has yet to live through a winter without resorting to a logistically intricate series of space heaters. "It would have been easier to go to school for a few years and learn how to do the job myself," he says.

Since Alberto was coming to town anyway, he said he would stop by Casa Pascoli and bring me a special commemorative envelope that was canceled on October 15, 1995, the day marking the hundredth anniversary of Giovanni Pascoli's arrival in Castelvecchio. I am, you see, one of those strangely avid collectors of first-day covers. Pascoli is also my very favorite poet.

I had very much wanted to be in Castelvecchio for the Pascoli centenary celebrations. Friends who were spoke of readings and tributes and an exhibit of his published work that, in the words of my cousin Dacia, "dazzled the mind." But it was not possible, and so I have come here now to sit and wait.

I am surrounded by village women as I sip from my tall steaming glass, women bearing shopping bags filled with produce. Not one has anything but laments, albeit of the sort that would have made Pascoli sing.

"*O, Assunta, come stai?* I have not seen you since we ravaged the woods last year for those porcini—remember?"

"What can I do, Ombretta, my husband is sick with gastritis. God bless men when something is wrong with their health. One would think they were going any minute to die. *Insomma,* I have just returned from the market, where I bought a glorious piece of *baccalà* in order to make a pot of soup. When I was told the price, I almost became sick myself."

"I know, I know, but nowadays if you want to eat *baccalà,* that is what you have to do. Remember, Assunta, when we were children, when food cost nothing? *Baccalà* was something they threw at you in anger—remember? Now, one would think you were buying salmon. Christmas Eve we were seven, and I prepared a big pot filled with *cacciucco.* Do you know, I spent almost 100,000 lire?"

"No!"

"*Sì,* my husband almost killed me."

My instinct, apart from wondering how Pascoli would have treated this discourse, is to join in the conversation, to add my thoughts to the ridiculous situation about which they speak. They are quite correct in their indignation. In the last few years, Tuscany, like other places, has gone through a social metamorphosis, "discovering" (or, as some people put it, "stealing") poor people's foods—simple ingredients like *baccalà* and rabbit, elevating them to an aesthetic distinction worthy of Brunello wines and silver serving platters.

But now the women are leaving and I return to my coffee, pleased with the sun and the smell of pastries baking in the bar's kitchen, and congratulating myself for having had the intelligence this morning to journey to Castelvecchio, not only because of its colorful residents and the beauty of its green and solitary country, but because this is where many of Italy's greatest works of poetry were written. Works that were as dramatic in the struggles they portrayed as they were romantic in their attachment to poverty and the earth.

The greatest of the works (at least in my mind) were written by Giovanni Pascoli, who was actually born in Emilia-Romagna, although he lived a great part of his life here (from 1895 until his death in 1912). By his own request, Pascoli was buried in this town that now bears his name, in a tomb that once formed part of his house.

Pascoli came to the Garfagnana searching for *una becocca con attorno un po'd'orto e di selva*—a small hut surrounded by a bit of garden and some woods. His wish was to find "a valley that was as evocative as it was private, one that would be rich in voices, colors, light, and shadows."

To raise the money for the house, he sold five gold coins he had won in a Latin poetry contest in Amsterdam—a fact that enabled him forever after to facetiously claim that his house had been purchased with the help of Horace and Virgil. He moved to Castelvecchio with his sisters, Maria, and his dog, Guli, and settled into "an existence shielded between two mountains"—the Apuan Alps on one side, the Apennines on the other.

When I was little, I would sit around the holiday table listening to my mother and other members of my family recite Pascoli. Mother's favorite poem was "La Cavallina Storna," the gripping story of a horse that sees its master murdered and is beseeched by the mistress of the house to reveal the murderer by neighing when his name is spoken. The poem ends with these lines: *Mia madre alsó, nel gran silenzio un dito, disse un nome, e suonó alto un nitrito.* Amidst the great silence, my mother raised her finger and whispered a name, and a great neighing sound filled the room.

The only poem by Pascoli I ever actually learned by heart was one called "Nebbia" (Fog).

> *Nascondi le cose lontane,*
> *tu nebbia impalpabile e scialba*
> *tu fumo che ancora rampolli*
> *su l'alba*
> *da lampi notturni e d crolli*
> *d'aeree frane!*
> *Nascondi le cose lontane*
> *nascondimi quello che morto!*
> *Ch'io veda soltanto la siepe dell'orto,*
> *la mura ch'ha piene le crepe di valeriane.*
> *Nascondi le cose lontane:*

le cose son ebbre di pianto!
Ch'io veda i due peschi, i due melli,
soltanto,
che danno i soavi lor mieli
pel nero mio pane.
Nascondi le cose lontane
che vogliano ch'ami e che vada!
Ch'io veda l solo quel bianco di strada,
che un giorno ho da fare fra stanco
don don di campane. . . .
Nascondi le cose lontane,
nascondile involale al volo
del cuore! Ch'io veda il cipresso l solo,
qui, solo quest'orto, cui presso
sonnecchia il mio cane.

Hide from me what is far away
Thou fog, impalpable and pale
Thou morning mist who springs from the dawn
And protects it from lightning
And thunder.
Hide from me what is far away
Hide that which is dead
That I may see only the hedge in the kitchen garden
The walls, their cracks filled with valerian.
Hide from me what is far away
The things that bring tears to one's eyes
That I may see only the peach and the apple trees
Giving forth honey for my bread.
Hide from me what is far away,
Those things that force me to love and be of the world
So that I may only see the whiteness of the road
That I must inevitably travel
When the bells will toll don don.
Hide from me what is far away
Hide them, steal them quickly from my heart
That I may only see the cypress
Lovely there in the garden by which my dog is lying,
Dozing.

I continue to sit with a second order of *macchiato,* Alfredo now running twenty minutes late. Before long, I overhear another conversation, this one of a more intellectual bent than that of the women, although similar in the passion of its discourse. The topic, of course, is Pascoli, and, if I understand correctly, the two speakers have widely divergent views on the poet's stature. How many such conversations has this bar witnessed, I wonder.

They stand at the bar, the man with the plaid cap drinking a small glass of red wine. I check my watch, thinking how strange to see Tuscans drinking wine so early in the morning. The other man—Ettore, I think is his name—drinks tea and is much more elegantly dressed, with a proper coat and hat.

As he pours additional sugar into his tea, Ettore seems to feel a certain gratitude to Pascoli for such poems as "L'ora di Barga" (The Hour of Barga) and "La fonte di Castelvecchio" (The Essence of Castelvecchio), two glorious tributes to the radiant charms of the Garfagnana.

But his words have caused a certain amount of turmoil on the part of his companion. The man with the cap (I think his name is Alfonso) is now sputtering and waving his hands wildly. "You call those odes to the beauty of the Garfagnana?" he bellows. "Apart from '*Al serchio,*' which has a few passages alluding to beauty, Pascoli's work deals almost exclusively with death, tragedy, and solitude. *Grazie,* but we Garfagnini can do without such tributes!"

He finishes the wine in a violent gulp. "And then there was "Il gelsomino notturno" (Nocturnal Jasmine), the poem he wrote when his sister married. His epitaph, some people say. *Si, propio un epitaffio.* To me, it was nothing more than the perverted work of an impotent. A grown man raging with jealousy over his sister's marriage—who ever heard of such a thing? *Ascoltami a me, Ettore*—listen to me, Ettore—a truly great poet does not need to revert to such topics. If Pascoli cannot find any other way than to air his dirty laundry in public, then he should have the decency to say what he means without hiding his lurid intent beneath flowerly images of moonlit nights and fragrant flowers."

"Alfonso, you clearly don't know what you are talking about. Pascoli's genius lies precisely in the way he layered his meaning, using beautiful words to communicate dark, forbidden feelings. Why, he is studied by children in school. Ask any *fanciullo* about Pascoli and he'll recount wonderful stories of animals and flowers and walks through the woods. Only when we become adults do we understand what he *truly* meant. But that is what poetry is for; if everybody said what they meant, poetry would not exist."

Alfonso tries to break in, smiling in anticipation of the points he will gain with his next rejoinder, but Ettore charges ahead with: "Pascoli was the most human poet the world has ever seen. A man who lived in a world of unimaginable darkness choosing the exquisitely sweet perfume of nocturnal jasmine as a screen—the paradox alone is enough to warrant veneration!"

With that, Ettore buttons his coat and the two walk toward the exit and out of my range of hearing. The last thing I hear Alfonso grumble is: "Pascoli should have kept his perversity to himself, beautiful language or no beautiful language."

I bid a silent *arriverderci* and thank them, not only for the entertainment value of the argument itself, but for the way in which they *conducted* the argument—the voices, the hand gestures, the ebb and flow of their inflection.

My mind meanders to thoughts of my friend Jerry from New York. Jerry loves Tuscany and travels to this region every chance he gets. A few years ago, he also began studying the language, hoping to enhance his travel experiences by interacting with Tuscans in their own language. But at a certain point, he became discouraged.

"I may eventually learn the words," he said. "But I will never learn to use them with such passion. To fully invest myself in every expression, to think of each phrase as a performance, to *sing* my sentences in the same way Pavarotti sings 'Nessun Dorme.'"

To Jerry, the Tuscan language requires an energy that is somehow missing from English. "Americans speak the way they live, which is more on an even, middle plain than Tuscans, who always seem to be either laughing or crying," he says. "It would be impossible for me to take a sentence like 'This soup is very good,' and invest it with the energy necessary to say it like a Tuscan. *E buonissima questa zuppa,* they would say, and the expression would, of necessity, end with an exclamation point, whether written or spoken."

My reverie is interrupted by the arrival of Alfredo, whose first two words, *Lasciami spiegare,* lets me know that he doesn't have my Pascoli envelope. *Lasciami spiegare,* he says. Let me explain. "I went up to Casa Pascoli and rang the bell for five straight minutes, but no one answered, and so I went around to the back and rang some more, but it is really out of season and I'm not sure if the caretakers are there."

The long and short of it is that we are going to go back together after he has concluded his business with the contractor. By now it is almost lunchtime, so I tell him I will wait at Zi'Meo, a restaurant named after one of Pascoli's dear friends. Originally a cow barn, Zi'Meo's menu is filled with the hearty fish soups so loved by the poet—*zuppa di baccalà, minestra d'aragoste, zuppa di seppie.* In fact, I decide to honor Pascoli's memory and—despite what I know will be an unfavorable reaction from the waiter—order soup as both a first and second course. I am not disappointed, either in my expectation of the reaction or in the delight of feasting on such wonderful culinary creations.

Having finished my wonderful repast, I reunite with Alfredo and we point ourselves to the top of the hill. Alfredo parks the car at the foot of the drive leading to Casa Pascoli, and on our way up the cobblestone path he encounters his good friend Ennio, who, it just so happens, is a good friend of the caretaker. Alfredo explains our dilemma and Ennio offers to intercede on our behalf.

What that means is that Ennio knocks on the door and it is promptly answered by the caretaker, who not only produces a copy of the canceled envelope without further adieu, but offers to give us a personal tour of the museum and the gardens. I'm not entirely sure the same thing wouldn't have happened had we knocked on the door ourselves, but this is the Garfagnana, and in the Garfagnana it is always better to have an insider mediating on your behalf.

Once the country mansion of the Cardosi-Carrara family, Casa Pascoli is the beautiful stone house where Giovanni Pascoli wrote many of his most famous collections, among them, *Myricae* (1903), *I primi poemetti* (1897), *I canti di Castelvecchio* (1903), and *Poemi conviviali* (1904), which was written in Latin. When Pascoli died in 1912 he left the house and its furnishings to his sister, Maria. She, in turn, upon her death donated them to the Barga Town Council, which maintains them intact. Encompassed within the eight rooms are Pascoli's completed manuscripts, his library, and an archive. There is also a quiet garden with lilac trees and fountains, a loggia with views of the Paniá and the Corsonna valleys, and, adjoining the house, a chapel where Pascoli lies side by side with his sister.

When we have taken our leave of Ennio and the caretaker, Alfredo and I walk for a while on a stone pathway behind the house. At a certain point we come to the ruins of what, Alfredo says, was once a bread-baking oven used by Pascoli as well as other local residents. Why outdoors? I ask.

"So that they could use the least amount of wood to heat the largest amount of space. Ten or more breads fit into an oven this size—enough, probably, to feed the whole village for days."

He points to a piece of wood laid against the rusted metal door of the oven. When I move closer, I see that the wood is burnished with a piece of a poem by Pascoli about bread.

> *And you, Maria, with your smooth gentle hand*
> *Knead the dough, stretching and spreading*
> *Until there it is, thin like a sheet and big*
> *As the moon.*
> *With opaque hands*
> *You offer it to me, laying it down soft*
> *On the hot earthenware bricks.*
> *You distance yourself and I nudge it*
> *Near the flame*
> *Until it screams*
> *And grows into a ball*
> *And the house is filled with the odor of bread.*

ABOUT FISH

There are many who say that the taste of fish soups varies greatly according to where they were prepared; that even if the type of fish used is the same, the individual waters in which they swim impart a unique flavor that is impossible to duplicate. While that is undoubtedly so, a more important element in the diversity of flavors is the fact that many of the fish used by the Garfagnini are not elsewhere available.

That having been said, the following recipes offer great flexibility in the choice of fish and will unquestionably result in delicious—albeit somewhat differently flavored—soups, but only if the fish is fresh. Note that, in the Garfagnana, many fish soups are served over bread, which adds both bulk and—because the bread is first rubbed with garlic—flavor. Polenta squares and focaccia are also used. The soups themselves often have very little liquid.

The most important factor in creating excellent fish soups is to cook with the very freshest of fish. When choosing fish, the following five criteria should be used to determine freshness:

1. The eyes must be clear and bulging, not receding and glazed over.
2. The scales should have a high sheen and be firmly attached to the skin.
3. The gills must be reddish, not gray.
4. The flesh, when pressed, should be firm to the touch.
5. There should be no offensive odor, especially around the gills or belly.

Remember that many fish stores sell previously frozen fish with no indication that it should be used at once and not under any circumstances be subjected to refreezing. Also, remember that whitish surfaces are a clear indication that the fish is old and has begun drying out. If you are in doubt, place the fish in cold water. A newly caught fish will float.

Cleaning Fish

Small Fish

To clean small fish like smelts and sardines, spread open the outer gills, hold the inner gills with thumb and forefinger and give a firm but gentle pull. All the parts to be discarded should come out together in one hearty pull. To cut the fish into fillets, remove the head and tail and cut the flesh cleanly away on both sides of the backbone and dorsal fin. The ventral or belly fin is then removed by cutting around the backbone in one single piece.

Large Fish

To prepare a large fish, begin by spreading several layers of newspaper on the work surface. If the fish needs to be scaled, cut off the fins with scissors first in order to avoid skin abrasions. Wash the fish in cold water before starting; scales are easier to remove when the fish is wet.

Grab the fish by the tail; if it is too slippery, grab it with a cloth. Starting at the tail end and using a very sharp 8- or 10-inch knife, lift the scales up and scrape them off as you would a carrot. Make sure to also remove the scales around the base of the head and the fins. When this part is completed, lift the fish, wrap the first layer of newspaper around the scales, and discard.

Next, cut the entire length of the belly from the vent under the tail to the head. Remove the entrails, which are all contained in a pouchlike receptacle that is easily freed from the flesh. Now cut around the pelvic and ventral fins on the underside of the fish and remove them. To remove the head, cut above the collarbone and break the backbone with a strong snap of the knife. If the pectoral fins were not already cut off, they will come off with the head. Wrap and discard the entrails.

Wash the fish in cold running water, carefully removing any blood or membranes. Remove also the blood line under the backbone.

To remove the odor of fish from utensils and dishcloths, use a solution of 1 teaspoon baking soda to 1 quart water. To remove odors from the hands, rub them with lemon juice or vinegar before washing.

HERB POLENTA

To make herb polenta, you need ¼ cup coarse polenta, salt and freshly ground black pepper to taste, 1 medium onion, chopped, 5 tablespoons extra-virgin olive oil, and ¼ cup assorted fresh chopped herbs (basil, parsley, rosemary, thyme, sage, oregano, or any combination thereof). Whisk the polenta and ½ teaspoon salt into 4 cups water simmering in a saucepan; cook over low heat until the polenta is dense enough to hold a spoon upright. Remove from heat and scrape into a mixing bowl. In the meantime, sauté the chopped onion in 3 tablespoons of the oil until soft. Stir into the polenta along with the herbs and the remaining oil. Pour into an oiled baking pan and cook in a 350 degree oven for 45 minutes. Cool and cut into wedges.

Discussions of Pascoli are passionate. "You call those odes to the beauty of the Garfagnana? Grazie, we can do without such tributes!"

ZUPPA DI COZZE E VONGOLE
Soup Made with Mussels and Clams

The Garfagnini refer to mussels and clams as "the oysters of the poor," which aptly illustrates the historic pragmatism of a people used to elevating that which is available to a status approaching nobility. Until recently, both of these common (and delectable) mollusks were available in great quantity in the waters of the Tyrrhenian. Now, while still relatively inexpensive, they come from such faraway places as Sweden and Indonesia. Truth be told, they make a much better soup than their more elegant pearl-bearing cousins.

5 tablespoons extra-virgin olive oil
5 cloves garlic, 3 cloves minced and 2 cloves halved
1 dried red chili pepper, crushed
1 pound mussels, scrubbed under cold running water and
   debearded
1 pound Manila clams, scrubbed under cold running water
1 cup dry white wine
1 cup canned Italian plum tomatoes, squeezed until shredded and
   with liquid reserved
3 cups Basic Fish Broth (see page 13)
Salt and freshly ground black pepper to taste
4 ¾-inch-thick slices peasant-style bread, toasted
1 cup chopped fresh parsley

1. Heat the oil in a soup pot over medium heat. Sauté the minced garlic and chili pepper over medium heat for 1 to 2 minutes; do not allow the garlic to brown. Add the mussels and clams, cover, and cook for 5 minutes.

2. As soon as the shells have opened, add the wine and cook, uncovered, until the wine has evaporated. Add the tomatoes and their liquid and cook for 5 minutes.

3. Add the broth to the pot and cook for 10 minutes, or until the sauce is reduced to a slightly dense consistency. Add salt and pepper.

4. Rub both sides of the bread with the garlic halves. Divide the slices among 4 bowls. Pour the shellfish and soup over the bread, and serve hot, sprinkled heavily with the parsley.

ZUPPA DI BACCALA DI VENERDI ◖

Friday Codfish Soup

Although the religious observance of meatless Fridays is now a thing of the past, old habits die hard, and on Fridays there is not a store in Garfagnana that does not prominently display a case of dried baccalà. *Another reason for the regional popularity of* baccalà *is that, in the olden days, fresh fish was both relatively hard to find and prohibitively expensive. And so the Garfagnini would buy a nice large piece of their adored* baccalà *and use it for various dishes, including the following soup.*

3 tablespoons extra-virgin olive oil
1 medium red onion, diced
2 stalks celery, diced
2 leeks (white part only), washed, dried, and chopped
1 cup dry white wine
4 cups Basic Fish Broth (see page 13)
1 cup chopped fresh parsley
1 bay leaf
5 very ripe Italian plum tomatoes, chopped
Salt and freshly ground black pepper to taste
3 small red potatoes, peeled and diced
¼ teaspoon dried thyme
1½ pounds *baccalà* (dried codfish), soaked in several changes of
    water for up to 48 hours (use a glass, enamel, or stainless-steel
    pan)
4 large wedges *focaccia*

1. Heat the oil in a soup pot over medium heat. Sauté the onion, celery, and leeks for 3 minutes or until the onion is translucent. Add the wine and cook until evaporated.

2. Add the fish broth, parsley, bay leaf, and tomatoes, stirring to mix well. Add salt and pepper. Add the potatoes and thyme.

3. Drain and rinse the *baccalà*. Remove the skin and chop into 1-inch chunks. Add to the soup and cook, uncovered, over medium heat for 15 minutes, stirring often but with caution to avoid flaking the fish.

4. Divide the *focaccia* among 4 bowls. Pour the soup over and serve hot.

ZUPPA DI GAMBERI, SCAMPI, E PEPERONI

Shrimp, Prawns, and Pepper Soup

This recipe is also frequently referred to as "sea and mountain soup" (zuppa mare monti) because its preparation unites two succulent crustaceans from the Tyrrhenian Sea with fresh vegetables from the gardens of the Garfagnini.

   5 tablespoons extra-virgin olive oil
   1 leek (white part only), cleaned and diced
   1 medium onion, diced
   1 large red pepper, cored, seeded, and sliced into thin slivers
   1 small cucumber, peeled, seeded, and cut into thin semi-circles
   1 bay leaf
   1¼ pounds medium-sized shrimp, cleaned and deveined
   1½ pounds prawns, cleaned and deveined
   1 cup dry white wine
   4 cups Basic Fish Broth (see page 13)
   Salt and freshly ground black pepper to taste
   1 cup finely chopped fresh parsley
   4 wedges herb polenta (see page 204)

1. Heat the oil in a soup pot over medium heat. Sauté the leek and onion for 3 minutes or until the onion is translucent. Add the red pepper, cucumber, and bay leaf and cook until the vegetables are soft.

2. Increase the heat to high and add the shrimp and prawns. Stir to mix well.

3. Pour in the wine and continue to cook until it has almost evaporated. Add the fish broth, salt, and pepper, then cover, and cook for 10 minutes. Sprinkle with the parsley.

4. Divide the polenta among 4 bowls. Pour the soup over and serve hot.

ZUPPA COI NICCHI E POMODORI

Baby Clams and Tomato Soup

It has been said that zuppa coi nicchi *is the* cacciucco *of the poor—a fact that, according to Castelvecchio's Signora Malva Montigni, is just not true. "For one thing," she says, "it is very hard nowadays to find baby clams. So this soup has about it an air of rarity. For another, it is served in some of our best restaurants. Whoever says otherwise simply doesn't know what they're talking about."*

3 tablespoons extra-virgin olive oil

5 cloves garlic, 3 cloves minced and 2 cloves halved

1 dried red chili pepper, crushed

2 pounds Manila clams, scrubbed under cold running water

1 cup canned Italian plum tomatoes, squeezed until shredded and
   with liquid reserved

1 cup dry red wine

Salt and freshly ground black pepper to taste

1 cup finely minced fresh parsley

4 thin wedges peasant-style bread, toasted

1. Heat the oil in a soup pot over medium heat. Sauté the minced garlic and chili pepper for 1 to 2 minutes; do not allow the garlic to brown. Add the clams, cover, and cook for 5 minutes.

2. As soon as the clams have opened, add the tomatoes, their liquid, and the wine. Discard any unopened clams. Cook, stirring frequently, until the sauce is thoroughly blended. Add salt and pepper and sprinkle with the parsley.

3. Rub both sides of the bread with the garlic halves. Divide the slices among 4 bowls. Pour the soup over and serve hot.

CACCIUCCO ALLA GARFAGNANA ◒

Garfagnana Fish Stew

Cacciucco is the Italian version of bouillabaisse (although, as Castelvecchio's Rafaela Lunardini contends, "a highly superior version"), and like its French counterpart is prepared differently in every ten square meters of the country. Following is a distinctly Garfagnini version in its liberal use of the tomatoes that grow in every villager's garden.

⅓ cup extra-virgin olive oil

6 cloves garlic, 4 cloves minced and 2 cloves halved

1 dried red chili pepper, crushed

1 pound assorted fish fillets, such as snapper, Chilean sea bass, halibut, or true cod, cut into large chunks

2 cups dry white wine

1 can (32 ounces) Italian plum tomatoes, squeezed until shredded and with the liquid reserved

8 ounces mussels, scrubbed under cold running water and debearded

1 pound Manila clams, scrubbed under cold running water

½ cup water

4 ounces shrimp, peeled and deveined

Salt and freshly ground black pepper to taste

8 ¾-inch-thick slices peasant-style bread, toasted

1 cup finely chopped fresh parsley

1. Heat the oil in a soup pot over medium heat. Sauté the minced garlic and chili for 1 to 2 minutes; do not allow the garlic to brown. Add the fish pieces and cook for another 2 minutes. Pour the wine over the fish and allow to evaporate.

2. Add the tomatoes and their liquid to the pot and cook for 5 more minutes, stirring carefully with a wooden spoon to mix well.

3. Place the mussels, clams, and water in a skillet. Cover, and cook over medium heat for 4 minutes or until the shells begin to open. Remove the mussels and clams with a slotted spoon, discarding any that have not opened. Remove half from their shells and place both shelled and unshelled in the soup pot. Filter the broth through a paper towel–lined

sieve to remove any sand and add the broth to the soup.

4. Add the shrimp to the pot, cover, and cook for 5 minutes or until the seafood is done and the flavors are thoroughly blended. Add salt and pepper.

5. Rub both sides of the bread with the garlic halves, 2 slices per garlic half. Divide the bread among 4 bowls. Pour the soup over and serve hot, sprinkled liberally with the chopped parsley.

COMITATO CELEBRAZIONI DEL
CENTENARIO PASCOLIANO

CIRCOLO CULTURALE «GARFAGNANA»

1895–1995 CENTENARIO PASCOLIANO

★ 15 Ottobre 1995 ★

CASTELVECCHIO PASCOLI (LUCCA)

Xilografia di A. BALDUINI

Serie da 1 a 1000   N? 603

EUROPA PACE E LIBERTÀ
1945–1995
ITALIA 750

55030 CASTELVECCHIO PASCOLI (LU)
15.10.1995
CENTENARIO PASCOLIANO

15 OTTOBRE 1995
Castelvecchio Pascoli

The special commemorative envelope canceled on the day marking the hundredth anniversary of Pascoli's arrival in Castelvecchio.

ZUPPA DI SEPPIE E BIETOLA

Soup Made with Squid and Swiss Chard and Served over Herb Polenta

Swiss chard is a popular winter ingredient in the Garfagnana, not only for the sweet flavor it imparts to any food with which it is paired, but for its large leaves which, in this historically poor region, were once a supremely important factor.

4 tablespoons extra-virgin olive oil

4 cloves garlic, minced

1 dried red chili pepper, crushed

2 pounds squid, cleaned and sliced into rings

1 cup dry white wine

1 cup canned Italian plum tomatoes, squeezed until shredded and with liquid reserved

Salt and freshly ground black pepper to taste

8 ounces Swiss chard, washed, dried, and chopped

4 large squares herb polenta (see page 204)

1. Heat 2 tablespoons of the oil in a soup pot over medium heat. Sauté the garlic and chili pepper for 1 to 2 minutes; do not allow the garlic to brown.

2. Add the squid and stir to mix well. Stir in the wine, tomatoes, salt, and pepper.

3. Add the chard to the pot, cover, and cook for 10 minutes.

4. Meanwhile heat the remaining 2 tablespoons of oil in a skillet over medium heat. Sauté the polenta squares until browned on both sides. Place each square in a bowl, pour the soup over and serve hot.

ZUPPA DI GAMBERONI E CARCIOFI CASALINGA

Country-Style Shrimp and Artichoke Soup

⬤

The following recipe is a perfect marriage between the sweetness of shrimp and the tartness of artichokes. At one time, however, it was only prepared in the home because, in general, restaurateurs were reluctant to pair elegant foods such as shrimp with vegetables that were considered peasant food. Fortunately, times have changed.

1½ pounds baby artichokes, outer leaves and chokes removed, cut into quarters
Salt
3 tablespoons extra-virgin olive oil
3 cloves garlic, minced
1 dried red chili pepper, crushed
16 large shrimp, peeled and deveined
1 cup dry white wine
4 large squares *focaccia*
1 cup finely chopped fresh parsley
Freshly ground black pepper

1. Blanch the artichoke quarters for 5 minutes in a saucepan of boiling salted water. Drain.

2. Heat the oil in a soup pot over medium heat. Sauté the minced garlic and chili pepper for 1 to 2 minutes; do not allow the garlic to brown.

3. Add the shrimp and cook until browned (2–4 minutes), stirring constantly to coat the shrimp with the other flavors. Pour the wine over the shrimp, stir to mix well, and add the artichoke quarters. Cook for 10 minutes, adding a few tablespoons of boiling water if necessary to maintain the liquidity of the sauce. Add pepper.

4. Divide the *focaccia* squares among 4 bowls, pour the soup over, and serve hot, sprinkled liberally with the chopped parsley.

ZUPPA DI TOTANI ALLA PASCOLI ●

Pascoli's Cuttlefish Soup

According to the letters housed in Casa Pascoli, this soup was one of Giovanni Pascoli's favorites, largely because he considered it a suitable blend of mare e monte—sea and mountains—what with its many herbs, among which was his beloved basil.

3 tablespoons extra-virgin olive oil
8 chopped fresh basil leaves
¼ teaspoon fresh thyme
½ teaspoon chopped fresh oregano
½ teaspoon chopped fresh sage
1 dried red chili pepper, crushed
5 cloves garlic, 3 cloves minced and 2 cloves halved
1½ pounds cuttlefish or small squid, cleaned and sliced
16 crayfish or large shrimp, shelled and deveined
1 cup dry white wine
1 cup drained canned Italian plum tomatoes, squeezed until
    shredded
Salt and freshly ground black pepper to taste
1 cup Basic Fish Broth (see page 13)
8 ¾-inch-thick slices peasant-style bread, toasted
1 cup chopped fresh parsley

1. Heat the oil in a soup pot over medium heat. Sauté the basil, thyme, oregano, sage, chili pepper, and minced garlic for 1 minute. Add the squid and continue to cook until the fish is slightly tender, stirring constantly (approximately 5 minutes).

2. Add the crayfish and stir to mix well. Add the wine and continue to cook until it has largely evaporated. Stir in the tomatoes, salt, and pepper.

3. Add the broth and cook, covered, for 5 more minutes.

4. Rub both sides of the bread with the garlic halves, 2 slices per garlic half. Divide the slices among 4 bowls. Pour the soup over and serve hot, sprinkled liberally with the chopped parsley.

MINESTRA DI ARAGOSTE   ◖

Lobster Soup

Originally the Garfagnini used what is called European lobster in making this soup. Also known as spiny rock lobster and langouste, the European variety is smaller than its American or northern counterpart and has extra-long antennae but no claws. While some locals still use this variety, most Garfagnini have become enamored of the large-clawed type that reaches them frozen. Still others use a relative of the spiny rock that is exclusive to European waters and referred to by Italians as scampo. *Whatever version one uses, Castelvecchio's Signora Montigni cautions that it be the female of the species, which, she claims, has a sweeter, more refined taste. "Look underneath the lobster," she says. "The male will have bony, finlike appendages where the body and tail meet. The female will be soft and leathery."*

> 2 lobsters, about 1¼ pounds each
> Juice of ½ lemon
> 2 bay leaves
> 2 small carrots, scraped, one cut into 3 pieces and one finely diced
> 3 tablespoons unsalted butter
> 1 small onion, minced
> 1 stalk celery, diced
> 1 clove garlic, minced
> ¼ cup chopped fresh parsley
> 5 very ripe Italian plum tomatoes, peeled, seeded, and chopped
> Salt and freshly ground black pepper to taste

1. Boil the lobsters for 15 minutes in a pot of water to which the lemon juice, bay leaves, and cut carrot have been added.

2. Drain the lobsters. Detach the tail and claws, remove the meat, cut it into small chunks, and reserve in a covered bowl.

3. Crush the shells, place in a pan, cover with water, and cook over medium heat for 1 hour. Filter the broth through a sieve lined with a double layer of cheesecloth to remove all solids.

4. Heat the butter in a soup pot over low heat. Sauté the onion for 5 minutes or until soft. Add the celery, garlic, parsley, and diced carrot and continue to sauté for 3 more minutes.

5. Add the tomatoes to the pot, adjust for salt and pepper, and continue to cook over low heat for 20 more minutes.

6. Pour the filtered broth into the soup and stir to mix well. Cook for 5 minutes. Add the reserved lobster, adjust for salt and pepper, cook just until heated, and serve.

Hide from what is far away
Thou fog, impalpable and pale
Thou morning mist who springs from the dawn.

ZUPPA DI MARE AGLI ODORI

Fish Soup with Vegetables and Herbs

Literally speaking, odori *means a certain category of vegetables and herbs that creates an underlying flavor-base for most of the Garfagnini's cooking. Its connotation, however, is one of rustic home cooking and simple flavorful meals. This recipe makes use of the* odori *to create a dish that is simple to prepare and yet yields a surprisingly complex flavor.*

>   2 pounds assorted white fish fillets, such as monkfish, petrale sole,
>   Chilean sea bass, etc., cut into large chunks
>   1 ripe Italian plum tomato, cut in quarters
>   2 medium carrots, scraped and thinly sliced
>   1 medium onion, thinly sliced
>   12 ounces new red potatoes, peeled and cut into ½-inch chunks
>   4 cups Basic Fish Broth (see page 13)
>   Salt and freshly ground black pepper to taste
>   1 teaspoon chopped fresh thyme
>   ½ teaspoon chopped fresh rosemary
>   1 cup finely chopped fresh parsley
>   1 tablespoon chopped fennel fronds
>   16 croutons fried in oil (see page 66)

1. Place the fish pieces in a soup pot along with the tomato quarters, carrots, onion, and potatoes. Add the broth, cover, and simmer over low heat for 15 minutes.

2. Add the thyme, rosemary, parsley, and fennel fronds to the soup and continue to cook, uncovered, for 4 minutes. Add salt and pepper.

3. Divide the croutons among 4 bowls. Pour the soup over and serve hot.

ZUPPA ECONOMICA DI SARDINE
Economical Fresh Sardine Soup

Since fish soups have always cost more to prepare than a thick bean minestrone, they were generally served—if at all—only on Sundays or holidays. But the following recipe made use of sardines, which have always been abundant and economical and, as such, this delightful soup could be found on Garfagnina tables even on an ordinary Tuesday or Wednesday.

> 3 tablespoons extra-virgin olive oil
> 1 clove garlic, minced
> 1 medium onion, diced
> 3 very ripe Italian plum tomatoes, peeled, seeded, and chopped
> 1½ teaspoons chopped fresh thyme
> 1 bay leaf
> 1 teaspoon saffron diluted in ¼ cup hot water
> 10 ounces red potatoes, peeled and cubed
> 5 cups Basic Fish Broth (see page 13)
> 2 pounds fresh sardines, cleaned and boned
> Salt and freshly ground black pepper to taste
> 4 ¾-inch-thick slices peasant-style bread, stale or toasted

1. Heat the oil in a soup pot over medium heat. Sauté the garlic and onion for 3 minutes, then add the tomatoes, thyme, bay leaf, and diluted saffron. Stir to mix well.

2. Add the potatoes and broth. Heat to boiling over medium heat and continue to cook for 15 minutes.

3. Add the sardines, cover, and cook for 10 minutes over medium heat. Add salt and pepper.

4. Divide the bread among 4 bowls. Pour the soup over and serve hot.

ZUPPA D'INVERNO DI ZI'MEO

Zi'Meo's Winter Sole and Leek Soup

Leeks belong to that particular category of foods that possesses a unique power to transform simple dishes into works of art. In many cases they are preferred over onions because of their sweeter, less pungent flavor. Here they are paired with a variety of other ingredients to create a delicately complex fish soup that was one of Pascoli's favorites and is a mainstay of the menu at Castelvecchio's Zi'Meo.

4 fillets of sole, about 4 ounces each

3 tablespoons extra-virgin olive oil

2 medium carrots, scraped and diced

8 ounces leeks (white part only), washed, dried, and diced

8 ounces white mushrooms, cleaned according to directions on
    page 33, and cut into slivers

½ teaspoon chopped fresh thyme

1 cup dry white wine

4 cups Basic Fish Broth (see page 13)

16 large shrimp, peeled and deveined

1 pound assorted white fish fillets (i.e., monkfish, petrale sole,
    halibut, etc.), skinned and cut into large chunks

¼ cup heavy cream

Salt and freshly ground black pepper to taste

1 cup chopped fresh parsley

1. Roll each of the sole fillets into a cylinder and fasten with toothpicks.

2. Heat the oil in a soup pot over medium heat. Sauté the carrots, leeks, mushrooms, and thyme over medium heat for 3 minutes or until the leeks are translucent. Add the wine, and when it has reduced by half, add the fish broth. Stir to blend.

3. Heat the soup to boiling. Reduce the heat to low and add the fish chunks. Simmer for 5 minutes, add the shrimp and sole fillets and cook for 5 minutes longer.

4. Stir the cream into the soup being careful to keep the sole intact. Add salt, pepper, and the parsley. Blend all ingredients, heat through without boiling, and serve immediately, one sole fillet in each bowl.

VELLUTATA DI PESCE

●

Fish Velouté

Vellutata *(velouté) is a type of creamy* besciamella *(béchamel) soup also made with butter and flour, but instead of milk, broth is used to create the base. The following velouté is a delicately pureed soup that is best accompanied by a mixed green salad and dry white wine.*

1¼ pounds white fish fillets (Chilean sea bass, monkfish, halibut, etc.), skinned
4 cups Basic Fish Broth (see page 13)
4 tablespoons unsalted butter
2 tablespoons unbleached white flour
¼ cup heavy cream
Salt and freshly ground black pepper to taste
1 cup finely chopped fresh parsley
⅛ teaspoon paprika

1. Place the fillets and the fish broth in a soup pot and simmer over low heat for 10 minutes or until the fish begins to flake. Drain the fish, reserving the broth, and puree in a food processor with a ladleful or two of the broth.

2. Melt the butter in the soup pot over low heat. Whisk the flour into the melted butter a little at a time until blended and smooth. Pour the reserved fish broth into the pot and continue whisking until the *vellutata* is smooth and comes almost to a boil. Cook for 10 minutes, stirring occasionally.

3. Stir the pureed fish and heavy cream into the *vellutata*. Cook for 3 minutes more, stirring constantly to blend. Add salt and pepper. Serve hot, with a heavy sprinkling of chopped parsley and a pinch of paprika for each bowl.

VELLUTATA DI SOGLIOLE E MANDORLE

Sole and Almond Velouté

The following recipe combines two subtle flavors, sole and almonds, to produce a rich, creamy soup that is often served as the first course at Garfagnana weddings.

6 tablespoons unsalted butter

7 small fillets of petrale sole, about 3½ ounces each

½ cup dry white wine

2 tablespoons almond "flour" (see Note)

4 cups Basic Fish Broth (see page 13)

⅓ cup unbleached white flour

½ cup half-and-half

Salt and freshly ground black pepper to taste

½ cup unblanched almonds, finely chopped

3 tablespoons chopped fresh parsley

1. Melt 4 tablespoons of the butter in a skillet over medium heat. Sauté the sole fillets until they are lightly browned on both sides. Add the wine and cook for 5 minutes, turning the fillets 4 or 5 times.

2. Puree 3 of the fillets in a food processor along with the almond flour and 2 ladlefuls of fish broth. Reserve the remaining fillets, keeping them warm.

3. Melt the remaining 2 tablespoons butter in the skillet over low heat. Whisk the unbleached flour into the butter to form a thick paste. Cook and stir for 2 minutes, then add the remaining fish broth, whisking constantly until it is smooth and the *vellutata* comes almost to a boil.

4. Stir the sole puree and half-and-half into the *vellutata* and return to the near boiling point. Remove from the heat and add salt and pepper.

5. Pour the soup into 4 bowls and top each serving with a whole fillet. Serve hot, sprinkled with the chopped almonds and parsley.

Note: Almond "flour" can either be purchased from a baking supply store or made at home by pulsing whole almonds in a food processor 3 or 4 times on high speed. Do not grind to a paste.

MINESTRA DI FAGIOLI FRESCHI ⬤
E DATTERI DI MARE

Fresh Fava Bean and Mussel Soup

The following recipe was created by Antonio Garbari, Zi' Meo's chef, to celebrate the Pascoli centenary. "I only wish Pascoli were here to taste this," Garbari said at the celebration dinner. "There's no question he would have asked for seconds."

   2 pounds fresh shelled fava beans, peeled according to directions
      on page 170
   8 cups Basic Fish Broth (see page 13)
   3 tablespoons extra-virgin olive oil
   3 cloves garlic, crushed
   1 small onion, diced
   1 small carrot, scraped and diced
   1 stalk celery, diced
   6 tablespoons chopped fresh parsley
   2 pounds mussels, scrubbed and debearded
   ½ cup dry white wine
   Salt and freshly ground black pepper to taste
   8 ounces ditalini (little thimbles) or other small-cut pasta

1. Place the peeled fava beans in a soup pot with the broth, cover, and cook over medium heat for 30 minutes. Set aside.

2. Heat the oil in a skillet. Sauté the garlic, onion, carrot, and celery for 7 minutes or until the onion is lightly browned. Add half the parsley, mussels, and wine and cook, covered, over low heat for 6 to 8 minutes. Discard any mussels that have not opened.

3. Remove mussels from the shell, chop roughly, and add to the beans along with the salt, pepper, and the pasta.

4. Cook for 7 to 8 minutes or until the pasta is *al dente*. Serve immediately sprinkled with the remaining parsley.

Chapter Nine

THE VIRTUES OF MOUNTAIN AIR

Fornovolasco

ZUPPE DI CARNE
Meat Soups

I have often heard it said that life should be dictated by capricious whims; that it is a bad thing indeed to always have a purpose; that allocating one's time in small slots filled with enumerated responsibilities is bad for both the soul and the digestive system.

Well, today I have decided to heed that advice to the fullest. And so I have boarded the CLAP bus (yes, that is in fact the name of this bus line) headed toward Castelnuovo and plan—no, strike that word—*imagine* that I will get off wherever and whenever I am moved to do so by either the scenery, the populace, or, more likely, the need to eat.

The driver on this particular route is Sergio Zerbini; I know this because I have boarded the bus early and am sitting in the seat opposite his—and so, naturally, we strike up a conversation. At first we talk about the woman who, ten minutes ago, wanted him to go back to Lucca because she had left her bag of fish at the market. *Il mio pesce!* she screamed when she finally realized ten kilometers into the trip what had happened. *O lasciato il mio pesce! Sono quaranta mila lire—ferma!* The fish cost 40,000 lire—stop the bus!

Sergio had calmly explained that he couldn't go back, that her only option was to get off at the next stop and take another bus back to Lucca. She had done just that, but not happily.

"What did she want me to do, make a U-turn?" he grumbled to me since I was sitting in the very first seat.

From there, the conversation proceeds to what each of our names are and then where I am from and eventually, after a few dozen more kilometers, where I am going.

"I'm not sure," I answer proudly.

"Well, what does it say on your ticket?" he asks, somewhat confused by the glee in my voice.

"Castelnuovo, but I will probably be getting off before then. It's just that, right now, I'm not exactly sure where."

It is obvious that my remark has created a certain amount of agitation. He turns to look at me, probably to assess whether he has been conversing all this time with a lunatic. I smile brightly and explain that, just for today, I want to experience the feeling of having no plans whatsoever.

"Ah," he says studiously. And then his demeanor changes. "Then I'll take you to Fornovolasco. To my uncle's house, where you will see something you've undoubtedly never before seen."

I'm not sure what an experienced free spirit would do under these circumstances, but I say okay and congratulate myself for having agreed to this itinerary without knowing the exact specifics.

We change buses in Gallicano, where Sergio's route shifts westward onto a small local road whose end point is Gallatoio. Fornovolasco, which is where he lives, is conveniently located on this very road. "I will drop you off at my uncle's," he says. "And then I will come back when I am finished and you can tell me whether you made the correct choice."

The village of Fornovolasco is nestled in a cosy notch embraced by two gently sloping mountains. Its forty-two houses are built directly into the hillside and piled one on top of the other one like matchboxes. The air is clean and crisp in a way that makes one aware of each individual inhalation; every word seems more eloquent and colorful thrust onto its currents.

Walking through this village requires a constant navigation of the steps built to accommodate the uneven terrain; connecting streets generally burrow through archways containing someone's kitchen or bedroom. There are no cars in Fornovolasco—another reason for the cleanliness of the air.

The notch itself is bisected by a river containing crystalline, emerald-green water and untold legions of trout. When we were still on the bus winding through the valley on our way to Fornovolasco, in fact, Sergio had pointed out four enormous trout farms located along the road.

The village was once a haven for iron workers, but when the main plant closed in the early part of this century, most residents either emigrated to the States or turned to the kind of traveling handiwork that is still valued by older inhabitants of these remote places. Knife sharpeners, grain grinders, pottery repairers, chimney sweeps—all jobs that require a certain specific skill.

"I once had a cousin who used to go from town to town seeking work as a *spaccapietra*—a stone splitter," Sergio says as we walk toward his uncle's home. "He would break large boulders into the smaller ones used to make cobbled streets. Nowadays, of course, streets are made of tar, and when stones are needed for one thing or another, even the smallest towns use machines."

We cross the river over a small stone bridge and zigzag our way through a maze of tiny streets and alleys. "The uncle we are about to visit still travels from village to village, working as a *norcino*. Today he is here working for himself."

"What's a *norcino*?" I ask.

"A man who kills your pig and then turns it into sausages and prosciutto and *biroldo* and whatever else you want."

"Is that what you're taking me to see?" I suddenly begin having second thoughts.

"The sausage making, not the killing. This pig was killed yesterday."

Roberto Martinelli is a quiet, composed man of sixty-eight who has been dealing with pigs for a lifetime. According to Sergio, he is known throughout the region for his "superior knowledge and skill."

He welcomes me to his butchering shed and asks for my opinion of the village. "Tell the truth," he says without waiting for a response. "The air here is purer than down on the flatland—no?"

I nod my head, thinking how wonderful to have found a man so appreciative of the environment. But Sergio sets me straight.

"When you are a *norcino*," he says, "pure air is everything. Prosciuttos and sausages are cured in the open air after all."

"*L'insaccati*—the cured meats—made in Lucca have a completely different taste than those made here," Roberto adds. "Without good air, it makes no difference what combination of rosemary and salt you use."

Sergio asks for my decision—do I want to stay and watch—and when I nod my head enthusiastically, he tells Roberto that he will be back within half an hour to pick me up. My thoughts turn to the two people still on the bus, who, when Sergio asked if they minded his stopping for a few minutes in Fornovolasco, answered that he should take his time.

"It is only Arnaldo and his cousin Sirio from Alleva," he said when I questioned him about it. "What difference does it make to them if we get there at eleven-thirty or eleven-forty-five?"

I obviously have a long way to go in my education.

Roberto's shed is filled with vats, each containing various parts of the pig awaiting transformation. The one closest to the door is a vat filled with eight long, fat *biroldi*—sausages made with pig's blood that, throughout Tuscany, are considered to be a delicacy. "These will be ready to eat tomorrow," Roberto says. "Tonight I will boil them and let them cool overnight."

Farther into the room are vats of sausage meat and those containing chunks of fat that will be boiled to make *strutto,* or rendered lard. Then there are slabs of fatback, curing on the open shelf next to the mezzina and pancetta. The prosciuttos hang at the far end of the shed, four of them, big and meaty and twirling in the breeze whenever Roberto whisks by.

"I guess you're not a vegetarian," I tease him.

He throws back his head and laughs. *Madre di Dio, quei snaturati, come fanno a non mangiare il prosciutto?* Mother of God, those poor deviants. How do they go through life without eating prosciutto?

He suddenly looks up from his hacking and stares at me sternly. "If nature had assigned us a vegetarian destiny, our jaws would have evolved according to a far different design—he who dines on spinach and milk does not need canine teeth."

It is a good point.

"Read your history," he continues. "The people who have made the most difference in this world have *all* been big meat eaters—Count Cavour one of the biggest. It was Cavour who said: 'The soldiers who fought to create Italy shed much blood on the green grassy plains. But even more blood was shed on white linen tablecloths by negotiators feasting on haunches of roasted beef.'"

He looks at me slyly to see if his point has scored.

"And then there was that glorious day, on April 29, 1859," he says as if he himself had participated. "The day when the Austrian army was finally driven back from northern Italy and a satisfied Count Cavour turned to his army and said: 'Today we have made history. And now let us roast a pig.'"

Having said his piece, Roberto returns to his work. At the moment, he is screwing a metal contraption to the table. The contraption has a funnel on one end and a chute on the other. "For making sausages," Roberto says when he sees my questioning look. "Watch."

With the help of his nephew, Sauro, he drags the biggest of the vats over to the table and caps the chute with a long ribbon of what looks like rubber tubing but is, in fact, calf's intestines (which are both larger and more elastic than those of pig's). He then begins stuffing the funnel with the slightly pink sausage mixture, which, in addition to the meat, contains salt, pepper, spices, garlic, and Cognac. "Taste it," he says at one point. "There's no need to be afraid. It is all good healthy meat."

He takes a bite himself, but I demur and claim I've had too much breakfast, which he knows is a lie but lets pass. In general, I am known for fairly unlimited experimentation when it comes to food. But raw sausage is further than even I can go, this despite the fact that Tuscans often eat their sausages either completely raw, or grilled to a black-as-coal exterior enveloping an interior that is still virginally pink.

It is true that the hesitations I have about raw pork—the bacteria and parasites that infect animals raised for mass production—are not a factor here. In fact, Roberto tells me, by law, when you kill a pig, a veterinarian must be on hand to immediately afterward check the lungs, kidneys, liver, and heart for infection. Furthermore, he says, he feeds his pigs only oats, nuts, chestnuts, and the milk that is left over after having made cheese.

However, I tell him when he asks again, my answer is still thank you, but no.

As Sauro churns one end of the sausage machine, Roberto guides the meat into the intestine and the sausage soon extends across the table in a long continuous tube that gives off a pungent odor of rosemary, garlic, and sage. When the table is filled with approximately twenty such tubes, the door opens and Sergio is back.

"So?" he asks when he notices that I have made myself at home. In fact, I am sitting comfortably on a garden chaise next to the sausage table drinking wine and eating chunks of last year's prosciutto.

Tutto bene, I tell him.

He hopes I have not spoiled my appetite, he says, because he wants to take me to Fornovolasco's only restaurant, Ristorante La Buca, whose proprietor will definitely want to make my acquaintance.

Vito Mori is indeed as excited about meeting me as he is about meeting anybody from the States. As it turns out, he is not only the restaurant's proprietor but the town historian, this by virtue of a book in his possession tracing the whereabouts of the many people who emigrated from Fornovolasco when the iron mill closed. They all, it seems, moved to California and are documented, along with those who remain, in a book written by Janet Pisenti called *Thirty-eight Cousins from Italy* (Northwestern Graphics).

"Look," Vito says, flipping through the pages. "This section talks about *my* family."

Having pointed out his brothers and sisters and uncles and cousins and—since Sergio is standing right there—Sergio's family tree as well, he synthesizes the rest of the book into two highlights: New Mexico Senator Pete Domenici's mother comes from Fornovolasco—page 83 in the book—and so does his cousin, Joe Rochioli, who now owns a rather large winery in Healdsburg, California.

I tell him there is also a Bianchi winery in California, although they are no relation to me, and he asks copious questions about my background and ancestry and whether it would be possible for me to call some of his relatives when I get back to the States to say that he is well. I would be delighted, I tell him, and then Sergio breaks in to say he is starving.

Our lunch consists of foods that Vito makes especially for us, since the restaurant is otherwise closed for the Feast of the Immaculate Conception. We feast on *minestra al prosciutto e basilico* (soup made with prosciutto and basil), *coniglio alla griglia* (grilled rabbit), and, for dessert, *macedonia con grappa* (fruit salad drizzled with grappa).

The restaurant itself is a warm, cozy room located on the site of an old *osteria*—an inn—dating back to the 1700s. Held together with nails made by the iron workers of centuries past, the front door is flanked on both sides by huge stone wheels once used to grind flour—the one on the right used for wheat and the one on the left for chestnuts. The stoneware crock at the foot of the stairs says 1756. It was used, Vito says, to hold salt pork. Now it holds a yellow rose bush.

When lunch is over and we have said good-bye to both Vito and Roberto, Sergio tells me it would be a shame if I left without seeing Fornovolasco's leading claim to fame, La Grotta del Vento—the Wind Caves—just down the road. If I want, he says, he will take me there by car and then I can catch the last bus home.

I am quite pleased with how things have turned out so far on this "day of spontaneity," and so I readily accept his offer.

The Wind Caves of Fornovolasco are located in the Parco Regionale delle Alpi Apuane—the Apuan Alps Regional Park—and contain the most extraordinary varieties of stalactites and stalagmites seen anywhere in Europe. Of the four itineraries offered—all guided—we choose the second one, which lasts two hours and takes us past crystal-encrusted lakes, icicles made of alabaster, and polychromatic formations alive and glowing with the reflected colors of the waters continuously oozing over them. Our guide is wonderful, and at one point asks if we'd like to go even farther into the caves. Of course, we say, and he proceeds to take us down what seems like a vast underground canyon, past a number of underground rivers, vertical abysses, ancient fossil galleries, waterfalls, and bizarre forms of erosion.

We would have liked to have seen even more, to have gone on the third itinerary, a tour that, according to our guide, ventures into a dramatic series of underground canyons called Le Diramazione dell'infinito—The Crossroads of Infinity. But it is only for groups of twenty or more, and even then, advance reservations are required.

The trip takes somewhat longer than the two hours advertised, and there are only ten minutes left for me to catch my bus. Sergio races me to the stop and, to my surprise, the bus is actually there. "Thank you for a wonderful day," I say, climbing on board.

He hands me a bookmark containing a picture of the Wind Caves and what he says is an old Garfagnino proverb about embracing the unknown: *Quando vai incontro al vento, tieni gli occhi chiusi and la faccia girata verso il cielo.* When heading into the wind, keep your eyes closed and your face turned toward the heavens.

ABOUT MEATS

In Garfagnana, meat has always been food for royalty, witness *garmugia alla Lucchese,* the famous seventeenth-century soup that was served to nobles enfeebled by a long illness. But it is hardly necessary to go back to the 1700s to find a time when the Garfagnini ate meat rarely if at all. Until a few short years ago, anyone in the region who ate meat more than two or three times a year was considered extremely well-off. A typical household of four was lucky if, on a rare occasion, it could manage one slice of meat, which, of course, was divided into four equal portions.

Because of this chronic meat shortage, it became customary to flavor foods—especially soups—with small quantities of smoked pancetta or pork fatback in order to impart that richer, more full-bodied flavor that is rarely possible without using the real thing.

Christmas, Easter, and New Year's Day were exceptions. On Easter it was lamb, on Christmas chicken, and on New Year's capon or pheasant. Almost never did anyone eat veal or beef but instead rabbit, chicken, or duck—barnyard animals that reproduced easily. Most houses also had one or, more rarely, more than one pig, since these could also be raised in a barnyard setting.

Pigs were purchased between March and May when they were three or four months old. The lure of raising a pig had to do with the enormous quantity of meat derived from an animal that was so easy to care for. While they ate almost anything, pigs were generally fed a diet of chestnuts, fava beans, fruit, *farro* flour, and any leftover that would cause rapid fattening. In summers, everyone's pigs were entrusted to the care of a *porcaro,* who took them on a daily jaunt through the woods.

They were slaughtered in December, close to Christmas, and thus provided the basis for many of the foods traditionally consumed around that particular holiday: biroldo (blood sausage), prosciutto, sopresatta, fatback, sausages, salamis. . . . The quantity and variety of products were many, as is evidenced by the attitude that served as everyone's guiding dictum: *un si tira via nulla*—nothing gets thrown away.

Fatback

There is an ancient Tuscan proverb that says: *Tanta va la gatta al lardo che ci lascia lo zampino.* The more times the cat goes to steal some fatback, the more the probability she will get caught—an adage that speaks to lard's well-deserved appeal.

Fatback comes from the back of the pig, hence its name. Pure white in color, fatback is salted as soon as it is removed from the animal and cured for two or more weeks, after which it is *drogata*—drugged—with pepper, rosemary, and garlic and cured for another few days.

Once the curing process is complete, fatback is then used in a wide variety of Tuscan dishes. Throughout the province, the term *lardillare* refers to the practice of coating chicken or pheasants with it to both keep the skin moist while roasting and to impart flavor. Tuscans also eat fatback as a type of prized cold cut, called *lardo,* which is sliced paper thin and served as part of an appetizer platter that might also contain prosciutto and mortadella. The world's most famous fatback, in fact, is that which comes from Colonnata in the province of Massa Carrara.

Another popular usage—and the one called for in many of the recipes in this book—involves adding minced fatback to the initial sautée that underlies many of the Garfagnana's recipes—a sauté made up of carrots, onions, celery, herbs, and garlic.

Most butchers—even those in supermarkets—carry fatback. Pancetta (or for those with access to Italian specialty stores—*mezzina*) can be substituted if necessary.

Pancetta

There are two types of pancetta used throughout the Garfagnana: raw and smoked. The former comes from the belly fat of the pig and is made up of equal parts meat and fat. Immediately after butchering, it is salted and spiced with pepper, rosemary, and garlic and is rolled into the shape of a log. After curing for 20 to 30 days, it is ready to eat and sold either sliced as a cold cut or in chunks for use in various recipes requiring the melted flavor of pork.

The latter is marinated purely in water and salt and subjected to a light smoking. Butchers purchase it in sheets and sell it either in chunks or sliced in thicknesses that vary according to the customer's request. In Tuscany, as in the States, it is referred to as "bacon." Smoked pancetta is an essential ingredient in many of the soup recipes in this book.

Prosciutto

Prosciutto is the only completely natural pig product, says Roberto Martinelli. All others are manipulated in terms of added ingredients. Sausages are a certain combination of pork and spices; likewise salamis, *biroldi,* fatback, and pancetta. "Only prosciutto is as God made it. The only addition is salt."

Prosciutto is the thigh of the pig. As soon as the pig is butchered, the thigh is salted—½ pound salt for every 20 pounds of meat—and stored in a refrigerated compartment for 5 days. After 5 days, *norcini*—pig specialists—give it a vigorous massage to break down any veins, nerves, or fibers and then resalt and rerefrigerate it for another 17 or 18 days. At this point, they dust off the excess salt and store the prosciutto for a few months in a *cella di riposo*—a resting cell—at 4°C. Here it stays for 3 months, after which it is washed, sun-dried, and transferred to a curing room, with open windows to allow fresh air to circulate and begin the curing process. Says Roberto: "We regulate exposure according to the level of humidity in the air. Our prosciuttos are like fine violins, and they require the same type of care."

After 7 months in the curing room, the prosciutto is pierced four or five times in various locations to determine whether it has properly cured. Most of the Garfagnana's *norcini* use a fine, needle-like bone that comes from the leg of a horse because, as Roberto says, this particular bone loses its odor immediately and so can be used again and again. The meats are then cured for another 3 or 4 months, and only then, when they have lost approximately 28 percent of their original weight, are they ready to be eaten.

In the Garfagnina kitchen, prosciutto is not only eaten as a sublimely delicious cold cut but is used as an ingredient in many recipes as well. Its skin—*la cotiche*—is diced and sautéed with *l'odori* (the initial sauté of carrots, onions, and celery that underlies much of this area's cooking) and provides a welcome addition to bean, *farro,* and meat soups. The meat is also used in soups, diced and sautéed as indicated in many of the following recipes.

ZUPPA DI FAGIOLI CON COTICHE

Pork and White Bean Soup

According to Il Refugio's Vito Mori, when most of Fornovolasco's men worked in the local iron plant, they left their homes before sunrise and returned after sunset. And their wives, who worked equally long hours, but at home, would often prepare Zuppa di fagioli con cotiche, *simmering it on the stove for sometimes an entire day. The following recipe combines what I learned from Vito with my own modifications, chiefly the addition of nutmeg and the substitution of meat broth for water.*

⅓ cup dried *cannellini* beans, soaked according to directions on 169
⅓ cup dried *borlotti* (cranberry beans), soaked according to directions on page 169
¼ cup extra-virgin olive oil
1 chunk (2 ounces) smoked pancetta or bacon, diced
1 stalk celery, diced
2 small carrots, scraped and diced
1 medium onion, diced
2 cloves garlic, minced
3 tablespoons chopped fresh parsley
1 teaspoon chopped fresh rosemary
6 fresh basil leaves, chopped
⅛ teaspoon grated nutmeg
1 tablespoon tomato paste
8 cups Basic Meat Broth (see page 11)
Salt and freshly ground black pepper to taste
1 piece (⅛–¼ pound) pork skin
1 ham bone

1. Place both types of beans in a large saucepan with enough water to cover by 2 inches. Heat to boiling over medium heat. Cover, and cook for 2 hours, adding water if necessary. Salt at the halfway mark.

2. Heat the oil in another soup pot over medium heat. Sauté the pancetta or bacon, celery, carrots, and onion for 8 minutes, stirring constantly. Add the garlic, parsley, rosemary, and basil and stir to mix well.

3. Add the nutmeg and the tomato paste dissolved in one cup of the bean broth. Add salt and pepper and cook for 10 minutes, stirring occasionally.

4. Meanwhile, drain the beans, reserving the liquid. Pass half the beans through a food mill. Reserve the whole beans. Add the mashed beans, pork skin, ham bone, and the rest of the meat broth to the soup pot. Bring to a boil over low heat and cook for 2 hours, stirring occasionally.

5. Remove and discard the ham bone. Stir the reserved beans and bean cooking liquid into the soup and return to boiling. Serve hot.

Roberto Martinelli: "When you are a Norcino, pure air is everything. Prosciuttos and sausages are cured in the open air after all."

GARMUGIA ALLA GARFAGNANA
Garmugia Garfagnana Style

According to Mario Tobino, noted culinarian and cookbook archivist, garmugia dates back to the 1600s, when it was readily prescribed as a restorative for the well-to-do emerging from long illnesses. An unusually meat-rich soup, it was also considered effective in saving the souls of counts and baronesses struggling with what was then referred to as "temptation" but has since come to be redefined as depression. The best preparation, Tobino says, is the original one of cooking the soup slowly over burning red coals. An equally valid method is to cook it on a stove over low heat.

3 tablespoons extra-virgin olive oil

4 small onions, diced

1 chunk (4 ounces) prosciutto, diced

4 ounces ground beef

4 ounces ground veal

1 pound fresh shelled fava beans, peeled according to directions on
   page 170

½ cup fresh or frozen peas

4 medium artichokes, outer leaves and chokes removed, cut into
   slivers

4 ounces asparagus tips

4 cups Basic Meat Broth (see page 11)

Salt and freshly ground black pepper to taste

1. Heat the oil in a soup pot over medium heat. Sauté the onions and prosciutto for 7 minutes or until the onion is lightly browned. Add the ground beef and veal and continue to cook for 5 minutes, stirring constantly to break up the meat.

2. Add the fava beans, peas, and artichokes. Stir to mix well and cook for 3 minutes. Add the asparagus and cook for another 2 minutes, stirring frequently.

3. Add the broth and cook for 10 minutes or until the vegetables are tender. Serve hot.

MINESTRA TRE COLORI
"Three-Color" Soup

To Roberto Martinelli, this soup stands for the Italian flag: the whiteness of the chicken broth, the red of the prosciutto, and the green peas. Apart from being patriotic, he says its delicate flavor is exquisite in either summer or winter.

> 1½ cup fresh or frozen peas
> Salt
> 6 cups Basic Chicken Broth (see page 12)
> 12 ounces cooked chicken breast, thinly sliced
> 2 ounces prosciutto, cut into thin slivers
> ¼ cup freshly grated Parmigiano-Reggiano
> Freshly ground black pepper to taste

1. Heat a small amount of salted water to boiling in a saucepan over medium heat. Add the peas and cook for 10 minutes or until tender. Drain.

2. Place the broth in a soup pot and heat to boiling over medium heat. Add the peas, chicken, and prosciutto and cook for 2 to 3 minutes until just heated. Add salt.

3. Serve immediately, dusted with the grated Parmesan and plenty of freshly ground black pepper.

MINESTRA DI SELVAGGINA AL MARSALA

Meatball and Marsala Wine Soup

This recipe was literally pulled from the mouth of Fornovolasco's Velia Antinori. We had been talking about various types of meat and I commented on the fact that they were used in very few first course recipes. The Signora agreed although she did say that some people make polenta with chicken or rabbit and serve it as a first course in small portions. But then, perhaps because she heard me say that I was compiling soup recipes for a book to be published in the U.S., she invited me into her kitchen and, for the next few hours, we experimented with a number of meat soups, of which the following is my favorite—perhaps because of its unusual method for creating the tiny meatballs.

1 pound leftover roasted meat (beef, veal, game, or pork), very
    finely diced
2 ounces marsala
½ small onion, very finely diced
½ small carrot, scraped and very finely diced
½ celery stalk, very finely diced
1 whole clove
8 cups Basic Meat Broth (see page 11)
1 egg yolk
Salt and freshly ground black pepper to taste
⅛ teaspoon nutmeg

1. Using a mortar and pestle, pound the meat into a mash, adding the marsala one teaspoon at a time. Placed in a covered bowl. Wash and dry the mortar and pestle.

2. Place the onion, carrot, celery, and clove in the bowl of the mortar. Using the pestle, grind the vegetables into a dense mash similar to the meat.

3. Place both the meat and vegetable mashes in a soup pot. Add the broth, stirring to mix well. Heat to boiling over medium heat. Reduce the heat to low, cover, and cook for 1 hour.

4. Strain the broth through a sieve lined with a double layer of cheese-cloth, returning the broth to the soup pot and placing the strained meat and vegetable mash in a bowl. Keep the broth at a simmer.

5. Add the egg yolk, salt, pepper, and nutmeg to the mash in the bowl. Beat with a fork to blend thoroughly. Pinch off enough of the mixture to form a small, cherry-size ball and roll between the palms of the hands until the ball is firm and smooth. Continue until all the mixture is used up.

6. Divide the balls among 4 bowls, cover with the simmering broth, dust with black pepper, and serve immediately.

Vito Mori, owner of Ristorante La Buca *and town historian.*

POLPETTINE IN BRODO ○
Tiny Meatballs in Chicken Broth

In days gone by, Garfagnina women would make large meat loaves using basically the ingredients listed below. These would be cooked in water for an hour or two, thereby creating both a first-course broth and a meat loaf entree that would generally be served with potatoes and marinated vegetables. In today's more refined kitchen, the meat loaf has given way to tiny, dainty meatballs cooked in meat broth flavored with chopped escarole. Best when accompanied by a chilled Vernaccia de San Gimignano.

    4 ounces ground veal
    4 ounces ground beef
    2 medium eggs, lightly beaten
    3 ounces unflavored bread crumbs
    3 tablespoons chopped fresh parsley
    ¼ cup freshly grated Parmigiano-Reggiano
    Salt and freshly ground black pepper to taste
    8 cups Basic Meat Broth (see page 11)
    1 large head escarole, cleaned and roughly chopped

1. Place all ingredients except the broth and escarole in a large bowl. Mix by hand until well blended. Pinch off walnut-size pieces and roll between the palms to form small balls. Place the balls side by side on a platter.

2. Heat the broth in a soup pot over medium heat until boiling. Add the escarole and cook, covered, for 3 minutes. Add the meatballs, dropping them one at a time into the simmering broth. Cook, uncovered, for 10 minutes. Serve immediately.

MINESTRA CON QUADRI DI LATTUGA RIPIENA

○

Soup with Veal-Stuffed Lettuce Bundles

Roberto Martinelli calls this recipe evidence of his wife's newfound leisure time. "In the past, who would have had time to fill each lettuce leaf and roll them so carefully into tiny bundles?" he asks. "If we had made this soup at all, we probably would have mixed all the ingredients directly into the soup." He gives a sly wink. "Much better this way."

4 heads *lattuga* (Boston-type lettuce)
8 ounces ground veal
3 tablespoons extra-virgin olive oil
1 small carrot, scraped and diced
1 small onion, diced
1 celery stalk, diced
2 tablespoons freshly grated Parmigiano-Reggiano
½ cup dry white wine
¼ cup unflavored bread crumbs
1 egg, lightly beaten
Salt and freshly ground black pepper to taste
6 cups Basic Meat Broth (see page 11)

1. Remove 6 of the largest outer leaves from each head of lettuce, discarding any that are damaged or torn. Reserve the remainder of the heads for use another time.

2. Boil 1 gallon water in a large soup pot. Place the leaves in the boiling water for 5 to 6 seconds or until limp. Drain. Using a small knife, remove any spines that are still tough but be careful to leave the body of the leaf intact.

3. Heat the oil in a skillet. Sauté the carrot, onion, and celery for 7 minutes or until the onion is lightly browned. Remove to a bowl and cool for 5 minutes.

4. Add the veal, cheese, wine, bread crumbs, beaten egg, salt, and pepper to the cooled vegetables, mixing well.

5. Place a small quantity of filling into each lettuce leaf. Fold the sides one over the other left to right and then top to bottom. Press each bundle with the palm of the hand to flatten and pack.

6. Pour the broth into a soup pot. Place the lettuce bundles side by side in a steamer basket or colander. Suspend the basket over the broth and cook over medium heat for 15 minutes.

7. Remove the lettuce bundles from the steamer carefully, placing 6 in each of 4 bowls. Top with soup and serve.

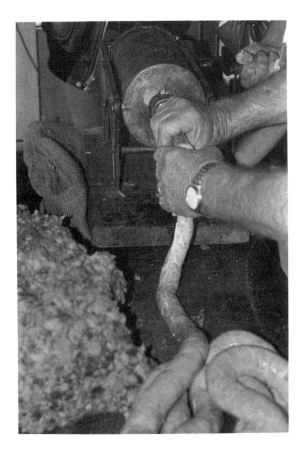

Roberto and his nephew making sausage the old-fashioned way.

ZUPPA DI SALSICCIA CON CECINA O
Sausage Soup Topped with Slices of Chickpea Torte

Cecina is a delightful Tuscan flat bread made from chickpea flour. Wonderful eaten as is, hot from the oven and sliced like pizza, it can also be used as a filling for sandwiches made with focaccia or as the top and bottom of a sandwich filled with, perhaps, a slice of prosciutto or mortadella. In the following recipe, it is sliced into wedges and used as a garnish for sausage soup. Chickpea flour (alternately called garbanzo flour) can be found at most Italian specialty stores.

> 1 cup water
> ⅔ cup chickpea flour
> Salt and freshly ground black pepper to taste
> 6 tablespoons extra-virgin olive oil
> 1 tablespoon chopped fresh rosemary
> 1 medium onion, chopped
> 2 cloves garlic, crushed
> 1 medium carrot, scraped and diced
> 3 tablespoons chopped fresh parsley
> 3 links fennel sausage, removed from casings and crumbled
> 8 cups Basic Chicken Broth (see page 12)

1. Place the water in a large bowl. Stir in the flour, add salt and pepper and let sit for 3–4 hours, skimming off the froth once or twice during that period.

2. Preheat the oven to 500 degrees. Oil a pizza pan with 3 tablespoons of the oil. Skim the final froth off the bowl, and pour into the pan to a ¼-inch depth. Scatter the rosemary over the top and bake for 20 minutes or until the *cecina* is cooked through.

3. Heat the remaining oil in a soup pot over medium heat. Sauté the onion, garlic, and carrot for 5 minutes or until the onion is soft. Add the sausage and parsley and continue to cook for 5 more minutes, stirring frequently.

4. Pour the broth over the onion and sausage mixture, cover, and heat to boiling over medium heat. Reduce the heat to low and simmer for 20 minutes, covered.

5. Remove the *cecina* from the oven and cut into 8 wedges. Pour the soup into 4 bowls and serve, garnished with the *cecina* wedges.

ZUPPA DI FEGATINI E FUNGHI ○

Chicken Liver and Porcini Mushroom Soup

Roberto Martinelli refers to this soup as "the other use for chicken livers." What he means is that the Garfagnini generally only use them in making Crostini di Fegatini—*Chicken Liver Canapes*—*which are probably the area's most popular appetizer. "Everyone always says how much they love both the* crostini *and the* fegatini *soup," he says. "I don't know why we don't use chicken livers more. Perhaps we are stuck in our ways,* si?*"*

2 ounces dried porcini mushrooms
2 tablespoons extra-virgin olive oil
1 medium onion, chopped
3 cloves garlic, crushed
8 cups Basic Mushroom Broth (see page 15)
¼ pound chicken livers, whitish membrane removed, and coarsely
   chopped
2 tablespoons unsalted butter
1 teaspoon dried crumbled sage
16 croutons fried in butter (see page 66)

1. Place the mushrooms in a bowl and cover with warm water. Soak for 30 minutes, drain, and chop.

2. Heat the oil in a soup pot over medium heat. Sauté the onion and garlic for 5 minutes or until the onion is soft. Add the mushrooms and sauté for 3 minutes longer.

3. Pour the broth over the onions and mushrooms. Cover, and cook over low heat for 10 minutes.

4. Heat the butter in a skillet over medium heat. Sauté the chicken livers and sage for 5 minutes. Add to the soup pot, cover, and cook for 15 minutes over low heat.

5. Divide the croutons among 4 bowls. Pour the soup over the croutons and serve.

MINESTRA MARITATA
"Married" Soup

This recipe's name refers to the fact that it "marries" the pork to the vegetables in what is basically a one-dish meal. I have varied the original recipe by substituting pork loin for the traditional blood sausage and by adding garlic, which adds a spicier flavor.

1 pound chicory, washed, dried, and chopped
1 pound escarole, washed, dried, and chopped
1 small head savoy cabbage, cored and chopped
Salt
1 chunk (2 ounces) pork fatback, diced
4 cloves garlic, chopped
1 chunk (4 ounces) salami
1 chunk (4 ounces) prosciutto
1 chunk (4 ounces) smoked pancetta or bacon
1 chunk (4 ounces) boneless pork loin
6 cups Basic Chicken Broth (see page 12)

1. Blanch the chicory, escarole, and cabbage in a soup pot filled with salted boiling water for 5 minutes. Drain and reserve.

2. Heat the fatback in the soup pot over medium heat until the fat is rendered out. Sauté the garlic for 2 minutes; do not allow to brown. Add the chunks of salami, prosciutto, pancetta, and pork and brown in the rendered fat for 1 minute per side. Add the blanched vegetables and broth and heat to boiling. Reduce the heat to low, cover, and cook for 2 hours, adding more water if necessary.

3. Remove the meats with a slotted spoon. Shred and return to the soup. Adjust for salt, cook for another 5 minutes, and serve hot.

MINESTRA AL PROSCIUTTO E BASILICO

Prosciutto and Basil Soup

This recipe has everything, says Il Refugio's Vito Mori. Meat, vegetables, cheese, and even the pasta without which most Garfagnini—and indeed most Italians— feel incomplete. But the secret, he says, is in the oil, "as it is in almost every dish we make."

 2 tablespoons extra-virgin olive oil
 2 cloves garlic, minced
 1 chunk (4 ounces) prosciutto, diced
 1 chunk (4 ounces) smoked pancetta or bacon, diced
 ½ cup canned Italian plum tomatoes, squeezed until shredded and
   with liquid reserved
 6 cups Basic Meat Broth (see page 11)
 4 ounces linguine, broken into 2-inch pieces
 2 tablespoons chopped fresh basil
 ½ cup freshly grated Pecorino Romano
 Salt and freshly ground black pepper to taste

1. Heat the oil in a soup pot over medium heat. Sauté the garlic, prosciutto, and pancetta or bacon for 4 minutes. Add the tomatoes, their liquid, and broth. Cover and heat to boiling over medium heat.

2. Add the linguine, return to boiling, and cook for 10 minutes. Remove from heat.

3. Stir in the basil, half the grated cheese, salt, and pepper. Stir to mix well and serve hot, dusted with the remaining cheese.

Prosciuttos hang at the far end of the shed, big and meaty and twirling in the breeze.

ZUPPA AL SUGO DI CARNE
Holiday Beef Soup

●

This was not an "everyday" soup recipe, but one used on holidays such as the feast day of a patron saint or New Year's Day. Its flavor comes, above all, from the dried mushrooms—mushrooms that were once religiously dried in summer and then wrapped in the ubiquitous yellow paper (made from corn) that was used for wrapping everything from purchased vegetables to school books.

2 ounces dried porcini mushrooms
3 tablespoons extra-virgin olive oil
1 small carrot, scraped and diced
2 medium onions, diced
8 ounces ground beef
3 cloves garlic, diced
3 fresh basil leaves
1 can (16 ounces) Italian plum tomatoes, squeezed until shredded
  and with liquid reserved
1 stick (4 ounces) unsalted butter
1 small head savoy cabbage, cored and shredded
Salt and pepper to taste
8 ounces carrots, scraped and cut into rounds
8 ounces celery hearts, sliced into rounds
8 ounces red potatoes, peeled and cubed
6 cups Basic Meat Broth (see page 11)
16 croutons fried in butter (see page 66)
4 tablespoons freshly grated Parmigiano-Reggiano

1. Soak the mushrooms in warm water for 20 minutes. Drain and chop; strain and reserve the liquid.

2. Heat the oil in a skillet over low heat. Sauté the diced carrot, half the onion, the beef, and garlic for 7 minutes or until the onion is lightly browned. Add the basil, chopped mushrooms, and the tomatoes with their liquid. Cover, and cook for 45 minutes, adding small amounts of the reserved mushroom liquid if necessary to maintain a dense saucelike consistency.

3. Heat the butter in a heavy soup pot over medium heat. Sauté the remaining onion until translucent. Add the cabbage and stir to mix well. Add salt and pepper.

4. Add the carrot, celery rounds, potato cubes, and broth. Cook over low heat for 1 hour.

5. Stir the meat and tomato sauce into the soup and cook for 10 more minutes.

6. Divide the croutons among 4 bowls. Pour the soup over and serve hot, dusted with the grated cheese.

VELLUTATA DI POLLO

O

Creamy Chicken Velouté

On Sundays, in the homes of those who were somewhat better off (which meant they had barnyard animals) women attempted to make something a little different while staying within the strict limits that defined even the lives of the benestanti—the comfortable. Vellutata di pollo fits that description perfectly: a soup fit for a king but using completely ordinary ingredients.

3 tablespoons unsalted butter
2 tablespoons unbleached white flour
8 cups Basic Chicken Broth (see page 12)
1 small chicken, about 2 pounds
1 medium onion, diced
1 stalk celery, diced
3 whole cloves
2 bay leaves
Freshly ground black pepper to taste
¼ cup heavy cream
Salt to taste

1. Melt the butter in a soup pot over low heat. Stir the flour into the butter until a thick paste is formed. Add the broth, one ladleful at a time, whisking constantly. Heat to boiling over medium heat.

2. Meanwhile, stuff the chicken with the onion, celery, cloves, and bay leaves. Add a dusting of black pepper, sew up the cavity, and place the chicken in the broth. Cook over low heat for 1 hour, partially covered.

3. Remove the chicken from the broth using a slotted spoon. Peel the skin away from the meat and discard. Discard the contents of the cavity. Detach the breast from the bone and slice into small slivers. Reserve, covered.

4. Remove the thigh meat from the bones and mash using a mortar and pestle. Place in a bowl. Slowly add the cream to the mashed meat, stirring constantly with a wooden spoon until most of the cream has been absorbed. Reserve the remainder of the chicken for another use.

5. Skim the fat from the broth and whisk in the chicken and cream mixture. Continue to stir until a creamy soup has formed.

6. Add the slivered breast meat, salt, and pepper to the soup. Heat the soup over low heat just until hot. Serve immediately.

Arnaldo and his cousin Sirio. "What difference does it make to them if we get there at 11:30 or 11:45?"

MINESTRA STRAPPATA CON OSSO DI PROSCIUTTO

Ham Bone Soup

Many of Garfagnana's most characteristic legends emanate from its long years of poverty. The one directly related to this recipe takes place in the Fornovolasco of the 1600s, when there were few people and even fewer houses and to possess a ham bone was a formidable accomplishment indeed, albeit one that left the owner wrangling with the moral duty to share his wealth. And so, after one minestra *was cooked, it became the custom to* strappare, *or wrest the bone away to the house next door, where it was used the following day. And so on until the* conditoio *(the seasoning element) had made the rounds of all the houses in the village.*

The Soup:

8 ounces fresh shelled *borlotti* (cranberry beans)
2 medium potatoes, peeled
½ cup canned Italian plum tomatoes, squeezed until shredded and
    with liquid reserved
5 tablespoons extra-virgin olive oil
1 chunk (2 ounces) pork fatback, finely diced
2 cloves garlic, minced
3 tablespoons chopped fresh parsley
5 fresh basil leaves, chopped
1½ teaspoons chopped fresh rosemary
1 ham bone
Salt and freshly ground black pepper to taste

The Pasta:

1 cup unbleached white flour
1 egg

1. Place the beans, potatoes, tomatoes, and 3 tablespoons of the oil in a large heavy-gauge soup pot with enough water to cover by 2 inches. Make a "pesto" of the lard, garlic, parsley, basil, and rosemary and add it to the pot along with the ham bone. Adjust for salt and pepper, cover, and cook for 2 hours over low heat.

2. Remove the bone and cut off the remaining ham. Return the ham slivers to the soup and discard the bone.

3. To make the pasta, create a dough with the flour, egg, the remaining oil, and salt to taste. Add a tablespoon or two of lukewarm water if necessary to create a soft, doughlike consistency. Roll the dough to a ⅛-inch thickness.

4. Cut the dough into irregular strips and add them to the soup.★ Cook for 10 minutes or until the pasta is done. Serve hot.

★A pasta machine can also be used to roll the dough to the appropriate thickness. It can then be cut by hand to create the "irregular" appearance.

ZUPPA DI VERZA E SALSICCIA

Sausage and Savoy Cabbage Soup

Says Roberto Martinelli of this soup: "It is my favorite for three reasons: one, it is easy; two, it uses sausage, which is the best of all the products I make; and three, it was taught to me by my mother, Dio la benedica (God bless her), who never had any sense of quantity and made enough to keep me happy for two or three days."

1 large head savoy cabbage, washed, cored, and cut into strips
8 cups Basic Meat Broth (see page 11)
3 tablespoons extra-virgin olive oil
3 tablespoons unsalted butter
¾ pound fennel sausage, removed from casings and crumbled
Salt and freshly ground black pepper to taste
3 tablespoons chopped fresh parsley

1. Place the cabbage strips in a soup pot with the broth. Cover, and cook over low heat for 1½ hours.

2. Add the oil, butter, and black pepper. Cook for 1 hour.

3. Add the sausage and cook for another 20 minutes. Add salt. Serve hot sprinkled with the parsley.

CREMA DI ASPARAGI AL
PROSCIUTTO COTTO

Creamed Asparagus Soup Cooked with Ham

The Garfagnini of old used wild asparagus in making this soup. Prolific growers, asparagus stalks could always be found—and in many places, can still be found— in olive groves and mountain fields.

1 pound asparagus tips
8 cups Basic Chicken Broth (see page 12)
4 tablespoons unsalted butter
2 tablespoons unbleached white flour
Salt and freshly ground black pepper to taste
1 egg yolk
2 ounces heavy cream
3 tablespoons chopped fresh parsley
½ cup fresh grated Parmigiano-Reggiano
1 chunk (½ pound) cooked prosciutto (ham), finely diced
16 croutons fried in olive oil (see page 68)

1. Place the asparagus tips in a pot with the broth. Cover, and cook over medium heat for 10 minutes. Drain and reserve the cooking liquid. Place the asparagus tips in a bowl and keep warm.

2. Melt the butter in a saucepan. Stir the flour into the butter until a thick paste has been created. Pour the asparagus broth in a steady stream over the butter-flour mixture, whisking constantly. Adjust for salt and pepper and bring to a boil.

3. Beat the egg yolk with the cream, stir the parsley and half the cheese into the cream mixture and continue beating until well blended. Place in a soup terrine.

4. Pour the soup into the terrine, whisking to blend all ingredients. Add the asparagus tips and the diced ham. Stir to blend.

5. Divide the croutons among four bowls. Pour the soup over the croutons, dust with the cheese, and serve immediately.

Acknowledgments

As usual, this book would not have been possible without the help and support of many people. Let me first—and again—thank Sandra Lotti, researcher extraordinaire, for assisting with the gathering of the recipes and selection of the villages as well as for her limitless knowledge of just about everything. This is not the first book we have done together, and I very much hope we will go on to do many more.

Thanks also—and again—to my mother, Maria Valleroni, who welcomed me back each evening from the Garfagnana with charm and forbearance and a table set with foods more wonderful than I can possibly describe.

To Douglas Hatschek, who combed the mountains and plains of the Garfagnana in search of the photographs that grace the pages of this book, *grazie*. You stood your ground when I thought we had more than enough shots and wanted to go for pizza. And it shows!

Thank you, Tom Gelinne, for reviewing each of the recipes and ensuring that when I said a cup, I really meant a quart.

Special thanks to Amerina Castiglia, for proofing the manuscript to ensure the linguistic integrity of my "Tuscanisms."

Thank you, Ombretta Lotti, Luigi Lenchoni, Leila Melani, Erico Martelli, Ernesto Carmassi, and Alderigo Triglia, for providing many of the contacts and a great deal of the information. Special thanks to Marco Franceschoni, who chauffeured us from village to village (and sometimes back again) with a patience and good humor that I might not have had in his stead.

Thank you, Daniel Halpern, Alan Turkus, and all the other people at Ecco for doing as wonderful a job on this book as you did on my previous one.

And finally, an enormous thank-you to all the people of the Garfagnana and especially to those mentioned in these pages. Your history and traditions have tantalized me since childhood, and I am grateful finally to be able to hold you up in front of those whose experience of Tuscany has been limited to more eastern provinces and say with great pride, "You have missed the very best part."

A

Ancient Lima Bean Soup Made with Apples and
   Butternut Squash in the Old Garfagnini Style, 183
Angel-Hair Pasta in Vegetable Broth, 24
Artichoke Soup, 50
Artichoke Velouté, 87
Asparagus Tip Soup, 57
Autumn Vegetable Soup, 47

B

Baby Clams and Tomato Soup, 208
Barga, 27-57
Basic Chicken Broth, 12
Basic Fish Broth, 13
Basic Meat Broth, 11
Basic Vegetable Broth, 14
Basil Pesto, 10
Basil Tortellini in Broth, 21-22
"Bastard" Soup, 180
Bean soups, 163-193
  about, 168-170
  Ancient Lima Bean Soup Made with Apples and
    Butternut Squash in the Old Garfagnini Style, 183
  "Bastard" Soup, 180
  Black-Eyed Pea Soup, 193
  Chestnut and White Bean Soup, 192
  Country-Style Minestrone with Thick Egg Noodles,
    188-189
  Earth and Sea Soup, 172-173
  Fava Bean and Potato Soup, 185
  Fresh Cranberry Bean Soup, 171
  Fresh Fava Bean and Cardoon Soup, 186-187
  Fresh Fava Bean Soup, 184
  Hearty Kale and White Bean Soup, 177-178
  Il Casone's Minestrone Rustico con Taglierini
    all'Uovo, 188-189
  Invernale della Signora Elda, 174
  Minestra di Fagioli Minuti, 193
  Minestra di Fave e Cardi, 186-187
  Minestrone di Castagne e Fagioli Secchi, 192
  Minestrone Garfagnana Style, 190-191

  Minestrone Garfagnina, 190-191
  Oven-Baked Bean and Salami Soup, 179
  Ribolitta Garfagnina, 181
  Sbroscia della Vecchia Garfagnana, 183
  Signora Elda's Winter Soup, 174
  Soup Olive Presser-Style, 175-176
  Twice-Cooked Bean Soup, Garfagnana-Style, 181
  White Bean and Escarole Soup, 182
  Zuppa alla Frantoiana, 175-176
  Zuppa Bastarda, 180
  Zuppa di Fagioli, 171
  Zuppa di Fagioli e Salame Cotta in Forno, 179
  Zuppa di Fave e Patate, 185
  Zuppa di Fave Fresche, 184
  Zuppa di Scarola e Fagioli Bianchi, 182
  Zuppa di Terra e Mare, 172-173
  Zuppa Sostanziosa, 177-178
Beans
  peeling fava beans, 170
  soaking, 169-170
  types of, 169
Black-Eyed Pea Soup, 193
Bread, xvii
Bread soups,
  Everyday Bread Soup, 69-70
  Minestra di Pane di Tutti I Giorni, 69-70
  Pancotto, 68
Bread soups, purees, and cream soups, 59-89
  about, 66
Bricks, use of, xvi-xvii
Brodetto con Ditalini, 113
Brodi. *See* Broths
Brodo al Funghi, 15
Brodo con Bricioletti, 25
Brodo con Tortellini di Basilico, 21-22
Brodo di Carne, 11
Brodo di Cereali, 16
Brodo di Pesce, 13
Brodo di Pollo, 12
Brodo di Vegetali, 14
Brodo di Vino, 20

Brodo di Vongole, 17
Brodo Estivo, 18
Broths, xv, 3-25
   Angel-Hair Pasta in Vegetable Broth, 24
   Basic Chicken Broth, 12
   Basic Fish Broth, 13
   Basic Meat Broth, 11
   Basic Vegetable Broth, 14
   Basil Tortellini in Broth, 21-22
   Brodo al Funghi, 15
   Brodo con Bricioletti, 25
   Brodo con Tortellini di Basilico, 21-22
   Brodo di Carne, 11
   Brodo di Cereali, 16
   Brodo di Pesce, 13
   Brodo di Pollo, 12
   Brodo di Vegetali, 14
   Brodo di Vino, 20
   Brodo di Vongole, 17
   Brodo Estivo, 18
   Capelli d'Angelo in Brodo, 24
   Cereal Grains, made with, 16
   Chicken Broth with "Crumbled Ricotta," 25
   Chicken Broth with Tiny Semolina Gnocchi, 19
   Clam, 17
   clarifying, 9-10
   Creamy Marsala Broth, 20
   Egg Drop Soup, 23
   Gnocchetti di Semolino in Brodo, 19
   Mushroom Broth, 15
   removing fats from, 9
   as soup base, xix
   Stracciatella, 23
   Summer Broth, 18

C

Cacciucco alla Garfagnana, 209-210
Cacciucco di Ceci, 156
Canned tomatoes, 34
Capelli d'Angelo in Brodo, 24
Castelnuovo di Garfagnana, 91-119
Castelvecchio Pascoli, 195-221
Castiglione di Garfagnana, 59-89

Ceci, Mele, Salsiccia e Patate alla Garfagnana, 157
Ceci e Funghi alla Daniella, 158-159
Cheese, xvii
Chestnut and White Bean Soup, 118-119, 192
Chestnut soups. *See* Grain soups
Chestnuts, about, 99
Chicken Broth with "Crumbled Ricotta," 25
Chicken Broth with Tiny Semolina Gnocchi, 19
Chicken Liver and Porcini Mushroom Soup, 243
Chickpea Soup with Penne and Gorgonzola, 160
Chickpea Stew, 156
Chickpeas, 141-161. *See also* Lentil and chickpea
   soups
   about, 147-148
   soaking, 149
Chickpeas, Apples, Sausage, and Potatoes Garfagnana-
   Style, 157
Chilled Tomato Soup, 72
Clam Broth, 17
Country-Style Chickpea Soup, 155
Country-Style Minestrone, 106
Country-Style Minestrone with Thick Egg Noodles,
   188
Country-Style Shrimp and Artichoke Soup, 212
Cream of Fennel Soup, 82
Cream of Potato and Rutabaga Soup, 84-85
Cream Soup with Red and Yellow Pepper Pesto, 88
Cream soups
   Artichoke Velouté, 87
   Cream of Fennel Soup, 82
   Cream of Potato and Rutabaga Soup, 84-85
   Cream Soup with Red and Yellow Pepper Pesto, 88
   Creamy White Fish Soup, 86
   Crema con Pesto di Pepperoni, 88
   Crema di Finocchio, 82
   Crema di Patate e Barbe, 84-85
   End of Season Tomato Soup, 83
   La Fine di Agosto, 83
   Vellutata di Carciofi, 87
   Vellutata di Pesce, 86
Creamed Asparagus Soup Cooked with Ham, 253
Creamy Chicken Velouté, 248-249
Creamy Marsala Broth, 20

Creamy White Fish Soup, 86
Crema con Pesto di Pepperoni, 88
Crema di Asparagi al Prosciutto Cotto, 253
Crema di Finocchio, 82
Crema di Lenticchie, 153
Crema di Patate e Barbe, 84-85
Croutons, making, 66-67

D
Daniela's Chickpea and Mushroom Soup, 158-159
Denseness, xviii
Dolce di Castagne, 116

E
Earth and Sea Soup, 172-173
Economical Fresh Sardine Soup, 217
Egg Drop Soup, 23
End of Season Tomato Soup, 83
Essential Soup, 108
Everyday Bread Soup, 69-70

F
Farinata di Farina di Riso, 105
Farinate, xv
Farro, about, 127-130
    preparing, 130
Farro and Butternut Squash Minestrone, 138
Farro and Chickpeas, 134
Farro and Shellfish Soup, 131
Farro e Ceci, 134
Farro, Sausage, and White Wine Minestrone, 137
Farro soups, 121-139
    Farro and Butternut Squash Minestrone, 138
    Farro and Chickpeas, 134
    Farro and Shellfish Soup, 131
    Farro e Ceci, 134
    Farro, Sausage, and White Wine Minestrone, 137
    Farro, Vino e Salsiccia, 137
    Guido's Farro Soup, 135-136
    Il Farro di Guido, 135-136
    Minestra di Pazienza e Farro, 132
    Minestrone col Farro, 133
    Minestrone di Farro e Zucca, 138

Minestrone with Farro, 133
    Soup Made with Patience and Farro, 132
    Zuppa di Farro e Frutti di Mare, 131
Farro, Vino e Salsiccia, 137
Fatback, 230-231
Fava Bean and Potato Soup, 185
Fava beans, peeling, 170
Field Vegetable Soup, 49
Fish Broth with Ditalini,8 113
Fish, about, 202-204
    choosing, 203
    cleaning, 203-204
Fish Soup with Vegetables and Herbs, 216
Fish soups, 195-221
    Baby Clams and Tomato Soup, 208
    Cacciucco alla Garfagnana, 209-210
    Country-Style Shrimp and Artichoke Soup, 212
    Economical Fresh Sardine Soup, 217
    Fish Soup with Vegetables and Herbs, 216
    Fish Velouté, 219
    Fresh Fava Bean and Mussel Soup, 221
    Friday Codfish Soup, 206
    Garfagnana Fish Stew, 209-210
    Lobster Soup, 214-215
    Minestra di Aragoste, 214-215
    Minestra di Fagioli Freschi e Datteri di Mare, 221
    Pascoli's Cuttlefish Soup, 213
    Shrimp, Prawns, and Pepper Soup, 207
    Sole and Almond Velouté, 220
    Soup Made with Mussels and Clams, 205
    Soup Made with Squid and Swiss Chard and Served
        over Herb Polenta, 211
    Vellutata di Pesce, 219
    Vellutata di Sogliole e Mandorle, 220
    Zi'Meo's Winter Sole and Leek Soup, 218
    Zuppa coi Nicchi e Pomodori, 208
    Zuppa d'Inverno di Zi'Meo, 218
    Zuppa di Baccala di Venerdi, 206
    Zuppa di Cozze e Vongole, 205
    Zuppa di Gamberi, Scampi, e Peperoni, 207
    Zuppa di Gamberoni e Carciofi Casalinga, 212
    Zuppa di Mare Agli Odori, 216
    Zuppa di Seppie e Bietola, 211

Zuppa di Totani alla Pascoli, 213
Zuppa Economica di Sardine, 217
Fish Velouté, 219
Flavor bases, xvi
Food mills, xviii–xix
Fornovolasco, 223–253
Fresh Basil Soup, 53
Fresh Cranberry Bean Puree with Savoy Cabbage, 71
Fresh Cranberry Bean Soup, 171
Fresh Fava Bean and Cardoon Soup, 186–187
Fresh Fava Bean and Mussel Soup, 221
Fresh Fava Bean Soup, 184
Friday Codfish Soup, 206

G
Garfagnana Fish Stew, 209–210
Garlic Soup, 39
Garmugia alla Garfagnana, 235
Garmugia Garfagnana Style, 235
Gnocchetti di Semolino in Brodo, 19
Grain soups, 91–119
    about, 98–99
    Brodetto con Ditalini, 113
    Chestnut and White Bean Soup, 118–119
    Country-Style Minestrone, 106
    Dolce di Castagne, 116
    Essential Soup, 108
    Farinata di Farina di Riso, 105
    Fish Broth with Ditalini, 113
    Grated Pasta Soup, 114
    Intruglia, 102–103
    La Minestra della Signora Virginia (Sensa Pesce), 107
    La Minestra di Rape della Signora Rosa, 109
    Manafregoli, 117
    Many Ingredients Soup, 100–101
    Mescola alla Garfagnana, 100–101
    Minestra con Pane Grattato alla Povera, 112
    Minestra di Pasta Grattata, 114
    Minestra di Riso e Limone, 104
    Minestra di Uoua e Pangrattato, 111
    Minestra Essenziale, 108
    Minestrone di Castagne e Fagioli Secchi, 118–119
    Minestrone Rustico, 106

    Polenta, Savoy Cabbage, and Red Bean Soup,
        102–103
    Poor People's Dumpling Soup, 110
    Poor People's Wine Soup, 115
    Rice and Lemon Soup, 104
    Rice Flour Soup, 105
    Sheepherder's Chestnut Soup, 117
    Signora Rosa's Broccoli Raab Soup, 108
    Soup Made with Eggs, Cheese, and Bread Crumbs,
        111
    Sweet Chestnut Soup, 116
    Vinata alla Povera, 115
    Virginia's Soup (Without Fish), 107
    Wheat Berry Soup, 110
    Zuppa di Frumento, 110
Grated Pasta Soup, 114
Guido's Farro Soup, 135–136

H
Ham Bone Soup, 250–251
Hearty Kale and White Bean Soup, 177–178
Herb Battuto, 10
Herb Polenta, 204
Holiday Beef Soup, 246–247

I
Il Casone's Minestrone Rustico con Taglierini all'Uovo,
    188–189
Il Castello's Fresh Fish and Tomato Soup, 75
Il Farro di Guido, 135–136
Il Passato del Pesce del Castello, 75
Intruglia, 102–103
Invernale della Signora Elda, 174
Isola Santa, 141–161

L
La Fine di Agosto, 83
La Mascherata della Signora Bertolani, 73–74
La Minestra della Signora Virginia (Sensa Pesce), 107
La Minestra di Rape della Signora Rosa, 109
Leek Soup, 38
Lenticchie e ceci. See Lentils and chickpeas
Lentil and chickpea soups

Cacciucco di Ceci, 156
Ceci, Mele, Salsiccia e Patate alla Garfagnana, 157
Ceci e Funghi alla Daniela, 158-159
Chickpea Soup with Penne and Gorgonzola, 160
Chickpea Stew, 156
Chickpeas, Apples, Sausage, and Potatoes Garfagnana-Style, 157
Country-Style Chickpea Soup, 155
Crema di Lenticchie, 153
Daniela's Chickpea and Mushroom Soup, 158-159
Lentil Soup with Anchovies, 152
Lentil Soup with Fresh Walnut Paste, 154
Lentil Soup with Tomatoes and Prosciutto, 151
Minestra di Ceci con Penne e Gorgonzola, 160
Minestrone di Lenticchie al Pomodoro, 150
Minestrone with Lentils and Tomatoes, 150
Thick Lentil Cream, 153
Zuppa di Ceci Rustica, 155
Zuppa di Lenticchie al Pomodoro e Prosciutto, 151
Zuppa di Lenticchie con Battuto di Noce, 134
Zuppa di Lenticchie con le Acciughe, 152
Lentil Soup with Anchovies, 152
Lentil Soup with Fresh Walnut Paste, 154
Lentil Soup with Tomatoes and Prosciutto, 151
Lentils and chickpeas, 141-161
    about, 147-148
    soaking, 149
Lettuce, 34
Lobster Soup, 214-215

M
Manafregoli, 117
Many Ingredients Soup, 100-101
"Married" Soup, 244
Matilda's Butternut Squash Soup, 45
Meat soups, 223-253
    Chicken Liver and Porcini Mushroom Soup, 243
    Crema di Asparagi al Prosciutto Cotto, 253
    Creamed Asparagus Soup Cooked with Ham, 253
    Creamy Chicken Velouté, 248-249
    Garmugia alla Garfagnana, 235
    Garmugia Garfagnana Style, 235
    Ham Bone Soup, 250-251

Holiday Beef Soup, 246-247
"Married" Soup, 244
Meatball and Marsala Wine Soup, 237-238
Minestra al Prosciutto e Basilico, 245
Minestra con Quadri di Lattuga Ripiena, 240-241
Minestra di Selvaggina al Marsala, 237-238
Minestra Maritata, 244
Minestra Strappata con Osso di Prosciutto, 250-251
Minestra Tre Colori, 236
Polpettine in Brodo, 239
Pork and White Bean Soup, 233-234
Prosciutto and Basil Soup, 245
Sausage and Savoy Cabbage Soup, 252
Sausage Soup Topped with Slices of Chickpea Torte, 242
Soup with Veal-Stuffed Lettuce Bundles, 240-241
"Three-Color" Soup, 236
Tiny Meatballs in Chicken Broth, 239
Vellutata di Pollo, 248-249
Zuppa al Sugo di Carne, 246-247
Zuppa di Fegatini e Funghi, 243
Zuppa di Salsiccia con Cecina, 242
Zuppa di Fagioli con Cotiche, 233-234
Zuppa di Verza e Salsiccia, 252
Meatball and Marsala Wine Soup, 237-2386
Meats, about, 229-232
Mescola alla Garfagnana, 100-101
Minestra, xv
Minestra al Prosciutto e Basilico, 245
Minestra con Pane Grattato alla Povera, 112
Minestra con Quadri di Lattuga Ripiena, 240-241
Minestra di Aragoste, 214-215
Minestra di Ceci con Penne e Gorgonzola, 160
Minestra di Fagioli Freschi e Datteri di Mare, 221
Minestra di Fagioli Minuti, 193
Minestra di Fave e Cardi, 186-187
Minestra di Pane di Tutti I Giorni, 69-70
Minestra di Pasta all'Uovo e Piselli, 55
Minestra di Pasta Grattata, 114
Minestra di Patate alla Garfagnina, 41
Minestra di Pazienza e Farro, 132
Minestra di Punte d'Asparagi, 57
Minestra di Riso e Limone, 104

Minestra di Riso e Piscialetto, 37
Minestra di Selvaggina, 237-238
Minestra di Uoua e Pangrattato, 111
Minestra di Verdure Primaverile, 52
Minestra Essenziale, 108
Minestra Maritata, 244
Minestra Strappata con Osso di Prosciutto, 250-251
Minestra Tre Colori, 236
Minestra Verdissima, 54
Minestre, xv
Minestrone, xv
Minestrone col Farro, 133
Minestrone di Castagne e Fagioli Secchi, 118-119, 192
Minestrone di Farro e Zucca, 138
Minestrone di Lenticchie al Pomodoro, 150
Minestrone Estivo, 56
Minestrone Garfagnana Style, 190-191
Minestrone Garfagnina, 190-191
Minestrone Rustico, 106
Minestrone with Farro, 133
Minestrone with Lentils and Tomatoes, 150
Mushroom Broth, 15
Mushrooms, 33

N
Noodle Soup with Fresh Peas, 55

O
Odori, xvi
Onion Soup with Milk, Garfagnana-Style, 51
Over-Baked Bean and Salami Soup, 179

P
Pancetta, 231
Pancotte, passate, e Creme. *See* Bread Soups, Purees,
    and Cream Soups
Pancotto, 68
Parsley, 33-34
Pascoli's Cuttlefish Soup, 213
Passate. *See* Pureed soups
Passato con Verdura Grigliata, 76-77
Passato del Pastore, 78
Passato di Borlotti con Verza, 71

Passato di Festa Reale, 78-80
Passato di Pomodoro alla Panna, 72
Pasta, about, 98
Piazza al Serchio, 121-139
Polanta, about, 98
Polanta, Herb, 204
Polenta, Savoy Cabbage, and Red Bean Soup, 102-103
Polpettine in Brodo, 239
Poor People's Dumpling Soup, 112
Poor People's Soup Made with Field Herbs, 46
Poor People's Wine Soup, 115
Porcini Mushroom Soup, 35
Pork and White Bean Soup, 233-234
Pot, the proper, xv-xvi
Potato Soup Garfagnina Style, 41
Potato Soup in the Style of the Monks of Soraggio, 40
Prosciutto, 231-232
Prosciutto and Basil Soup, 245
Pureed Soup for the Convalescing, 81
Pureed soups
    Chilled Tomato Soup, 72
    Fresh Cranberry Bean Puree with Savoy Cabbage, 71
    Il Castello's Fresh Fish and Tomato Soup, 75
    Il Passato del Pesce del Castello, 75
    La Mascherata della Signora Bertolani, 73-74
    Passato con Verdura Grigliata, 76-77
    Passato del Pastore, 78
    Passato di Borlotti con Verza, 71
    Passato di Festa Reale, 79-80
    Passato di Pomodoro alla Panna, 72
    Pureed Soup for the Convalescing, 81
    Royal Festival Soup, 79-80
    Sheepherder's Sunday Soup, 78
    Signora Bertolani's Vegetable Masquerade, 73-74
    Vegetable Puree Served over Roasted Vegetables,
        76-77
    Zuppa Frullata per Convalescenti, 81

R
Recipe variation(s), xix-xx
Ribollita Garfagnina, 181
Rice, about, 98
Rice and Dandelion Soup, 37

Rice and Lemon Soup, 104
Rice Flour Soup, 105
Rice soups. *See* Grain soups
Royal Festival Soup, 79-80

S

Salt, xviii
San Pellegrino in Alpe, 3-25
Sasso Rosso, 163-193
Sausage and Savoy Cabbage Soup, 252
Sausage Soup Topped with Slices of Chickpea Torte,
   242
Sbroscia della Vecchia Garfagnana, 183
Sheepherder's Chestnut Soup, 117
Sheepherder's Sunday Soup, 78
Shrimp, Prawns, and Pepper Soup, 207
Signora Bertolani's Vegetable Masquerade, 73-74
Signora Elda's Winter Soup, 174
Signora Rosa's Broccoli Raab Soup, 109
Soffrito, xvi
Sole and Almond Velouté, 220
Soup Made with Eggs, Cheese, and Bread Crumbs, 111
Soup Made with Mussels and Clams, 205
Soup Made with Patience and Farro, 132
Soup Made with Squid and Swiss Chard and Served
   over Herb Polanta, 211
Soup Olive Presser-Style, 175-176
Soup terrines, xix
Soup with Veal-Stuffed Lettuce Bundles, 240-241
Soups, about, xv-xx
Spring Vegetable Soup, 52
Squash Blossom Soup, 48
Stracciatella, 23
Summer Broth, 18
Summer Minestrone, 56
Summer Salad Soup, 42
Sweet Chestnut Soup, 116

T

Temperature, xviii
Terrines, soup, xix-xx
Thick Lentil Cream, 153
"Three-Color" Soup, 236

Tiny Meatballs in Chicken Broth, 239
Tomatoes, canned, 34
Twice-Cooked Bean Soup, Garfagnana-Style, 181

V

Vegetables, about, 33-34
   canned tomatoes, 34
   lettuce, 34
   mushrooms, 33
   parsley, 33-34
Vegetable Puree Served over Roasted Vegetables, 76-77
Vegetable soups, 27-57
   Artichoke Soup, 50
   Asparagus Tip Soup, 57
   Autumn Vegetable Soup, 47
   Field Vegetable Soup, 49
   Fresh Basil Soup, 53
   Garlic Soup, 39
   Leek Soup, 38
   Matilda's Butternut Squash Soup, 45
   Minestra di Pasta all'Uovo e Piselli, 55
   Minestra di Patate alla Garfagnina, 41
   Minestra di Punte d'Asparagi, 57
   Minestra di Riso e Piscialetto, 37
   Minestra di Verdure Primaverile, 52
   Minestra Verdissima, 54
   Minestrone Estivo, 56
   Noodle Soup with Fresh Peas, 55
   Onion Soup with Milk, Garfagnana-Style, 51
   Poor People's Soup Made with Field Herbs, 46
   Porcini Mushroom Soup, 35
   Potato Soup Garfagnina Style, 41
   Potato Soup in the Style of the Monks of Soraggio,
     40
   Rice and Dandelion Soup, 37
   Spring Vegetable Soup, 52
   Squash Blossom Soup, 48
   Summer Minestrone, 56
   Summer Salad Soup, 42
   Very Green Soup, 54
   Wild Herb Soup, 43-44
   Woodcutter's Soup, 36
   Zuppa alla Boscaiola, 36

Zuppa alla Povera con Erbe di Prato, 46
Zuppa d'Insalata, 42
Zuppa dei Frati di Soraggio, 40
Zuppa dei Prati, 49
Zuppa della Signora Matilde, 45
Zuppa di Aglio, 39
Zuppa di Basilico Fresco, 53
Zuppa di Carciofi, 50
Zuppa di Cipolle al Latte alla Garfagnana, 51
Zuppa di Erbe Legate, 43-44
Zuppa di Fiori di Zucca, 48
Zuppa di Funghi Porcini, 35
Zuppa di Porri, 38
Zuppa di Verdura Autonnale, 47
Vellutata di Carciofi, 87
Vellutata di Pesce, 86, 219
Vellutata di Pollo, 248-249
Vellutata di Sogliole e Mandorle, 220
Very Green Soup, 54
Vinata alla Povera, 115
Virginia's Soup (Without Fish), 107

W

Wheat Berry Soup, 110
White Bean and Escarole Soup, 182
Wild Herb Soup, 43-44
Woodcutter's Soup, 36

Z

Zi'Meo's Winter Sole and Leek Soup, 218
Zuppa al Sugo di Carne, 246-247
Zuppa alla Boscaiola, 36
Zuppa alla Frantioiana, 175-176
Zuppa alla Povera con Erbe di Prato, 46
Zuppa Bastarda, 180
Zuppa coi Nicchi e Pomodori, 208
Zuppa d'Insalata, 42
Zuppa d'Inverno di Zi'Meo, 218
Zuppa dei Frati di Soraggio, 40
Zuppa dei Prati, 49
Zuppa della Signora Matilde, 45

Zuppa di Aglio, 39
Zuppa di Baccala di Venerdi, 206
Zuppa di Basilico Fresco, 53
Zuppa di Carciofi, 50
Zuppa di Ceci Rustica, 155
Zuppa di Cipolle al Latte alla Garfagnana, 51
Zuppa di Cozze e Vongole, 205
Zuppa di Erbe Legate, 43-44
Zuppa di Fagioli, 171
Zuppa di Fagioli con Cotiche, 233-234
Zuppa di Fagioli e Salame Cotta in Forno, 179
Zuppa di Farro e Frutti de Mare, 131
Zuppa di Fave e Patate, 185
Zuppa di Fave Fresche, 184
Zuppa di Fegatini e Funghi, 243
Zuppa di Fiori di Zucca, 48
Zuppa di Frumento, 110
Zuppa di Funghi Porcini, 35
Zuppa di Gamberi, Scampi, e Peperoni, 207
Zuppa di Gamberoni e Carciofi Casalinga, 212
Zuppa di Lenticchie al Pomodoro e Prosciutto, 151
Zuppa di Lenticchie con Battuto di Noce, 154
Zuppa di Lenticchie con le Acciughe, 152
Zuppa di Mare Agli Odori, 216
Zuppa di Porri, 38
Zuppa di Salsiccia con Cecina, 242
Zuppa di Scarola e Fagioli Bianchi, 182
Zuppa di Seppie e Bietola, 211
Zuppa di Terra e Mare, 172-173
Zuppa di Totani alla Pascoli, 213
Zuppa di Verdura Autonnale, 47
Zuppa di Verza e Salsiccia, 252
Zuppa Economica di Sardine, 217
Zuppa Frullata per Convalescenti, 81
Zuppa Sostanziosa, 177-178
Zuppe di carne. *See* Meat soups
Zuppe di fagioli. *See* Bean soups
Zuppe di farro. *See* Farro soups
Zuppe di grano. *See* Grain soups
Zuppe di pesce. *See* Fish soups
Zuppe di verdure. *See* Vegetable soups

About the Author

Anne Bianchi is a food writer who divides her time between New York and the Tuscan province of Lucca, where she also runs a cooking school called Toscana Saporita, located in Campo Romano, a five-hundred-year-old farmhouse-turned-agriturismo. She has written a number of books, of which the most recent is *From the Tables of Tuscan Women: Traditions and Recipes,* also published by The Ecco Press. Currently, she is working on a collection of stories and recipes from the Maremma area of Tuscany, which was once the home of the Etruscans.

10/96

I M P O R T A N T

Leave cards in pocket